MAN

AGAINST MYTH

BY BARROWS DUNHAM

LITTLE, BROWN AND COMPANY

BOSTON · 1947

TO MY MOTHER AND FATHER

. . . by whom came life
and the happiness of life

Acknowledgement is due the Clarendon Press, Oxford, for permission
to quote from *The Testament of Beauty* by Robert Bridges; and to
Houghton Mifflin Company for permission to quote from *You, Andrew
Marvell* by Archibald MacLeish.

PREFACE

I first conceived the analysis of social myths as a series of lectures. It was Ella Winter who suggested to me the possibility of a book, and I must attribute to her whatever originality the plan may possess. To her husband, Donald Ogden Stewart, I owe grateful thanks for a warmth of encouragement which is said to be rare in successful authors, but which is bountifully present in him. As a research assistant in the gathering of materials for this book Mrs. Irma Spritz Lustig has served with great intelligence and skill.

But my chief help has come from my wife, Alice Dunham, who has borne with fortitude the rather terrifying lot of living with a nascent author. Whatever my doubts and anxieties, her patience has never flagged. And I add (with her permission) that, though she is not by nature inordinately given to listening, she has lent to these pages a generous and candid ear.

My indirect indebtedness is too much to state in detail. Of the great thinkers, I owe most to Spinoza, Hume, Marx, and Whitehead, in which company, I suppose, Hume served as a sort of philosophical conscience. To all my teachers, of whom Whitehead was one, I owe a wholly unpayable debt; but perhaps I can offer some return by acknowledging the debt here, and by freeing them of any blame for the form their influence has taken in this book.

Lastly, there are many persons who have taught me much by their example, by the splendor with which their own lives exhibit the moving presence of ideals.

I think, for instance, of Mr. Philip D. Jacobson, a dealer in real estate and a disciple of Henry George, who, when I observed that a Georgian economy would put him out of business, replied very simply, "In a reasonable society I can always find something to do." I think of Orestes Stephano, the defender of Greek freedom; of Frank Kai-Ming Su, a herald of the new China. I think of my Negro friends, Mr. Allan Freelon, whose breadth of culture I should be happy to possess, and Miss Carolyn Bird, whose help and counsel have smoothed away many a difficulty in my life. I should like to think that this book reflects some of the cordial humanity which all these persons have taught me to admire.

The book has grown from the leisure moments of more than two years. I have written for the most part with pleasure, but sometimes with that mild agony which accompanies the extraction of ideas from the brain. And although, over the interminable months, I have longed for an end of labor, I confess I feel a little sorry that the work is done.

One day at lunch, my son Clarke and his friend Tommy, two nine-year-olds, fell to talking about this book. "Your father's writing something?" asked Tommy. "Yes." "What's the story about?" "It isn't a story; it's about social superstitions." Tommy pondered this awhile. Then he said, "Gee whiz."

I feel that way about it myself.

BARROWS DUNHAM

Cynwyd, Pennsylvania
March 1, 1947

CONTENTS

Time eateth away at many an old delusion,
yet with civilization delusions make head;
the thicket of the people wil take furtiv fire
from irresponsible catchwords of live ideas,
sudden as a gorse-bush from the smouldering end
of any loiterer's match-splint, which, unless trodden out
afore it spredd, or quell'd with wieldy threshing-rods
wil burn ten years of planting with all last year's ricks
and blacken a countryside.

Robert Bridges: *The Testament of Beauty*, I: 599–607.

Haec sunt, quae hic notare suscepi, praejudicia.
Si quaedam huius farinae adhuc restant, poterunt
eadem ab unoquoque mediocri meditatione emendari.

Spinoza: *Ethics*, Part I, Appendix, last sentences.

(These are the prejudices which I undertook to point out.
If some grains of them are still left, anyone can disperse
them by means of a little thought.)

CHAPTER I INTRODUCTION: MYTHS AND THE PHILOSOPHERS

"YOU ARE a philosopher, Dr. Johnson," said Oliver Edwards. "I have tried too in my time to be a philosopher; but, I don't know how, cheerfulness was always breaking in." The two old fellows, sixty-five and sixty-seven respectively, were renewing their college acquaintanceship. I dare say that the Doctor's learning seemed as formidable as it was vast and as solemn as it was formidable. Poor Oliver, a man who had "gone through life without experience," could scarcely avoid mistaking gloom for philosophy; and, moreover, it is true that a certain number of philosophers have spent their time in explaining how to make the best of a very sad world.

Now, Dr. Johnson is not to be classed among professional philosophers, who have a rather different vocation and whose wisdom is sometimes noticeably less than his. And it was, I fancy, not cheerfulness alone which prevented Oliver Edwards from becoming a philosopher. The men to whom that still august title belongs have place in an admired tradition. Over its beginning lies the shadowy greatness of Thales; over its present stage lies a shadow, but of whom? Of Dewey, Russell, Santayana, Wittgenstein? One's tongue trips over the names and cannot utter them. For the shadow is not one man's shadow; it is the world's.

The world's shadow, of course, is what we mean by night. I do not wish to press this metaphor too hard, because the present state of philosophy and human thought in general is not as yet

> . . . a darkness which no stars redeem,
> A wall of terror in a night of cold.

Rather, it is that ambiguous gloom which may perhaps be twilight and may perhaps be dawn. The professional philosophers exhibit a lot of confidence in their own opinions, but not much confidence in philosophy. Some of them, indeed, are frank to say that they do not know just what philosophy is. This notion is much less startling than the fact that men are willing to utter it. For what can be more absurd than to confess, at the end of a lifetime of intellectual labor, that one has no idea what the labor has been about?

One reason for this curious state is that philosophy, in what might be called its official sense, has been a self-perpetuating tradition. Every philosopher feeds upon his predecessors, and is likely to consult Hegel or Kant before he consults reality. There results a steady elaboration of inherited ideas, a strife of systems, and a cautious play of individual fancy. In this process, some theories are improved and others are destroyed. It takes about an equal amount of philosophic effort to do either.

A second reason is that philosophy deals with the

larger generalizations, and therefore seems remote and even terrible. If you say to yourself, "I shall have whole-wheat bread for dinner," and proceed accordingly, you are dealing with a particular loaf and a particular dinner, and everyone will find the business understandable. Now, if you further say, "I shall have whole-wheat bread for dinner because it is nourishing," you remain perfectly understandable, though you have passed into dietetics. If, next, you detail the reasons why whole-wheat bread is nourishing, you enter a number of sciences like chemistry and physiology, and you become noticeably less understandable — at any rate, less familiar. Pausing a little at this point, you will say perhaps, "Well, anyhow, the more nourishing my diet, the healthier I shall be." Here you add medicine to the sciences you have already skimmed, and your generalization has, accordingly, a yet wider range. To this generalization everyone will assent — and not out of ignorance, either. But now suppose it occurs to you or to someone else to ask, "How is it possible that a collection of plant seeds, winnowed and milled and baked and eaten and digested, can transform themselves into bone and tissue?" You will hardly know that you are asking the same question which Anaxagoras asked, twenty-five centuries ago, "How can hair come from what is not hair, or flesh from what is not flesh?" How can it, indeed? Evidence, as gathered by the sciences, seems to show that it does. But how does it? The answer lies beyond the sciences in philosophy.

Let us come at the thing in another way. You have just said, "The more nourishing my diet, the healthier I shall be." Suppose, now, that an irreverent friend replies, "So what?" In this remark appears what commencement speakers like to call a "challenge." (They have been challenging me for the past twenty years, in the same deep voice drawn from the same deep paunch.) You have to answer, and your answer will surely be, "It is a good thing to keep healthy." "A good thing for you or for everybody?" continues the relentless catechizer. "For everybody," you say, not wishing to hold a purely self-interested position. Now, it is clear that you were driven into ethics the moment you answered the question, "So what?" And you were driven into a certain kind of ethics the moment you said, "For everybody." Ethics being a part of philosophy, you necessarily find yourself philosophizing even before the bread has entered your mouth.

Any last doubts will vanish if we allow the dialogue to continue a bit longer. "Why," says the questioner, who perhaps fancies himself a Socrates, "why is health a good thing for everybody?" "Because," you reply, "you feel good when you're healthy." "Ah," says the questioner, revealing himself not as Socrates but as an American college professor, "I perceive you are a hedonist; and since you evidently want the greatest amount of pleasure for the greatest number of people, you are a utilitarian." "Is there anything wrong in that?" you ask in some alarm. "There are many things wrong with it: the hedonistic paradox, for example." You begin to feel the ground sliding from under you; better look about for a rock. Ah, here it is: "I think that everyone has a duty to keep healthy." But the rock splits open: "Sir," says the professor, "you have changed your ground. You are now a Kantian. But do you really think that health-seeking can be inferred from the categorical imperative?" No safety here; better make one more try. "Well, pleasure or no pleasure, duty or no duty, everybody wants to be healthy." The avalanche comes down in a professorial sigh: "Dear me, dear me, now you are confusing fact and value. It's the most elementary mistake possible." "Professor, have another slice of bread."

Shall I tell you how you should have gone about it? The first thing is to seize the initiative. When the professor asked, "Why is health a good thing for everybody?" you should have replied, "There is a presumption in favor of the view. It's up to you to show that the view is false." This maneuver reverses the roles: you are now the questioner, he the answerer. He pauses to survey the battleground, and you can disturb his meditations with an icy "Well?"

Now, the professor knows very intimately all the difficulties in the various ethical theories, and he doesn't want to take a position which you can speedily sap. His next move is tentative: "It's not easy, you know, to say what the term 'good' means." "Of course not," you reply, "but is that a reason for our not trying?" "I suppose not," says the professor, neatly outflanked; "I'm inclined to believe, however, that Professor George E. Moore is right in saying that 'good' is indefinable." You haven't heard of George E. Moore, but you must stick to your strategy: "Do you mean to say that 'good' means something, but that one cannot say what?" "The view is somewhat paradoxical," sighs the professor. "I think it more likely that when you call something 'good,' you're simply expressing your personal approval. It's like saying something in a certain tone of voice." "Like a pig grunting his approval over the trough?" you ask. "Well, roughly that, though I wouldn't have chosen just that analogy."

You are ready now for the *coup de grâce:* "Then, when I say that health is a good thing for everybody, I am merely grunting?" "Yes, if you *must* put it that way." "And if somebody else thinks that ill-health is a good thing, he is merely grunting too?" "Yes." "Professor, give me back that slice of bread." "But you just now gave it to me." "Sorry, but I've changed my grunts."

Unknown to you, the professor was what is called a Logical Positivist, one of the strangest of philosophical sectaries, whose doctrines we shall examine in a later chapter. The point is, however, that he, as questioner, put you through, and you, as questioner, put him through, a fairly arduous process of determining exactly what each of you meant. You were finally revealed as not knowing exactly what you did mean; he was finally revealed as confessing that he didn't mean anything.

Now, this is the philosophical process *par excellence.* It is the analysis of concepts. From it three results are obtainable: (1) we discover whether a term or statement has any meaning; (2) we discover what that meaning ultimately is; and (3) we discover what other statements must be presupposed, if the given statement is to be true. It is possible, of course, to undertake the process with an excessive zeal, and thus reduce it in the end to hair-splitting and casuistry. Nevertheless, if you do not carry the process as far as time and patience will permit, you are bound to fall short of knowing the world and your relation to it.

For instance, it is not really obvious, though it seems so, that health is a good thing for you or for everybody. We can find a sense in which the statement will be true; namely, that health is one among many other values. But if it is said that health is the highest of all values, then the statement is quite probably false. Health evidently takes its value from other "more valuable" values which it serves. We should want to know what a man does with his health before congratulating him upon having it. And there are some quite healthy people whose actions are so nefarious that we may deem them unworthy of continued life, let alone continued health.

Thus all attempts to work out the meaning and the presuppositions of statements, as far as thought can carry them, are philosophical. I do not mean that you have to be a professional philosopher to do this. On the contrary, anybody can do it, if he is equipped with intelligence and the necessary analytical technique. It is desirable, indeed, for everybody to try, so that the professional philosophers may be drawn away from contemplating their own tradition, and that the rest of mankind may be lifted toward philosophy. If we make of the effort a co-operative enterprise, it is very likely that most of us will get there in the end.

PHILOSOPHY AND THE SCIENCES

The Greeks understood philosophy to be an organized system of all man's knowledge of the world. There were subdivisions in it, of course. There were philosophies of nature, of ethics, of politics, of logic, of the "soul," of the heavenly bodies, and indeed of medicine. Moreover, a single man, if he had sufficient opportunity for study, could hope to speak authoritatively on all these subjects. Plato, for example, seems at least twice to have condensed within the limits of one work his entire range of knowledge and conjecture.[1] Aristotle's collected works are a kind of one-man encyclopedia.

Such glories are no longer possible, for there is much too much to be known. Nowadays, a biologist, for example, not only does not know all of science, but he does not even know all of biology. He knows only his own "field" — botany, perhaps, or parasitology or genetics — and possibly but a section of that. It looks like a deliberate narrowing of range. The converse, however, is true: it is not that the scientist's individual range is narrowed, but that the total range of knowledge has grown inconceivably vast. The scientist's mind is still stretched to capacity, but he just can't get all of science into it. The bottle which once held all man's knowledge of the world is now as a pint to an ocean.

I know that it is fashionable to cry down specialization and to cry up the merit of "broad views," to depreciate analysis and excessively appreciate synthesis. But, unless I am much mistaken, the loudest admirers of broad views possess views which are broad but empty, and the most zealous advocates of synthesis have (in the absence of analysis) nothing which they can synthesize. A scientist, being forced to specialize if he is to know anything in detail, can surrender his specialty only on pain of surrendering also all the knowledge he

[1] In the *Republic* and in the *Timaeus*.

has, together with the further knowledge he may get.

The fact of specialization indicates triumph, not defeat. It proves the immensity of man's knowledge, not the poverty of it. And just as I think we cannot regret this fact when it holds for individual men, so I think we cannot regret it when it holds for individual disciplines. The long centuries during which philosophy embraced all the knowledge there was (and there wasn't much) gave way to a time when the young sciences, leaving the ancestral home, took what they needed and left the rest to philosophers. Thus "natural philosophy" became physics, chemistry, astronomy, and so forth; "political philosophy" became sociology; and "mental philosophy" became psychology. This last occurred as recently as forty years ago, amid the most horrid clamor of threats and imprecations and a free distribution of wounds, which are even yet not altogether healed.

Historically speaking, the content of philosophy is what is left over after the sciences departed. Nobody took ethics, not even the sociologists; nobody took logic; nobody took esthetics; nobody took (for who would want?) metaphysics. These subjects, therefore, remain part of philosophy's content, despite the fact that the mathematicians eye logic covetously and the gentlemen of the fine arts would like to ravish esthetics. The subjects themselves, I am happy to report, have thus far resisted all blandishments.

But we can get at the matter another way. Obviously, each scientific discipline has its limits. Physics and chemistry, for example, are very closely allied, but there must come a time when you are no longer talking physics but are talking chemistry. Chemistry and biology are also allied, but again there must come a time when you are talking biology and not chemistry. Now, each science contains large and small generalizations, the large ones being attempts to organize that entire body of knowledge. But what about generalizations which are larger than any single science? Well, when these involve two or three sciences (say, mathematics and physics or chemistry and biology) we can still leave it to the appropriate scientists to deal with them. As a matter of fact, scientific borderlands are developed in this way, and you get mathematical physics and biochemistry. But what about generalizations which exceed *all* the sciences? Any scientist could have something important to say about these, but no scientist could deal with them decisively on the basis of his own discipline.

Are there such generalizations? Of course there are, and we human beings deal with them almost every moment of every day. Take, for instance, the Second World War, which for several years involved every one of us in the most intimate manner possible. We had to make up our minds about that war, whether it was just or an unmitigated evil. Now, some people held it to be an unmitigated evil on the ground that it was exactly like the First World War, which also had been an unmitigated evil. When pressed for proof, such people might perhaps have said, "Well, history always repeats itself, and is doing so now." If we had asked, "What evidence is there for that?" they might perhaps have replied, "As a matter of fact, the whole universe behaves like a machine, doing the same thing over and over again."

Here we have a generalization, which is certainly

familiar enough, to the effect that all change is mechanical and repetitive. Now, the concept of change is something no single science can exhaust, since it is a phenomenon that all sciences have to deal with. Moreover, the different sciences give somewhat different accounts of change: change looks like "energy" when you are studying inorganic substances and like "life" when you are studying organisms. But the question actually set by opponents of the Second World War was really this: is change merely repetitive or is it the constant introduction of novelty into the world? If it is the latter, then the possibility exists that the Second World War was radically different from the First, and an entirely different evaluation might follow.

The question which began as a dispute over a social issue is now seen to have passed entirely into philosophy. No single science can answer the question. The sciences all together cannot answer the question, though their evidence would be very important. The question can be answered only by someone (who could be almost anyone) able to examine all the evidence from a point of view embracing all the evidence. That point of view would be, I think, genuinely philosophical. And if I am right in thinking so, then it will likewise be true that never, at any time, can the philosophical enterprise be wholly irrelevant to human life.

Thus there need be no great difficulty in deciding when an inquiry is philosophical. It is so whenever we deal with generalizations which exceed the reach of any science or combination of sciences. It is so whenever we deal with problems involving the nature of logic and scientific method. It is so whenever our problems involve the determination of moral values, as in fact most of our problems do in some way or other. Perhaps, to sum it all up, we can say that it is philosophy which tells us what we mean when we are talking, or whether, while talking, we indeed mean anything.

THE UTILITY OF MYTHS

"The unhappiness of man," wrote Baron d'Holbach, "is due to his ignorance of nature." It is a profound truth, and the future of mankind undoubtedly turns upon it. Knowledge is, of course, a satisfaction in itself. We are likely to feel that even if we cannot avoid the blows of circumstance, there is some consolation in knowing what hit us. Yet how much greater the satisfaction would be if we had no need to be consoled, if our knowledge of the given circumstances were transformed, by further knowledge, into control over it!

With respect to the physical universe this has very largely happened, and the achievement of it is the great gain of the past three hundred years. There is no need for us to recount here the extraordinary breadth of man's mastery over nature. It will suffice to say that the mastery is now so great that the earth's entire population can have its wants adequately supplied. We can guard ourselves against any natural catastrophe which may reasonably be expected, and we can perceive no limit to the abundance which our technology makes possible. The performance of modern men proves beyond doubt that it is knowledge, not faith, which moves actual mountains.

But when we turn to society, to man's relations with his fellows, we find no such beneficent control. The bounties drawn so skillfully from nature are not well shared, and the failure so to share them has, by a fatal reaction, impeded the producing of them. When depressions occur, we find ourselves poor for having created much. Our machines, instead of saving the labor of all, bestow leisure with wealth upon some and leisure with poverty upon many.

Wars consume and destroy us. Whole populations are tormented and enslaved because they or their territories possess desired treasures. Democratic countries, watching the rise of fascism elsewhere, have discovered in their own respectable citizens an itch for the same brutal delights. Lastly, science itself and all the techniques of impartial study confront in fascism a remorseless enemy, which spreads deceit and error as its natural breath.

At the same time, it is certainly true that we have some knowledge of human nature and of society. We have, in fact, a great deal; but it is limited, hampered, and indeed corrupted by the attempt of small and privileged groups to maintain their power. Such an attempt requires the deception of large masses of men. Accordingly, beliefs are chosen and propagated not for their conformity with science, but for their effect on human behavior. Generally speaking, truth has been suffered to exist in the world just to the extent that it profited the rulers of society. There was a time — and not so very long ago — when these rulers could not afford the knowledge that the earth is round.

In the learned world there exists a hierarchy of sciences, with mathematics and physics at the top and psychology and sociology at the bottom. Scientists in the upper ranks are lordly and secure; those in the lower ranks are partly humble and partly rebellious. The test which sustains these gradations is the test of exactness. It is commonly supposed that a discipline grows more exact as it grows more mathematical, and that there is a precise correspondence between exactness and truth. I think that this test is not without ambiguity, but in any case it is not the real reason for the hierarchy. The real reason is that the physical sciences are fairly neutral politically, while the social sciences are full of dynamite. It therefore becomes desirable to prevent the latter from acquiring prestige, and even to assert that there can be no such thing as a social science at all. Beguiled by the criterion of exactness, many physical scientists have helped to propagate just this view.

It is also true, however, that infection sets in in the social sciences themselves. I do not refer to those scholars who, having gratified their economic ambitions, obediently devote their lives to the production of arguments *ad hoc*. I refer to the fact that scholars are subject to pressure, that they are disposed to sweeten unpalatable truths, and that they bring to the study of society a point of view already conditioned by the society which is to be studied. All these difficulties can be overcome, or at any rate mitigated; but while they exist, they have the effect of making the science much less of a science than it would otherwise be. Psychology, for example, would be much more of a science if there were not so many scholars anxious to show that wage earners have relatively low I.Q.'s and that subject peoples are psychologically incapable of self-government. Sociology would be much more of a science if there were not the embarrassing necessity of playing down the effect of economics on social behavior. While axes are being ground, science cannot speak.

The physical sciences, however, need not contrive too flattering an unction out of the awe and reverence accorded them. For there was a time in history when they stood in precisely the same position as the social sciences do now. The aristocrats, who ruled feudal society (as was then believed) by divine appointment, buttressed their own dominion with an elaborate structure of myths concerning the nature of the physical universe. They looked with no tolerance whatever upon the early scientific discoveries. Bruno was burned and Galileo was threatened, not because they said true things about the world, but because the saying of true things about the world was incompatible with the lordship of aristocrats. Physical science was one of the weapons which the middle class forged against the aristocracy; the aristocracy had therefore to do all in its power to prevent the weapon's being forged. For Galileo to assert that the earth is a sphere rotating upon an axis, when feudal myth held it to be stationary and flat, was as "subversive" as for a sociologist to assert today that wars originate from the nature of capitalism. Against Galileo was launched the might of Inquisitors. Against the indiscreet sociologist is launched the might of administrators and of un-something-or-other committees.

Along with the chastening lesson that "we were once what you are now," the physical scientists might also begin to be aware that their own labors are subtly limited by economic interests. It is true that no demands are made upon them, as scientists, for the creation of myths: I have never heard any of them argue that the nature of the atom is such as to produce, when organized into human form, a profit-seeking animal. Nevertheless, during the controversy over atomic research, scientists found that they had to unite against various attempts to limit or indeed erase the entire field of study. The discovery and especially the publication of truth is always in some peril. The hierarchy of sciences will have to be resolved into an equality of partnership, if science as a whole is to prosper.

Plenty of myths still survive about the nature of the universe. There is a conviction that a leaning ladder requires to be walked around, that warts may be removed by application of a strip of bacon fried and fastened under a full moon. The daily newspapers, impartial disseminators of objective truth, still supply their readers with guidance by infallible astrology. These gentle illusions, however, have no place in physical science as such. It is different with social studies. Myths abound concerning the nature of society; and these myths will be found, stretched screaming over many a long volume, in the very heart of the science itself. There can be few tasks more important than to remove these myths, and thus to instill health and vigor into man's most valuable study — that of his own nature and destiny.

Now, myths do not profit mankind as a whole, and what is needed is rather the knowledge which can remove the causes of suffering. Nor are myths particularly profitable to any section of mankind as objects of belief by the members of the section. But myths can very well be profitable to one group when belief in them exists throughout the rest of the community. Thus, although it might be indifferent to an aristocrat whether the earth was flat or not, it was extremely important to him that his enemy, the merchant, should not know it to be round and thereupon seek out the riches of global trade. In our day the motive is the same, although the context of course is very different.

There are three main characteristics of modern society which it is the purpose of myths to conceal or excuse:

First, there is the deliberate denial of abundance. Except in wartime, we do not produce the enormous quantity of goods which our technology makes possible, and we do not develop our technology as rapidly as we might. In other words, we produce abundantly only when the purpose is destructive. When the purpose is constructive, our economy creaks and clatters to a halt.

Second, there is gross inequality in the distribution of what we do produce. The tremendous concentration of wealth at one end of the social scale is matched (perhaps overmatched) by a concentration of poverty at the other end. A dazzling prosperity in the urban rich hardly conceals the infamous and degrading lot imposed upon colonial peoples abroad and upon special victims (like the American Negro) at home. No man can look upon this scene with clear eyes and then suppose that justice is being done.

Third, there is the fact that, despite our democratic political institutions, we, the citizens of the United States, do not control our national economy. That economy is administered by a rather small group of men, and the mode of administration is fixed by the nature of the economy itself. That is to say, goods are produced, and can be produced, only if the production of them is a source of profit. It is more usual for our political institutions to obey the commands of our economy than for our economy to obey the commands of our political institutions.

If you carefully examine these three conditions, you will discover that they are such as to make myths necessary. No one in his senses would, for example, deliberately reject a society of abundance, for that would mean rejecting good housing and food and clothing and medical care and education, all of which he now spends his life trying to get for himself and his family. If men are to be prevented from moving into a society of abundance, they must be dissuaded by certain doctrines which undertake to show either (1) that the goal is impossible to attain, or (2) that the goal is undesirable.

Suppose that, undertaking point (1), you try to show that a society of abundance cannot be reached. You will not be able to argue that abundance is technologically impossible, for we have ample means to produce it and our means will grow yet more ample. No Malthus could now convince anybody that the population must necessarily outrun the food supply. The statement that abundance is impossible must therefore be made to rest upon some other basis. You might say, for instance, that human nature is ineradicably selfish and warlike, that therefore men cannot be brought to think of abundance for all, still less to work for it; but that men must be left to go on starving, torturing, and killing one another to the end of time — or of the human race. Or you might say that human nature is incapable of planning a society of abundance: there are so many "inferior" minds, and even the "best" minds cannot adequately deal with so vast a problem. In all this, you would be saying that, although abundance is technologically possible, it is psychologically impossible. Anyway, impossible.

Again suppose, undertaking point (2), you attempt to show that a society of abundance is undesirable. Now, the goal of abundance, with the ease and peacefulness of life which it would bring, is so obviously desirable that arguments to the contrary can scarcely be imagined. Nevertheless there are several. It can be said, for example, that "freedom" is better than "security," that the production of a few tough, adventurous spirits is better than the production of a multitude of pampered groundlings. It can be said that "inferior" peoples do not deserve abundance, that they wouldn't appreciate it, and that they don't want it. It can be said, further, that since there are two sides to every question, abundance probably has its disadvantages: for instance, the "soul" might drown in a bath of sensuous pleasure, if there were no rigors for it to endure. I think you will discover that men who object to abundance for all are remarkably concerned with the spiritual welfare of the underprivileged.

The other two characteristics of modern society — inequality and economic privilege — generate myths in precisely the same way. The myths about inferior races and the biologically unfit are obviously calculated to show that there can be no social or economic equality throughout mankind. The myth "That thinking makes

it so" reduces equality to a private and whimsical concept of the individual mind, and the myth "That all
problems are merely verbal" explains equality entirely
away as a meaningless term. Similarly, the myths "That
you can't change human nature," "That the rich are fit
and the poor unfit," "That you have to look out for
yourself," all contrive to justify the rule of the few
over the many. Most social myths are antidemocratic,
which is another way of saying that truth is on the side
of democracy. Most social myths are aimed at freezing
the *status quo,* which is another way of saying that the
future belongs to mankind.

What are the groups which profit by social myths?
Well, plainly they are the ones profiting by the present
organization of society. They are the monopolists and
cartelists whose wealth derives from the labor of domes-
tic and colonial populations. I shall refer to these groups
sometimes as "reactionaries" and sometimes as "fascists."
The distinction is perhaps subtle, but it is certainly important. Reactionaries are men who maintain their
privileged economic position within a context of political democracy; fascists are men who propose to overthrow political democracy on behalf of their privileged
economic position. Obviously there is a shift from the
one group into the other: Krupp the reactionary had
no difficulty in becoming Krupp the fascist. The shift
is accelerated whenever democratic institutions are
used to limit the power of reactionaries. For the freedom which reactionaries admire is the freedom to produce cheaply and sell dear; the equality which they
admire is that of equally low wages; and the fraternity
they admire is that of millions of obedient workers,

toiling contentedly from sunrise to sunset at machines which they do not own, making goods they will never possess.

THE ANALYSIS OF MYTHS

It would be a mistake to think of these myths as sheer inventions whose purpose existed already in the mind of the inventor. Rather, they are more likely to be notions which have lain around in various works and in various minds until their propaganda value is suddenly discovered. Take, for instance, the idea that individual things are real but that classes and systems are abstractions — an idea which Mr. Stuart Chase propounded in *The Tyranny of Words*. This doctrine is very old. It can be found in Greek philosophy, but especially it is the medieval theory called Nominalism, which had in its day a very revolutionary effect. The theory was never true. Its effect in the fourteenth century was revolutionary, because it was then directed against the feudal system. As Mr. Chase used it in the twentieth century, its effect was reactionary, because it was used to paralyze the anti-fascist struggle.[2]

Or take Herbert Spencer's belief that poverty is a sign of biological unfitness. It cannot be said that Spencer produced this theory with the conscious intent of justifying economic competition. He was merely struck with the analogy between jungle life and the economic behavior of the mid-nineteenth century. It seemed to him

[2] See *infra*, Chapter IX.

that the laws of the former might not unreasonably be transferred to the latter, and he worked out his idea accordingly. His results were greeted by acclaim, but I imagine that to the end of his life he never had the faintest notion that he had been all along a propagandist.

Some of the myths, moreover, contain a core of truth, but are overlaid with so much ambiguity and misapplication that the core is altogether obscured. The myth, however, retains a sort of atmosphere of being true. Such myths have a considerable advantage over the others, which have to be tremendously heated before they will display a convincing fire. There is, for example, a true sense in which human nature never changes, and there is a true sense in which every question has two sides. But the inferences which would flow from these true senses are precisely contrary to the inferences sought. The myth-makers who ride these doctrines, therefore, will find them very unreliable mounts, which are capable of unseating the rider at the least mistake.

In a sense, this is the case with all myths, whether half-true or wholly false. One of the pleasantest tasks of the critic is to show that, even if the myth were true, it would either not prove what is desired to be proved, or would prove exactly the opposite. Consider the doctrine that life is a struggle in which the fit survive and the unfit perish. This doctrine is supposed to show that we ought not to have doles and social insurance generally, because such measures help the unfit to survive at the expense of the fit. Spencer himself opposed public education on just such grounds. Well, now, suppose that life *is* a struggle, and suppose that the impoverished masses of mankind join their forces and overthrow the power of the rich. It would follow (would it not?) that the impoverished masses had demonstrated in a most convincing way that *they* were the fit, and the rich the unfit. In other words, Spencer's doctrine will justify revolution as well as the *status quo*. When you justify violence as a general condition of things, you are not entitled to pick the winners in advance. At all events, a theory which provides equal justification for precisely opposite actions must be in its essence nonsensical.

But, though the myths have various origins, they have a common means of propagation. In all their forms they pour through the avenues of communication: the press, the radio, the library, the lecture platform. They constitute the points of view from which the news is impartially interpreted. Everybody examines the news, and nobody examines the views. The idea that there are two sides to every question will be accepted as reasonable, if vague, and on the basis of it our commentator proceeds to show the good things among the bad on the reactionary side and the bad things among the good on the democratic side. The idea that human nature never deviates from selfishness will also be accepted as reasonable, and on the basis of it our commentator proceeds to eliminate from the news every trace of nobility, self-sacrifice, or social-mindedness — at least among democrats.

Indeed, the whole profession of news-interpreter is founded upon the supposition that people do not mean what they say. If the words of public figures could always, or often, be taken at their face value, there would be nothing for the interpreters to interpret except the actual course of historical events. But this would require them to have a knowledge of history and would abolish their status as men of "inside information." Now there cannot be an inside unless there is an outside, and there cannot be hidden truths unless there is a cover which conceals them. The news interpreters must therefore assume the existence of that cover, and must persuade their listeners that it was placed there by the natural mendacity of man.

The results are striking. In the course of one year, a columnist will write perhaps 350 columns, allowing for paid vacations. In ten years, he will have written 3,500 columns; and in twenty years, 7,000. At the rate of 500 words per column, he will have achieved a total of 3,500,000 words, and still be going strong — or, if not strong, at least going. Now, there are columnists who have reached these heights without even once, in all the 7,000 columns and the 3,500,000 words, saying a single adjectival kind or cordial thing about the human race. Word after word, sentence after sentence, the lines of print have crept like elongating serpents about the world, and now stretch out to set their teeth upon the stars. But in no word or sentence, and in no line of print, have these writers ever once sided with men against the oppressors of men, ever once hinted so much as a twinge of sympathy for the weak and the monstrously abused. "Shall we," they will say, "bite the hand that feeds us?" They would not if they could, and they could not if they would, for satiety weakens the jaws.

Since social myths provide the background against which interpretations are presented and policies described, it is clear that we shall never rightly understand either the interpretations or the policies until we have erased the illusory background and substituted one of truth. This task is one for which philosophers are peculiarly fitted, and it is one which they have thus far studiously declined. As a result, their books are largely unread, and their classrooms are embarrassingly empty. For who wants to meditate upon the question whether values are "ingrained in the structure of the universe," while editors and commentators and politicians are expressing doubt whether the common man deserves a quart of milk each day? And who wants to debate the question whether the universe is friendly, while diplomats are fondling the atomic bomb?

In thus expending their energies upon irrelevant issues, philosophers have forgotten their own tradition, especially that part of it which flowered in the seventeenth and eighteenth centuries. For this was a time when philosophers great and small busied themselves with tearing to pieces all the myths which supported feudal society. Of that fabulous structure, whose base sprang out of earth and whose top touched heaven, they left not one stone upon another. From the time when Descartes sapped the main gate to the time when Kant exploded the powder magazine, the work went forward carefully, eagerly, and even gaily. The defenders of the citadel were frantic but powerless, nailed each to his own place of shelter by the deadly small-arms fire of Voltaire and the Encyclopedists.

How was the ruin accomplished? By showing the inner absurdity of the myths and their lack of correspondence with fact. By stripping from the physical universe and from human history all notions of miraculous events. For, obviously, the real existence of miracles, which are contraventions of the normal course of things, would turn the world from a system into a chaos, would wrench it from human control, and would place it at the whim of some supernatural being, whether deity or devil. Such a world would respond to witchcraft but not to science. The sorcerer would triumph over the physicist.

The social myths of the twentieth century are comparably miraculous. If, for example, a man with a "white" skin were really to be, for that very reason, more virtuous and more valuable than a man with a "black" skin, that would be a prodigy surpassing even Jonah's sojourn within the whale. If it were really true that biological evolution had toiled from the ancient Reptilia, through myriad intermediate forms of life, toward the ultimate creation of industrial magnates, that would be a miracle more astounding than ever Joshua achieved with the obedient sun. If it were really true that truth is what anyone thinks it is at any given time, or that problems can be solved by application to a dictionary, the entire world would become so thoroughly miraculous as to obliterate all means of recognizing anything, including the miracles themselves.

A philosophical analysis of social myths would proceed in the manner I suggested toward the beginning of this chapter. It would undertake to establish the actual meaning of the myth, if in fact the myth has a meaning. It would compare this meaning with objective data drawn from all the relevant sciences. It would reveal what statements the myth presupposes and what statements the myth further implies. And lastly, it would be careful to show the effect of the myth upon human behavior, by asking what anyone would do who held the myth to be true. The general result is to make it quite plain that the myth is out of accord with fact, that it assumes absurdities or implies them, and that it either paralyzes action toward a better world or stimulates action toward a worse one. In other words, myths make the believer an escapist or a storm trooper.

The myths I have assembled and analyzed in this volume are far, of course, from exhausting the possible choices. I think, however, that they may claim to be both widespread and fundamental. They are genuinely philosophical in that they are among the larger generalizations, and from them flow a multitude of specific applications. They involve, moreover, many of the classic philosophical problems, so that anyone who is acquainted with the history of thought will readily perceive the machinery which is used to construct them.

Two of the myths, "That You Cannot Mix Art and Politics" and "That You Have to Look Out for Yourself," are concerned with the theory of value, the first being an esthetic problem and the second an ethical. Four others, "That There Are Two Sides to Every Question," "That Thinking Makes It So," "That All Problems Are Merely Verbal," and "That Words Can Never Hurt Me," have to do with the theory of knowledge, and indeed they very nearly exhaust that subject among them. The remaining four are explicitly concerned with the nature of man and society. They are somewhat smaller generalizations than the others as regards the whole range of human knowledge, but in their area they are basic. That is to say, if they were truths instead of myths, they would suffice to overturn what is now recognized to be knowledge in that area.

And now, I suppose, one may invite the reader inward, whether he be philosopher by choice, by chance, or by instinct. I cannot, perhaps, hope to have slain so many dragons. If any are left stirring amid their wounds, it would be generous for you yourself to dispatch them.

CHAPTER II THAT YOU CAN'T CHANGE HUMAN NATURE

CONCERNING the world and all that is in it man has had many strange opinions, but none more strange than those about himself. From time to time he has been thought the victim of chance or of fate, the sport of gods or of demons, the nursling of divinity or of nature, the "rubbish of an Adam" or evolution's last and fairest animal. He has spun mythical genealogies and embroidered those that were actual. He has mourned lost Edens, golden ages, states of nature; and with equal conviction he has awaited new heavens, new paradises, and new perfections. He has explored the cosmos, and he has mastered the atom. He has seemed to know everything except himself.

One reason is that knowledge is manifested in control. If a man builds a bridge capable of sustaining all sorts of traffic, you will readily believe that he understands engineering. But evidence of this sort, which is the living testimony of practice, is singularly absent in social affairs. We have already had occasion to observe that, however much men may control the physical universe, they exert far less conscious, planned control over their relations with one another. In these, the most important of all matters, men seem more ignorant than perhaps they really are.

This seeming ignorance can be found, also, in the anarchic state of psychological theory. There is no single, reigning doctrine to which psychologists assent, as physicists do to the theory of relativity. On the contrary, there are various doctrines which compete for acceptance. Some of them, like the Freudian, hold that human behavior is decisively conditioned by inborn impulses; others, like the Behaviorist, hold that it is decisively conditioned by environmental influences. This welter of opinion suggests that the science is still immature and that its assemblage and analysis of data is very incomplete.

Immature as psychology may be, there is no reason to suppose that it will not grow, or that successful generalizations about the data will never be made. Further study will presumably reveal such generalizations, and an increasing stability in man's social relationships would undoubtedly speed the process. Meanwhile, one must look with some caution upon all psychological theories, including, I suppose, the one I shall present in this chapter.

The unsettled state of psychology, however, is favorable to the perpetuation of myths; and the myths, so long as they survive, retard the progress of the science itself. Men who have their social conclusions already in mind can borrow freely from what appears to be scientific data, there being no doctrine of sufficient authority to prevent such practices. Moreover, we are all of us men living among men, and our experiences of one another generate, almost unsolicited, certain convictions about human nature. That is to say, we are all of us amateur psychologists, and we bestow upon our views the sort of mystical accuracy which a believer in home remedies opposes to the advice of physicians.

In such a climate illusions multiply, and among them there is, I suppose, none more ubiquitous than the idea that "you can't change human nature." This ancient platitude might long ago have been relegated to a home for superannuated ideas, were it not so constantly useful. It has been voiced by a motley congregation of sinners and saints, rulers and slaves, philosophers, monks, theologians, psychiatrists, journalists, statesmen, and professors. Everyone has said it; many have believed it; few have understood it.

Its uses are multifarious. Is there poverty in the world? That's because men are naturally improvident. Are people unemployed? That's because men are naturally lazy. Are there wars? That's because men are naturally belligerent. Do men cheat, injure, and bankrupt one another in economic competition? That's because men naturally act on the profit motive. Have some men been slaves when others were slaveowners, or serfs when others were kings? That's because they were all born to be so, each in his kind.

Or again: Do we wish to prevent the development of criminals and to rehabilitate those already made? It's no use: you can't change human nature. Do we wish to enact justice and equality among races? It's no use: you can't change human nature. Do we wish to spread the enlightenment of science to all mankind? It's no use: you can't change human stupidity.

Or again, a much more cautious variant: Do we wish to extend the suffrage to millions now without it? Impossible: they must be educated first. Do we wish to abolish the several discriminations against Jews and Negroes? Impossible: people's "attitudes" must be changed first. Do we wish to make decisive improvements in the nature of society? Impossible: men's souls must first be changed, "materialism" giving way to "spirituality."

It may appear that the views in this last category assume the possibility of changing human nature. That appearance, however, is illusory, for the change which is assumed is completely divorced from the social milieu in which alone change can occur. It therefore becomes an abstract conception, floating agreeably in the minds of its possessors.

Take, for example, the disfranchisement of American Negroes. Our imaginary antagonist says that he is democratically fond of Negroes, but that he does not think they should vote until they have been educated. Very well, let us admire his democratic fondness. But the Negroes will not be adequately educated until they have adequate access to schools. They will not have adequate access to schools until there are adequate legislative appropriations. There will be no adequate legislative appropriations until legislators are elected who will really represent the disfranchised. Few such legislators will be elected until the disfranchised are allowed to vote. Thus our friend, in postponing the suffrage, postpones also the education which is supposed to qualify voters for the suffrage. The change he says he desires is one which he has rendered impossible, and cynics may surmise that he never really desired it.

It is easy enough to be an idealist so long as ideals are unrelated to action. Such men, when pressed with arguments or when confronted with the necessity of decision, will retreat into the assertion that there is no real change anyhow, that all we do is to tinker with externals. For the advocacy of impossible change is in fact the advocacy of no change at all. The third of our categories, then, reduces to the other two. These will repay study.

The opinions in the first category undertake to explain certain economic and political arrangements by asserting that men "naturally" act that way. This assertion is more than a simple statement of fact; it is an implicit justification. The point of view is what is hopefully called "realistic," and its holders may discourse largely, if not profoundly, upon the immutable laws which nature or nature's God have fixed in human affairs. The spectacle of planetary motion has always been watched with approval and indeed with awe. Transfer these feelings to a no less inevitable human motion, and you find that even the follies and brutalities of men begin to acquire a cosmic grandeur. The hard-headed realist (I use his own chosen title) gives rein to sentiment and surrenders himself happily to an invincible *status quo*.

The second group of opinions is very much like the first, except that it has abandoned ethics altogether. The proponents of these views disport themselves more blithely, being unencumbered by moral issues. Wars, they will agree, are certainly very bad, and so is starvation. But the question, they will say, is not what you want but what you can have; and, human nature being what it is, you must have wars and starvation. Equality is no doubt very admirable, but unluckily there is the "fact" that some people are inferior to others and cannot possibly be made equal with them.

Here we have the realist who would be an idealist if horse sense were not always neighing in his ear. He agrees fully with every principle found to be noble, by which agreement he assures you that his heart is in the right place, wherever that doubtful position may be determined to be. He does not entertain principles; they entertain him. He combines the pleasures of virtue with the comforts of inaction. One may imagine his happiness.

In all these varieties of opinion and temperament we can now detect a common purpose. That purpose is not the enlightenment of mankind through the radiance of a scientific fact. It is, on the contrary, the prevention of social change through the gloom of a disillusioning fiction. If men can be persuaded that between them and their hearts' desire lies an impassable barrier, they will (so it is thought) cease their struggles after improvement, and content themselves instead with such crumbs as circumstance vouchsafes them. Quieted by such a philosophy, they may work out their brief lives in the knowledge that toil, defeat, death, and all other disasters which beset them beset them naturally.

Now we can observe the bones on which this argument hangs its melancholy flesh. Human nature is said to be unalterable in certain respects, and these respects are such as to prevent any significant improvement in the condition of man. In other words, no matter how glamorous the prospects and persuasive the programs, men will go on acting in the old ways which have brought so much disaster. If such were really the case, then the only sensible thing to do would be to discard the programs and forget the prospects, even though the discarding and the forgetting mean an end to every human hope.

The respects in which human nature is said to be unalterable are mainly two: (1) that men are universally and incurably selfish, and (2) that in the mass men are stupid and ineducable, or at least that they have not sufficient intelligence to direct human affairs with any sort of wisdom. If the first of these statements is true, then undoubtedly it will follow that there can never be a stable, co-operative society among men. If the second is true, then mankind will never be able to protect itself against the evils of fortune or of social dislocations. The consequences are appalling. Are the statements really true? Let us see.

THE INCURABLE SELFISHNESS OF MAN

From Thrasymachus through Machiavelli down to their followers in the present day, a long line of dismal commentators has proclaimed this doctrine in accents of ill-concealed pleasure.[1] Acceptance of it is supposed to be the essence of wordly wisdom and even, theologically speaking, a means of salvation. It seems odd that

[1] For a detailed account see *infra.*, Chapter VIII.

one should expect to enter heaven upon the assumption that one is a creature of hell; but, unless I misread the authorities, this is precisely what they assert.

At any rate, the term "selfishness" means what is sometimes called man's inhumanity to man, the sacrifice of other people's interests to one's own advantage. The extreme example of this is the form of organized violence which is war. Accordingly, we hear on all sides the assertion that war can never be abolished, because it has its source in the unchangeable nature of man. Let us look at a few expressions of this view:

Man is a beast of prey. I shall say it again and again . . . Conflict is the original fact of life, is life itself, and not the most pitiful pacifist is able entirely to uproot the pleasure it gives his inmost soul.[2]

It was in his [Dr. Charles W. Mayo's] opinion absurd to imagine that it would ever be possible to abolish war. War is part of our human inheritance and hence lies beyond our control.[3]

Nothing done at San Francisco will alter the essential nature of man — in which are buried the complex causes of war.[4]

Mr. Baldwin proceeded to accept this "fact" with a stoicism worthy of a military analyst:

The guiding star still shines; it cannot be attained in a century or two. But it is nevertheless worth struggling for-

[2] Oswald Spengler: "The Return of the Caesars," *American Mercury*, Vol. 31, p. 137.

[3] John M. Fletcher: "Human Nature and World Peace," *Virginia Quarterly Review*, Vol. 20, p. 351. Mr. Fletcher takes the opposite view.

[4] Hanson W. Baldwin: "San Francisco Outlook," the *New York Times*, May 21, 1945, p. 10.

ward, pushing on; it would be worth the effort even if we knew the star was a mirage. Death is an accepted part of life. Yet death is no cause for despair. The whole philosophy of man is keyed to the conception of the ultimate triumph of life over death. Why, then, despair because war recurs?

Why despair? Because in war one's friends get killed, one's children get killed, and one gets killed oneself. Because everything one has built may be destroyed. Because it is idiocy to fight one war for the sake of fighting another later on. If human nature really does inevitably produce war, let us accept the fact without surrounding it with this comfortless nonsense.

One may take some encouragement from the fact that Mr. Baldwin thinks it worth while to chase after mirages. In other words, he thinks that some illusions are valuable for the entire human race. Now a man who thinks that some illusions are valuable is a man who will be a little careless of the distinction between illusion and reality. Perhaps, then, he is deceived about the connection between human nature and war. I think we shall find that he certainly is, and that Herr Spengler (the converted Nazi) and Dr. Mayo are deceived also.

I have said that war is an extreme case of man's inhumanity to man. It is, therefore, a limit to a certain kind of behavior. If we can show that this kind of behavior is not an essential part of human nature, then the limiting case will not be an essential part of human nature either. For example, extreme brilliance would be the limiting case of a burning light. Then, if it can be shown that the light does not necessarily burn at all, we can infer that the light does not necessarily have extreme brilliance.

Let us ask ourselves, then, whether everything that men do involves loss and sacrifice for other people. There is no question that *some* of the things men do are things which have this effect. But do *all* of them? The answer is plainly, no. So far as one's personal relations with one's fellows are concerned, the proportion of such acts is relatively small. On a social scale the proportion is rather larger; but even here the division of labor, which is a basic social fact, no matter how competitive the society may be, is a sort of unconsciously co-operative behavior on behalf of the general good. A society in which nobody ever did anything for the benefit of others would be one in which no division of labor could exist. It would, indeed, hardly be a society at all.

Well, then, we have established the fact that some of the things men do are things which benefit other people, although of course some of the things are not so. We can infer from this that behavior which benefits other people is at least as consistent with human nature as behavior which harms other people. This being true, it is plainly impossible to say that human nature is selfish in the sense that selfishness is present in all human actions.

Nevertheless, granting all this, it might still be true that selfishness exists in human nature side by side with social-mindedness, and that, as such, it is ineradicable. Expressed in concrete terms, such a view would mean that there are some things which men so profoundly need and desire that they will injure other people in order to get them. Apparently there are such things. But before you can predict that men will universally and inevitably commit these injuries for the sake of these gains, you must make one further and very important assumption: you must assume *that the gains are obtainable in no other way.* For if the gains are obtainable in some other way (by co-operation, for instance), what reason have you to suppose that men will not choose it? The only sufficient reason would be that human behavior is always selfish. But we have just established the falsity of that assertion. You have, therefore, no reason at all.

Suppose, now, it is said that all men have desires, that they seek to satisfy these desires, and that in this manner they constantly display an interest in themselves. Undoubtedly they do. No man has any desires except his own, and in satisfying them he may be said to display self-interest. But self-interest is not selfishness. Self-interest is the satisfaction of one's desires; selfishness is the satisfaction of one's desires at the expense of someone else. We may grant that self-interest is an essential part of human nature. I think, indeed, that it is. But we are still very far from being able to infer from this that selfishness is an essential part of human nature. We cannot possibly infer that it is so, unless we assume that all our desires are satisfied at cost to someone else. This concealed assumption, like the one previously discussed, is plainly false. We satisfy our desires in common with other people every day of our lives, and indeed the satisfaction of some of our desires *involves* the satisfaction of other people's. If this were not so, the institution of the meal, for example, would be wholly inconceivable.

Since we have now come to the question of desires, let us ask what it is that human beings may be said generally to want. If we set aside deceptive abstractions like "power," and if we attend to what may be called normal desires, as distinguished from manias and perversions (*i.e.* pathological states), we shall find that men chiefly want food, shelter, clothing, companionship, play, and sexual love. So far as one can tell from introspection into one's own behavior and from observation of other people's, both present and past, these desires are universal and basic. They are, furthermore, necessary conditions for the maintenance of the individual and of the race. It would make sense to say that human nature will always produce behavior in accordance with these desires.

But where is the "inevitable" selfishness? In themselves these desires certainly seem innocent, and at least two of them — companionship and sexual love — are social in their very essence. Upon so bland a substance how can the idea of human depravity be imposed? If such desires are in their own nature evil, then we shall be doing wrong every time we eat or play or put on a suit of clothes. Surely it is obvious that evil cannot exist in the desires themselves, but only in the way they are sometimes satisfied. The point of view which would consider these *desires* evil would be the point of view of a despot whose power is imperiled by the needs of common men. Indeed, it seems probable that precisely this is the social origin of the myth of human selfishness.

Let us recapitulate the argument. We have seen that

not all, but only some, of men's acts involve injury to other people and thus merit the adjective "selfish." The selfishness of these acts, however, derives not from the desires which prompted them, but the conditions under which they are performed. But if human nature were inherently selfish, then it would have to be so under any and all conditions. It is so, however, only under some conditions. Human nature, therefore, is not inherently selfish. This argument is a *modus tollens* to the greater glory of the human race.

We can now return to the limiting case from which we started. If, as we see, there is nothing in human nature which necessitates men's injuring one another, then there is nothing in human nature which necessitates war. War can occur under certain conditions, but there is nothing in human nature which renders inevitable the existence of such conditions. As far as human nature is concerned, those conditions need not exist. I think, in fact, that human nature is such that men will one day render such conditions impossible. For, as things now stand, either men will render war impossible or war will render men impossible.

It is worth while to observe, also, that war is far more repugnant to human nature than consistent with it. If war were consistent with human nature in the same sense in which companionship, for example, is consistent with human nature, then war would be a state in which men felt free and at ease. Exactly the reverse, of course, is true. War is in fact so repugnant to normal human behavior that men have to be drafted into it, and all modern armies provide staffs of psychiatrists to care for the psychological ills which war engenders. Happiness is a good test of what conditions are in harmony with human nature, and by that test war must seem to be unnatural indeed.

One thing more remains to be said. The doctrine that human nature is incurably selfish is not just an assertion about a supposed fact; it is also a moral judgment of condemnation. Like other social myths, it contains a fusion (not to say, a confusion) of scientific and moral concepts. We are told not only that men are what they are, but that they are bad, too. Apparently, to see is to disapprove, to know is to condemn. We may wonder, perhaps, how creatures so dyed in villainy were ever able to conceive the moral standards by which they condemn themselves, how sinners so inveterate could ever have thought that they might be improved. But the moral judgment has certain social effects of its own, and these require examination.

If human nature is unalterably selfish, then to the extent that it is so, all men share an equal guilt. "In Adam's fall we sinnéd all." But if it is true as a fundamental fact that all men are equally guilty, then no man and no group of men can be singled out as especially iniquitous. Furthermore, there is a feeling that one sinner has no right to condemn another. From these conditions two social results follow:

(1) It becomes impossible to identify any one man or any one group of men as the source of social injustice and therefore as a menace to human welfare. Such a man or such a group of men can hide behind the alleged common and equal guilt of all, and thus escape condemnation. The exploiter and the profiteer and the colonial imperialist can say, "I'm only being human."

In fact, that is exactly what they do say. The essence of Goering's defense at the Nuremberg trial was that he did exactly what anybody else would have done.

(2) It becomes impossible for any of us to claim the moral right to put an end to injustice. For if it is true that all men are equally sinners and that no sinner is entitled to condemn another, then none of us has the right to condemn profiteers and exploiters and imperialists. I well remember, during the Spanish Civil War, the assertions of the Reverend Mr. A. J. Muste that all nations had been guilty of aggression and that therefore no nation had the right to oppose German and Italian aggression in Spain. Such an argument is paralyzing. If we had taken it as our guide, we should simply have surrendered on high moral grounds to the Axis fascists.

Here, then, I think we have the true social reason for the doctrine of human selfishness. It exists because it has a special function to perform, not because it has any correspondence with fact. It exists because it conceals the men of power and their antisocial behavior. It exists because it robs us of the moral confidence necessary to attack them. It is, therefore, one of many ideological chains fastened upon mankind. Men may commit sins, but they can commit no sin so monstrous as believing themselves to be incurable.

THE INCURABLE STUPIDITY OF MAN

Although, as we now perceive, there is nothing in human nature to prevent by selfishness the attainment of a better world, there remains the possibility that men lack, and cannot acquire, the intelligence necessary to attain it. It might be the case that absolute stupidity reigns over mankind, or, to take a less extreme view, that human intelligence is weak by comparison with the problems it would have to solve if men were to control their own destiny.

The public journals are not lacking in comments of this sort. Writers (as I can testify) have a disposition to believe that passage into print necessarily involves a manifestation of intelligence. These manifestations, which are sometimes a little ghostly and sometimes a little ghastly, are thought to ennoble the writer above the reader, and immeasurably so above those who will not read. After this manner mused an essayist of the late 'thirties:

How do people who write, lecture, travel, entertain, and achieve positions of prestige and the front page suppose that a humble person occupies his time? He eats. He mates. He watches his children, a ball game, or a fight and talks about these matters. What else is there for him to do? [5]

The essayist must forgive me if I find the life of the "humble person," as she describes it, to be not without fullness and interest. Nor is there such a chasm between the humble and the famed. I do not know how many of the people who write, lecture, travel, entertain, and achieve positions of prestige go to ball games, but it is fairly well known that they are moderately given to mating. They may even have children, and, having chil-

[5] Eleanor R. Wembridge: "The Danger of the High Hat," the *Forum*, Vol. 94, p. 310. The next quotation is on p. 307.

dren, may even watch them. However, the essayist set forth these somber generalizations:

Do the ignorant repudiate wisdom because they do not understand it? Or is it because, understanding it, they are merely angered by it? I conclude that both these explanations are correct.

These statements may be taken to represent the snobbish, or merely vulgar, version of the presumed stupidity of mankind. There exists, however, another version, much subtler and more philosophical, which emphasizes not so much the general prevalence of stupidity as the fatal inadequacy of even the best human thought. When capitalism was rocked by its last depression, there arose various demands for a reconstruction of the system which would substitute social planning for the anarchy of individual planning. The demands were not unreasonable, and defenders of the older view, who nevertheless recognized reasonableness when they saw it, were obliged to assert that social planning, though desirable, could not be contrived. This assertion they based upon a melancholy comparison between the magnitude of the problem and the weakness of human mind. Mr. Walter Lippmann, whose views are sometimes less sedate than his style, expounded the theory at length and in very level language. Said he:

The essential limitation, therefore, of all policy, of all government, is that the human mind must take a partial and simplified view of existence. The ocean of experience cannot be poured into the little bottles of our intelligence. The mind is an instrument evolved through the struggle for existence, and the strain of concentrating upon a chain of reasoning is like standing rigidly straight, a very fatiguing posture, which must soon give way to the primordial disposition to crouch or sit down.[6]

The question of postures is interesting. One gets an impression of Mr. Lippmann writing his essays on the mantelpiece, and then, having thus thought and written, curling up on the sofa in honest fatigue. For my part, I must be candid enough to say that this entire book has been written from a crouch, which, primordial or not, I have found very comfortable. But perhaps Mr. Lippmann's title, "The Government of Posterity," refers not to later generations, but to a new anatomical location for thought.

The argument, as Mr. Lippmann states it, is analogical; and all analogical arguments are formally invalid. This one is by no means the best of a fallacious lot. For the question is not whether you can stand up indefinitely, but whether you can stand up long enough to achieve whatever purpose you had. You cannot, it is perfectly true, concentrate indefinitely upon a chain of reasoning. The question is, can you concentrate long enough to get the desired result?

At this point, I think one must be struck by the fact that the whole theory had to be shelved in wartime. Obviously no nation, and no coalition of nations, could prosecute a global war upon the theory that social problems are too vast for men to understand. To hold any such view would be to surrender to chance the achievement of victory and to paralyze with scepticism every strategic plan and political program. If social affairs can be well enough understood for whole peoples to be successfully mobilized for war, it will take a transcendental Lippmann to show that they cannot be so mobilized for peace. The man who told us in 1936 that "it is therefore an illusion to imagine a credible meaning in the idea that human evolution can be brought under conscious control" will have to tell us in 1947 that it is an illusion *not* to suppose such a meaning.

When an argument is thus refuted by the actual course of events, there must be something wrong with the argument. And there is. When Mr. Lippmann says that "the ocean of experience cannot be poured into the little bottles of our intelligence," he is thinking of each individual man (*quâ* bottle) singly facing the universe. Now, it is perfectly true that no individual man can comprehend the whole of reality, although the greatest of modern philosophers, Spinoza, thought even this possible. But the case is very different when we consider not one man trying to know the universe, but mankind trying to know it. Science is a social possession; that is to say, it belongs to all scientists taken in their relations with one another. The relatively small knowledge which each has acts upon the small knowledge of the others, and generates in time a true and universal knowledge like the theory of relativity, and a true and universal application like the development of atomic energy. It may well be that no single man can know society and the physical world sufficiently to control them, but there can hardly be any question that *mankind as a whole* can do both.

What has Mr. Lippmann demonstrated, then? He has shown that a society managed by individual wills, acting anarchically, will be a society in which the welfare of men is left very largely to chance. He has shown that, if we want to eliminate chance and to replace it with control, then mankind must manage its affairs co-operatively and together. It is true that he didn't stand up long enough to reach this conclusion. Perhaps, however, other people can.

It seems curious that Americans, whose own history testifies triumphantly to the achievements of mother-wit, should believe for one moment in the incorrigible stupidity of mankind. Not American history alone, but all history, refutes the notion. Men have seldom been more universally ignorant than they were in the Middle Ages, when the victims of disease were treated according to astrology, and the vicissitudes of life were attributed with equal improbability to the influence of saints, on the one hand, and of demons, on the other. Yet man has contrived to emerge at least partially from this state and to produce the science and technology of the modern world. And all this was accomplished in a vast school of social experience, where, from their own struggles and from the solving of immediate problems, men learned to know the world and to master it.

Finally, though you and I may continue to believe that man's intelligence is too weak ever to control his destiny, we had better remember that the actual rulers of society believe no such thing. On the contrary, they are fully convinced of their own ability to control society and manipulate it as they please. The myth is intended not for them, but for us. And whenever their acts produce an obvious social disaster, they use the myth exactly as they do the one about human selfishness, for it enables them to blame the disaster upon the alleged errors of mankind rather than upon their own. Thus:

We cannot prevent war unless we recognize that its final source, its ultimate cause, does not lie in the wickedness of rulers and diplomats, nor in the avarice of international financiers and armament makers, nor in "the contradictions of capitalism." The primary cause is the defective political judgment of the ordinary man and voter.[7]

So you see that diplomatic intrigues and the competition for markets have had nothing to do with these wars. The wars were our fault for having had such defective judgment. Perhaps there is some truth in this. But would the diplomats and the market-seekers like it better if our judgment were more keen?

HUMAN NATURE AND SOCIAL CHANGE

Besides concealing the misdeeds of rulers, the doctrine that you can't change human nature has a larger purpose: defense of the existing social arrangements. Since these arrangements are, throughout most of the world, capitalist in character, the doctrine undertakes to show that, human nature being what it is, capitalism is the inevitable form of society. If by the term "capitalism" we understand a society in which the land and the

[7] Sir Norman Angell: "Peace and the Common Man," *American Mercury,* Vol. 59, p. 251.

means of production are owned and controlled by individual men, whose incentive is profit, then the opposite of such a society would be one in which the land and the means of production are owned and controlled by society, with the incentive, not of profit, but of the simple production of goods. Accordingly, the doctrine that you can't change human nature has, as part of its purpose, the task of showing that, human nature being what it is, socialism is impossible. Here are three examples:

We believed that personal incentive and private initiative were fundamental to the continuity of progress, and that, whatever safeguards we might have to erect against a few lawless men and a few lawless enterprises, we must not destroy the dynamic that personal incentive and private initiative give to life and enterprise.[8]

There are only two motives that make human beings work. One of them is the fear of punishment and the other is the hope of reward. Fear of punishment is what drives the slave to toil under the lash of a superior or boss. The hope of profit or reward is the incentive that inspires the efforts of freemen. If you destroy the incentive system, what they call the capitalistic system, the profit system, you destroy the initiative of the American people. Instead of freemen toiling under the glorious inspiration of the hope of reward, we all become the slaves of the state, driven to our tasks by fear of punishment.[9]

[8] Glenn Frank: "The Outlook for American Institutions," *Vital Speeches,* Vol. 4, p. 52.

[9] From the remarks of the Hon. John Rankin, in the *Congressional Record* for June 17, 1943, p. 5978. Shades of Jeremy Bentham and the "two sovereign masters"! The philosophy of a man who advocated universal suffrage has descended to a man who defends the poll tax.

The chief defect of the socialistic method has been clearly demonstrated by the experience of the last few years. It does not take into account human nature, it is therefore outside of reality, in that it will not recognize that the most powerful spring of human activities lies in individual self-interest and that therefore the elimination from the economic field of this interest results in complete paralysis.[10]

Very well. Suppose, now, that we ask the questions: Which is "outside of reality," the Italian Fascist State or the Union of Soviet Socialist Republics? In which is the paralysis complete? Events have dealt very sadly with Rocco's assertions. Indeed, the continuing existence of the Soviet Union is a source of deep perplexity, for by all the reasoning of the best economists it ought to have vanished long ago, as inconsistent with human nature. The theory can now be harmonized with the facts only upon the supposition that the Soviet Union is a capitalist state after all. This supposition is easy enough to test: take a hundred thousand dollars with you into the Soviet Union, and see whether you will be permitted to build and equip a factory and to employ workmen. You will not get such permission, and that is exactly the difference between a socialist and a capitalist nation.

Instead of discussing the merits of the two systems, where they might have some reasonable arguments, opponents of the Soviet Union have for years encumbered themselves with the extraordinary paradox of

[10] Alfredo Rocco: "The Political Doctrine of Fascism," a speech delivered at Perugia in 1925. It is reprinted entire in D. O. Wagner's *Social Reformers,* Macmillan, New York, 1939. The quotation will be found on p. 654.

believing socialism to be at one and the same time dangerous and on the verge of collapse. They have invoked the "defensive" aid of boycotts, treaties, and armed intervention against a nation which their own theory demonstrated to be powerless. The theory was internally consistent, for, if socialism were profoundly contrary to human nature, it could establish no industrial system, raise and equip no armies, and achieve no popular support. But the theory turned out to have no correspondence with fact.

What was wrong in the theory was the act of defining human nature narrowly in terms of behavior characteristic of one social system only. The mistake could readily have been avoided, without regard to socialist antipathies, simply by recognizing that human nature had at one time been consistent with feudalism, at an earlier time with chattel slavery, and at a still earlier time with various patriarchal arrangements. There need not even have been an appeal to history: an anthropological survey of societies existing in the contemporary world would have sufficed to show that human nature is consistent with manifold social systems. It may well be that human nature requires incentives, but profit-making is by no means the only one, and, in its strict interpretation, does not even exist for a large part of mankind.

If, then, man has lived under various social systems and has been recognizably the same human animal under them all, it follows that you cannot deduce from human nature what a given social system will be. You can, however, deduce from human nature the fact that there will be social change. For social change occurs precisely because men have universally the same basic needs, and when they find they cannot satisfy those needs within a given social system, they change to another. In the course of these changes men also transform themselves. The primitive warrior has long disappeared, and neither imitation nor cynical jest can reconstitute him in a modern society. The patriarch, the Greek gentleman, the Roman noble, are gone. The medieval knight lies buried with his battle-ax. With each have disappeared — and somewhat to the world's relief — not simply bone and sinew, but a whole way of acting. The modern man does not act as a freeman or slave in a small city-state, nor as a serf or feudal lord. He acts as one who is a citizen of a nation and is about to become a citizen of the world.

Thus, the essence of social man is change. Viewed historically, mankind will appear a vast and shifting multitude, with a lifetime not of seventy years, as individuals may be said to have, but of perhaps 500,000. Its collective history includes the most diverse cultures, civilizations, economic systems, religions, technologies, and philosophies. Among all these there have been manifold interactions, which have constantly transformed them. The Romans conquered the Greek world, only to have their own culture Hellenized. The modern colonization of Africa has imposed changes on the native peoples not always (or indeed often) to their advantage, but the natives may be said to have taken gentle revenge in the influence which their arts have had on European painting and sculpture. The recent vogue of

Neo-Thomism shows how the philosophy of one economic system (feudalism) can be made to influence the thinking of another (capitalism).

There is no reason to suppose that the great process which is history will linger forever at its present stage. In our day, indeed, events have attained so formidable a tempo that a single lifetime, if one is lucky enough to prolong it sufficiently, will seem to contain more than there once appeared to be in history itself. The speed of events, however, is not altogether blinding. One can discern something of the direction and flow. One sees especially the common man, the "humble person" (as our essayist called him), moved by his very humanity, by the old unalterable need for food and shelter, into the acquisition of new skills, new knowledge, new modes of behavior by which his wants are now to be satisfied. One sees him discovering that when a more co-operative social behavior provides an ampler store, it is folly to persist in a jungle life of senseless competition. This transformation occurs not so much through the charm of abstract ideals as through the concrete needs of human nature and society. Human nature changes in some of its respects because it remains the same in others. The Old Adam is forever new because the New Adam is forever old.

Thus they are lost who placed their hope of personal dominion upon the changelessness of man. Perhaps, having now pursued them to the uttermost syllable, we may address them a final word:

The evil is not that you cannot change human nature. The evil is that human nature cannot change you.

CHAPTER III   THAT THE RICH
ARE FIT AND THE
POOR UNFIT

IT WAS two years after 1848. In that terrible year the
surface of European society had cracked open, kings
had tumbled from their thrones, and men of power
everywhere learned what it meant to hear the people
marching in the streets. In February, Paris and the fall
of Louis Philippe; in March, Vienna and the flight of
Metternich, Milan and the revolt against Austria, street
fighting in Berlin, royal abdication in Bavaria. From
the security of its island, the British aristocracy looked
first with surprise and then with horror at the sweep of
revolution on the Continent. There were Chartists in
England, and their strength seemed increasing.

On January 2, 1849, Mr. Charles Greville confided to
his invaluable diary a murmur of immense relief. Security stole back upon him, as if the people's power
had passed with the passing of the old year. "We have
seen," he wrote, "such a stirring up of all the elements
of society as nobody ever dreamed of; we have seen a
general Saturnalia — ignorance, vanity, insolence, pov-

erty, ambition, escaping from every kind of restraint, ranging over the world and turning it topsy-turvy as it pleased. Democracy and philanthropy have never before (or hardly ever) had their own way without let or hindrance, carte blanche to work out their great and fancy designs. This time they leave behind them — and all Europe exhibits the result — a mass of ruin, terror, and despair."

Such were the contemporary thoughts of "Punch" Greville, great-grandson of the fifth Earl of Warwick. And thus, with a simple gesture of mopping the brow, he dismissed as momentary man's efforts to live in plenty and in peace. He had not read the words of a German exile then also in London, who had observed a specter haunting Europe, and who reminded the oppressed that they had nothing to lose but their chains.

When the tumult of 1848 died away, when old monarchs had smoothed back their ruffled fur and new monarchs were posturing with appropriate decorum, the human elite began to refurbish its ideology. It was high time, for ideas grow obsolete like machinery, and one might as well hope to plow a modern wheat field with spades as maintain a modern government with feudal theories. The reader may, if he has taste for the experiment, attempt to see how many converts he can make to royalism by advocating the doctrine of the divine right of kings.

The ideas by which a ruling group maintains its power must be suited to the intellectual climate of the given epoch. Such a climate manifests not simply one and the same kind of weather, but an alternation of fair and wet, of calm and storm, of ice and heat. The rulers have, as it were, meteorologists, who provide different accounts of the different weathers, all seeking to show, however, that the climate is the best possible.

In the Middle Ages this enterprise flourished wonderfully, for then there was much mystery and little knowledge. But the rise of science, in which there is rather more knowledge than mystery, has set the modern maker of ideologies a difficult task. It is far easier to produce the sought conclusions from invented fancies than from the actual nature of things. Yet even science is adaptable, and it came to pass that the theory of evolution — that favorite offspring of nineteenth-century thought — served an inevitable term in the employ of power. The masters of mankind, who once derived their authority from gods, were now content to derive it from monkeys.

Accordingly, a brief two years after 1848, there appeared in London a book which, purporting to be a scientific study of social phenomena, explained just why it is that some men are rich while others are poor, just why it is that philanthropy involves a sentimental misconception of ethics, just why it is that governments are bad in proportion to the extent of their influence on human affairs. This book, which narrowly escaped the fearful title of "Demostatics," was in fact called *Social Statics* — a name scarcely less granite but now worn by time into a certain aspect of grace. The author was Mr. Herbert Spencer, and it was his first book.

Of the various ways by which one may feel at home in the world perhaps the simplest is to observe in one's own life a rhythm or a pattern which can also be found in the vast totality of things. The nineteenth-century

Englishman, at once a prophet and practitioner of industrial capitalism, rejoiced to find throughout the animal kingdom a struggle sharper even than his own. Among animals, assuredly, the race is to the swift, and victory to the strong. Even the joys of paternity, so far as these may be felt by less evolved nervous systems, go to males of superior biological allure. The successful financier, pausing after a day in the city to try a game of billiards at his club, could remark his kinship with organic nature in following competitive enterprise with competitive play.

For his part, Mr. Spencer was a man who saw things clearly. Once when George Eliot commented upon the absence of lines from his forehead, he observed, "I suppose it is because I am never puzzled." [1] He did not, so he tells us, undertake to solve set problems, but allowed generalizations to grow out of information absorbed sporadically. "And thus, little by little, in unobtrusive ways, without conscious attention or appreciable effort, there would grow up a coherent and organized theory." [2] As a method of inquiry, this technique was rather more pleasant than safe; and Huxley was moved to observe, somewhat tartly, that "Spencer's idea of a tragedy is a deduction killed by a fact." [3]

Undoubtedly, however, it was precisely by this method that Spencer evolved the theory which concerns us here. He gave the classic exposition of Social Darwinism exactly nine years before Darwin produced Darwinism. It is comforting to reflect that the social extension of

[1] Herbert Spencer: *An Autobiography,* Appleton, New York, 1904, Vol. 1, pp. 462–3.

[2] *Ibid.,* Vol. 1, p. 464.

[3] *Ibid.,* Vol. 1, p. 467.

evolutionary theory was made considerably before even its biological validity had been established. These are intimations of error which immeasurably lighten the critic's task. The "scientists" who still descant upon the glories of animal struggle and the tiger-virtues of the surviving fit would do well to recall that their theory arose in the unconscious cogitations of a man of unwrinkled brow and unpuzzled mind.

THE STRUGGLE FOR SURVIVAL

What, then, was the vision which Spencer saw so clearly? Throughout the tumultuous universe of organisms there reigns an inexorable law of struggle. Both species and the individual members of species strive to maintain their own existence, in the course of which enterprise they are forced to feed upon one another. Every organism lives under the disadvantage of being possible food for someone else. The worm exists as food for the bird; the bird, as food for the fowler. And the fowler himself? Well, he can escape his place in the dietary cycle, if he avoids the jungle or the haunts of cannibals. In any event, there is no denying the dependence of life upon food. He that survives must eat, and he that eats must kill.

The nineteenth-century intellectual thus looked upon a cosmic spectacle more awful than any ancient worshiper of Moloch could possibly have conceived — a spectacle of necessary selfishness, of inescapable brutality. It was "nature red in tooth and claw," before the sight of which Tennyson quailed. Spencer, however, viewed it imperturbably, and went on to draw a few lessons for society.

Sad as the spectacle is, he said, and unendurable for sentimental minds, it is not without its blessings. "It is much better that the ruminant animal, when deprived by age of the vigour which made its existence a pleasure, should be killed by some beast of prey, than that it should linger out a life made painful by infirmities, and eventually die of starvation." [4] One cannot resist imagining the argument by which the wolf explains to the superannuated lamb the benefit he is about to confer. It reminds one how Cardinal Bellarmine justified the burning of young heretics on the ground that the longer they were allowed to live, the more damnation they would acquire.

But there is another blessing. "Note further," says Spencer, "that their carnivorous enemies not only remove from herbivorous herds individuals past their prime, but also weed out the sickly, the malformed, and the least fleet or powerful." [5] Thus "all vitiation of the race through the multiplication of its inferior samples is prevented; and the maintenance of a constitution completely adapted to surrounding conditions, and therefore most productive of happiness, is ensured." That is to say, an animal society profits from the extinction of its unfit members. The predatory beast cannot avoid showering kindnesses wherever he prowls.

Without entering upon a discussion of these views, which is a matter I shall temporarily postpone, we may

---

[4] Herbert Spencer: *Social Statics*, Appleton, New York, 1888, p. 353.
[5] *Ibid.*

pause to contemplate the agreeable prospects thus opened to view. The tiger's venison dinner depends not only upon his teeth and claws but also upon his fleetness as compared with the deer's. The deer he catches will be one less fleet, relative to him, than other deer are. On the other hand, if there are no deer he can catch by speed or by stealth, then he proves himself a very unfit tiger, and he will not linger long to disgrace his tribe. In the great struggle for survival, then, the losers are the tiger that can't catch and the deer that can be caught. It is rather paradoxical. For it seems that if the tiger that can't catch met the deer that can be caught, he might get a meal and thereby survive; whilst the tiger that can catch, chasing the deer that can't be caught, has no chance of eating at all, and therefore ought to perish. Should these unseemly and un-Spencerian events occur, the fit would become unfit, and the unfit fit. No greater catastrophe can be imagined.

This argument is a play of the logical fancy. I shall add to it a serious argument: Suppose we grant that the fleetest deer and the fleetest, most voracious tigers will be the ones to survive. Suppose we grant, also, that by sexual selection they can transmit those admirable qualities to their descendants, who perfect them still further. Then, as generations pass, the contest between the fitter tiger and the fitter deer will become fabulously skilled and fabulously difficult. *Mutatis mutandis,* throughout the whole organic world, the annual slaughter of less talented animals would enormously imperil the safety of the survivors, who would be left to hunt animals more difficult to catch or to be hunted by animals more difficult to escape. The fleet young doe, escaping the tiger which caught her uncle, may later on fall a prey, precisely because there are no more uncles to be caught. Therefore, the final result of a magnificent evolutionary process would be great perfection in the midst of great insecurity. And the possessors of amazing talents would be no better off for the possession of them.

Now Spencer perceived, or thought he perceived, that the theory of animal struggle could be applied to human society. The social scene exhibits the enrichment of some men and the bankruptcy of others; it exhibits some men at work and others idle (except, oddly enough, in wartime); it exhibits some men ruling and others ruled, some men free and others slaves. It exhibits above all a desperate conflict for the possession of economic and social rewards, which are too few in number to be shared by all. Clearly, then, there will be some (perhaps many) losers, and the losers will be those who did not manifest the skills necessary to win. Failure in the economic struggle, moreover, entails the same hard consequences suffered by the deer that could be caught. Year by year, starvation and disease remove from society its unsuccessful members, leaving the conquerors to adorn and enlighten future generations.

And Spencer tells us just whom he means. "The poverty of the incapable, the distresses that come upon the imprudent, the starvation of the idle, and those shoulderings aside of the weak by the strong, which leave so many 'in shallows and in miseries,' are the decrees of a large, far-seeing benevolence." [6] You will have observed that in setting up these classes Spencer has managed to choose names which carry a certain amount of moral

[6] *Ibid.*, p. 354.

disapproval, and has thus smuggled into his argument an implicit justification which we shall later disentangle. But it is clear that by "the incapable" and "the idle" he means underpaid or unemployed workers, by "the imprudent" he means the people who took economic risks and lost, by "the weak" he means all those who somehow never manage to control their own social destiny. These are the people, unfortunate and unfit, whom that "large, far-seeing benevolence" gets rid of as soon as possible.

At least it will do so, if we don't interfere to slow down the process. Unluckily, so Spencer thinks, there are a lot of "spurious philanthropists" and "paupers' friends," who agitate for poor-laws, doles, unemployment insurance, and government work projects. Not only do these enterprises postpone the disappearance of the unfit, but they have the temerity to do so at the expense of the fit. Mr. Milliards, a genius of finance, is taxed to support Mr. Grimyhands (and family), who does not know the difference between stocks and bonds, having never seen either. Mr. Milliards has more money because he has more skill. He is taxed because he has more money. He is taxed, therefore, because he has more skill. It is most unjust. What are governments that they should thus violate the greatest law of life?

All this indignation, however, is a little misplaced. It happens that natural laws differ from moral or legal laws by being actually inviolable. If I undertake to defy the law of gravitation by stepping out of a tenth-story window, the consequent catastrophe is not a punishment upon me for breaking the law. The catastrophe is in fact due to my being unable to break it. Likewise with the law of survival: the most amiable philanthropy cannot prevent the weeding-out of the unfit; it can only delay the process somewhat and thus bequeath to the next generation a greater "burden" than would otherwise exist. But the process itself, says Spencer, "*must* be undergone, and the sufferings *must* be endured. No power on earth, no cunningly-devised laws of statesmen, no world-rectifying schemes of the humane, no communist panaceas, no reforms that men ever did broach or ever will broach, can diminish them one jot." [7]

The confusion of natural law with moral and legal law is one of the oldest of errors, and will be found in most of the logic books as a standard example of the fallacy of equivocation. But men still use it, undeterred by previous disasters. Thus:

While I am not notably a religious man, I have a profound respect for God's laws as I see them exemplified in Nature — laws which are equally apparent to Christian and pagan, to intellectuals and savages; laws which are superior to time, race, and geographical location; laws which laugh at the feeble efforts of Congresses and legislatures to nullify or dilute them. The law of gravity is one of them. Fortunately the legislatures thus far have let that alone. . . . The law of the selection of species or the survival of the fittest is another, and so is the law of supply and demand. Every conceivable kind of legislative body, from Congress to church synods, is fulminating against these. [8]

Mr. Linn is no nearer to a rational argument than Spencer was, but it is interesting to observe that he calls

[7] *Ibid.*, pp. 355–356. Spencer's italics.
[8] Walter Linn: "Social Insurance: Constructive Destruction,"*Annals of the American Academy of Political and Social Science,* Vol. 170, p. 8.

upon a far weightier authority, which is nothing less than the Deity Himself. It is perhaps even more interesting to juxtapose two further remarks. At the head of the article Mr. Linn placed the following note:

The author wishes to emphasize that in this article he is not voicing the views of any group with which he is or has been affiliated.

At the end of the article the editor placed the following note:

. . . Mr. Linn is a former newspaperman, who in 1913 became associated with Joseph R. Grundy in the Pennsylvania Manufacturers' Association. . . .

Such is political and social science in the twentieth century.

A LOOK AT THE ELITE

The argument, as thus far unfolded by Mr. Spencer and Mr. Linn, asserts two principles: (1) that no attempts to improve the general human lot can make any significant difference in the actual course of events; and (2) that the little difference they do make is undesirable, because it retards the weeding out of the unfit from among the fit. Thus it is the fate of all reforms to be both futile and dangerous.

Now, if we grant (as I, for one, do not) the existence of a social elite tossed up to their present eminence by the surge of evolution, it is natural to inquire of what persons this elite is composed. Obviously, in Spencer's view, it is composed of the winners in the economic struggle: the wealthy, the well-to-do, and perhaps men of modest competence. Among these will be persons whose power is mainly economic, others whose power is mainly political, and conceivably still others whose power rests on the possession of artistic or literary talents, although these last will have some difficulty in establishing their claims.

I sometimes think that historical epochs have a sardonic trick of burlesquing their own favorite ideas, as if events contained a hidden laughter which bubbles up to disturb the sober surface. The burlesque is achieved by a certain resolute, even desperate, literalness with which some personages of the time live out the content of the time's ideas. For every Saint Francis there appears to be a Friar Juniper, for every Napoleon a Louis Bonaparte. Now, the reigning idea of the modern age has been Individualism, with a potent and punning capital *I*. A host of authentic geniuses surge through modern history from the Renaissance to the Romantic Movement. Then the burlesque begins, and rises to an apogee of jest when clownish statesmen and learned buffoons announce themselves as evolution's best product, fit to prosper and fit to survive.

If Elizabeth's England displayed Individualism in the fiery splendor of its youth, Victoria's England displayed it as caricature. Individualism asserts an interest in mankind to be an interest in *persons,* history to be a pageant of heroes, freedom to be the movement of social atoms in a collisionless void. In his role of unconscious caricature, the post-Romantic individualist understood an interest in man to be an interest in his own personal problems, history to be a long suspense which had awaited his arrival, and freedom to be the flowering of wild eccentricities. "Gentlemen," an Oxford don was wont to tell his students in those days, "you have not only offended Almighty God, but you have also seriously displeased me!"

It is an amazing thing, this total unconcern of how the lordly *I* looks in a social situation. A British official in Ireland, St. George by name, having lost his hat while drunk, addresses a meeting of Irish Catholics: "Damnation to you all, I came to emancipate you and you've stolen my hat." [9] William IV, whose accession to the throne surprised nobody more than himself, signs the official declaration of grief for his brother's death, observing to his assistants, "This is a damn bad pen you have given me." A few days later, William greets a delegation of Freemasons: "Gentlemen, if my love for you equaled my ignorance of everything concerning you, it would be unbounded."

In the nineteenth century the fit were surely very odd. One thinks of old Carlyle and his "daily secretion of curses," inveighing against the "horrible, abominable state of things" and deploring, amongst other evils, the exhibition of monkeys in the London Zoo. One thinks of Dr. Arnold, startled to find in his carefree Rugbians "so much of sin combined with so little of sorrow," alarmed at the Trades' Unions — "a fearful engine of

[9] *Leaves from the Greville Diary*, edited by Philip Morrell, Everleigh Nash & Grayson, London, 1930, p. 86. The anecdotes about William IV are on pp. 99 and 105 respectively.

mischief, ready to riot or assassinate," and edified by the
"good poor" whom "it is most instructive to visit." One
thinks of Jeremy Bentham, bequeathing his own skele-
ton to preside over the centennial banquet of the
Bentham Society; of Oscar Browning, the Cambridge
don and lover of royalty, who observed that Wilhelm II
was "one of the nicest emperors I ever met"; of Lord
Panmure, "the Bison," Secretary of State for War and
intransigent foe of Florence Nightingale's reforms, who
complicated the Crimean campaign with telegrams like
the following: "Lord Panmure to General Simpson —
Captain Jarvis has been bitten by a centipede. How is
he now?" And there was Lord Curzon, the most reful-
gent of glittering snobs, who once informed a banquet
audience by way of compliment that he always made it a
practice to associate with his intellectual superiors. Starting out of momentary slumber at this remark, Lord
Houghton observed, somewhat loudly, "Gad, that
wouldn't be difficult." [10]

Yes, in the nineteenth century the fit were surely very
odd. Their more highly evolved descendants in the
twentieth century, men of immeasurable bombast and
illimitable lies, have pressed such traits far beyond the
border of ancestral dreams. Imagination boggled at the
sight of Goering and Goebbels sitting atop the crest of
evolution, as if the universe had labored for a billion
years in order to produce obesity and cunning. If, there-

---

[10] The anecdotes about Carlyle are from Spencer's *Autobiography*,
Vol. 1, pp. 440–3. Those about Dr. Arnold and Lord Panmure are from
Lytton Strachey's *Eminent Victorians*, Garden City, New York, pp. 233,
224, 223, and 168 respectively. Those about Oscar Browning and Lord
Curzon are from E. F. Benson's *As We Were*, Blue Ribbon Books,
New York, 1930, pp. 115 and 175 respectively.

fore, some of the fit are so strange and others are so evil, one may be pardoned for suspecting that there are errors in the theory.

INEVITABILITY AND ETHICS

The theory of evolution belongs to biology: it undertakes to explain how existing species came to be what they are. It is, therefore, simply a general explanation of assembled facts. What Spencer did, considerably before the theory reached definitive form, was (1) to apply it to human society, and (2) to merge it with ethics. That is to say, he argued that the same process which in the animal kingdom separates the biologically fit from the unfit also separates the economically successful from the unsuccessful in human society, and the good from the bad in the moral world. No other interpretation can possibly be made of that phrase about the "large, far-seeing benevolence." Thus, in human society, the biologically fit, the economically successful, and the morally good are all one and the same group of people. Their opposites must, accordingly, be one and the same, also: the biologically unfit, the economically unsuccessful, and the morally bad.

It is clear that Spencer must identify these three groups, if he is to justify, by evolutionary theory, the existing distribution of property. For if any of the economically successful are not biologically fit, then the "law" of evolution will not explain economic success; and if any of the biologically fit or the economically successful are not morally good, then it will be impossible to show that they *deserve* the property they have. By the same token, it will be impossible to explain economic failure on biological grounds, and it will be impossible to show that the poor deserve their sufferings.

When Spencer applied evolutionary theory to society and when he merged it with ethics, he took two tremendous leaps, which had no adequate machinery of flight. For it certainly is not obvious that a biological theory will also be a sociological theory, or that generalizations about the relations *among* species will also hold of relations *within* species. And it is far less obvious that scientific generalizations, which have to do with facts, can be transformed into moral generalizations, which have to do with values. You may say that the course of evolution was what it was and produced the results it produced, but you are still a long way from showing that the course of animal evolution has moral value or that its products are good products. Therefore, even if we were to grant that the rich and powerful are biologically fit, it will not follow that they are morally fit. They may be as physically fit as you please and still be morally deplorable. Animal evolution may, in the absence of any further argument, be moral devolution.

No such additional arguments are to be found in Spencer or, so far as I know, in any of the muscular defenders of the theory. What both they and Spencer seem to suppose is that once you have established the inevitability of certain events, you have also established their moral value. To say that a given society had to be what it is, and is what it had to be, may very readily convey a justification of it. The survivors of the economic struggle are in the nature of the case those that had the power to survive. It could not be otherwise, and we are to be content that it was so.

The meaning of inevitability is worth exploring. As Spencer and others use the concept, it means that certain events will happen regardless of what human beings *do*. Social inevitability, then, means human impotence in social affairs, and it is precisely the sufferings of common men which are powerless to be cured. The tide of historical events moves on, casting us little creatures where it will; and no one of us, with fragile tooth and brittle hand, may hope to carve a refuge in the neighboring rock.

Once it is established that social inevitability means human impotence, the question will arise whether there is in fact any basis for ethics at all. Ethics implies, and cannot exist without, the possibility of modifying environment in accordance with the choices made. Suppose I decide that I can best serve mankind by becoming a scientist. Now, if, in point of fact, I cannot acquire the necessary training, or if, having acquired the training, I have no opportunity to use it, my entire decision is nullified. It proves never to have been more than an idle speculation. Imagine, now, that this condition holds, not for one choice made by one person, but for all choices made by all persons. In such a case, ethics is completely defeated. Where nothing can be effected, nothing need be decided; and where nothing need be decided, attributions of worth or value have no significance at all. Such a world is neither good nor bad; it simply *is*.

If, therefore, we, like Spencer, regard existing society

as created and maintained by a power which human beings cannot control, we shall find that we have there an entity wholly unsusceptible of moral evaluation. Since ethics belong within the sphere of human potency, whatever lies outside that sphere is merely non-moral. If society is thus placed, it too becomes a non-moral entity like comets and earthquakes, which simply are what they are and do what they do. But if society is a non-moral entity, then neither its structure nor its parts can be said to be good or bad. Social events we shall be able to describe, but we shall never be able to say that they ought to have been or ought to be. This last, however, is precisely what Spencer's theory tries to do. It therefore must be said to have undertaken a task which its own argument rendered impossible. By regarding social relationships as inevitable it forever deprived itself of the means of justifying them. It can say that the rich are fit, but it cannot call them good; it can say that the poor are unfit, but it cannot call them bad.

There is another side to inevitability, which the theory quite overlooks. Negatively considered, inevitability is a limitation upon human power; but positively, it is an opportunity. It enables us to predict with confidence the results of our personal behavior and of our social programs. The knowledge of it frees us from the risks of mere conjecture, and so far from rendering us impotent, puts the universe within our power. Suppose we desire a certain object Y, and suppose we know that a certain act X will procure Y. Then, in order to get Y, we have simply to do X. Inevitability here lies in the connection between X and Y, and it is precisely this inevitability which makes possible the satisfaction of our desire. But what Spencer and others suggest is that, no matter what we do, we get Y; or, no matter what we do, we don't get Y. They thus construe inevitability purely in its negative sense, by which means they are able to render impossible the very changes that, from a moral point of view, are most desirable. It is the easiest of all ways of guaranteeing a favorite *status quo*.

This preoccupation with negative interpretations is characteristic of persons with a special stake in a special social order: it is their "everlasting Nay" to the prospect of change. In Spencer, however, it is fortified also by the cast of his temperament. "No one will deny," he tells us, "that I am much given to criticism . . . The tendency to fault-finding is dominant — disagreeably dominant." [11] Thus, for example, his tour through the Italian art galleries drew from him a long discourse upon the faults of the great masters and their deplorable inability to manage *chiaroscuro*. He decided that Wagner was "a great artist but not a great musician," which latter compliment he reserved for Meyerbeer. His father, from whom he thought he inherited this trait in a Lamarckian manner, was much given to lecturing other people upon their follies. On one occasion he visited some of this unsought moralizing upon a drunken fellow traveler. "Well, y' see, master," said the good-humored victim, "there mun be sum o' all sorts, and I'm o' that sort." There is, one perceives, much wisdom and tolerance to be found among the unfit.

[11] Herbert Spencer: *An Autobiography*, Vol. 2, p. 512. The anecdote about his father is in Vol. 1, p. 58. Spencer's honesty about himself is a very endearing trait. It is strange how these murderous theories are sometimes found in lovable men.

ARE THE FIT GOOD?

Thus, as we now see, this very un-Darwinian Darwinism smuggles ethics into science, while at the same time conceiving society in such a way as to render ethics inapplicable. Perhaps it will be useful to see how the smuggling was done.

The chief culprit in the argument is the term "fit." It happens that this word has had a deeply moral connotation ever since the time of the Greeks. Plato and Aristotle both regarded it as signifying a leading ethical concept (though not in a Darwinian sense) ; in Plato, indeed, fitness is raised to the height of a cosmic principle. These men, though they could not fix the meaning of the word for all time, did much to fix its tone. The words of dead philosophers very often survive as half-articulate echoes sounding again and again in common speech. And so it chances that whenever we call a thing "fit," we may quite unconsciously bestow moral approval upon it. If a thing is fit, we are inclined to believe, it must be good; and by the same token, if a thing is unfit, it must be bad. Thus, although the word "fit" has almost as many meanings as it has contexts, it seems in every context to have some suggestion, however faint, of moral praise. I should imagine that few of Spencer's followers (and none of Nietzsche's) ever perceived that "survival of the fittest" is a phrase whose ethical content is mere whisper and echo, without substance and without support.

This fact becomes perfectly apparent when we realize that, as scientific Darwinism uses the term, "fit" is applicable to men and plants and animals in precisely the same sense. If the term, taken in its scientific sense, really possessed any ethical content, we should be obliged to extend that content to plants and animals, and we should have to speak of good and bad lizards, good and bad oak trees. But this is obvious nonsense. Moral adjectives belong only to human beings or to things that have value or disvalue to human beings. The only respect in which moral merit can be attributed to the evolutionary process is that it finally produced beings who were capable of morality. But of surviving lizards all that can be said is that they had certain qualities which enabled them to survive.

We get a further view of the connection between evolution and ethics, when we examine the qualities which have, as they say, survival-value. These qualities are many and varied, for the list has been much extended since Darwin's time and now includes physical and chemical qualities as well as biological ones. The qualities more popularly known are strength, fleetness, intelligence, protective coloration, natural armor, and natural weapons (teeth, tusks, claws, and so on). One of the most important qualities is fecundity, since a species which produces a multitude of individuals obviously has a better statistical chance of survival. This quality accounts for the survival of rabbits, which have little other protection than their speed, and, I should suppose, for the survival of plants generally. But fecundity is never mentioned by the Spencerians. Since the poor are more fertile than the rich, the extension of this concept into society would lead to the conclusion that the poor are more fit than the rich — a conclusion to be avoided at all costs. The omission is deliberate, and nothing could more amply reveal the tendentious character of the entire theory.

Among the qualities assisting survival is one which Darwin emphasized and Spencer did not: co-operation. Says Darwin:

The most common mutual service in the higher animals is to warn one another of danger by means of the united senses of all. . . . Rabbits stamp loudly on the ground with their hind feet as a signal: sheep and chamois do the same with their forefeet, uttering likewise a whistle. Many birds and some mammals post sentinels. . . .[12]

Darwin goes on to mention other kinds of co-operation:

Social animals perform many little services for each other: horses nibble, and cows lick each other, on any spot which itches: monkeys search each other for external parasites.[13]

Co-operation extends to both attack and defense. Darwin quotes with admiration the story of the rescue of a young baboon by an old one, under assault from a pack of dogs.[14] The rescuer-baboon was evidently unacquainted with any law of nature requiring him to rejoice over the death of a weaker member of his tribe.

When you come to list the various qualities making for survival, it is curious how few are susceptible of ac-

[12] Charles Darwin: *The Descent of Man*, Modern Library Edition, p. 474.
[13] *Ibid.*
[14] *Ibid.*

quiring moral value. Strength perhaps, and fecundity perhaps; intelligence and co-operativeness certainly. Yet we find that none of these, not even co-operativeness, is intrinsically good; but each acquires value only in terms of the uses to which it is put. Is a Samson more valuable to society than a Newton? Is a crafty and thievish intellect more valuable than a mild but honest intelligence? Was the co-operation of the Axis nations more valuable than the world's refusal to co-operate with them? All these qualities tend to assist the survival of species and individuals, but otherwise the qualities are sometimes good and sometimes bad. Their contribution to survival will not justify them unless the survival itself is a good thing, and it will not be a good thing unless the individuals show by their actions that they are worthy to survive.

The biologically fit, then, are not necessarily the morally fit. Neither are they necessarily the economically successful. Strength, intelligence, fecundity, and co-operativeness do not on all occasions produce economic success. We all know examples in which weakness, stupidity, sterility, and selfishness seem to be crowned with wealth and position. Moreover, so far as these qualities do influence economic success, their influence varies with different social systems. In a pastoral, patriarchal society fecundity is of great importance: there the contest between Leah and Rachel is constant and acute. But in modern society fecundity is more of a drain on income than a contribution to wealth, and Rachel is somewhat more the model of a desirable wife than Leah could expect to be. Physical strength, too, is of no great economic value in a machine age. Intelligence has rather more. Co-operativeness? Well, that seems to have value mainly for overlords, when it is practiced by underlings.

If thus, the biologically fit are not necessarily the morally good or the economically successful, then the identification of the three groups breaks down, and Spencer's theory is lost. The identification of the unfit, the poor, and the undeserving breaks down likewise. The people whom Spencer calls idle and imprudent and incapable are what they are much more because of their position in society than because of any inherited traits. They are idle because there is no work for them, they are imprudent because competition demands risks of them which they are in no position to take, and they are incapable (whenever they really are so) because they have had no access to training or because they have been forcibly deprived of skills they had acquired. It is not evolution which casts a strong, intelligent, skilled mechanic upon the scrap heap at the age of forty-five. And the people who cast him there are not the fit and the good, though they may be the successful.

Furthermore, the theory conceals this paradox: the wealth of the wealthy and the power of the powerful depends directly upon the poverty of the poor and the weakness of the weak. Wealth is acquired precisely by the extraction of profits from the labor of employees. If there were no employees, there would be no profits, no wealth; and if the condition envisaged by Spencer really did exist, the rich would be forced to struggle might and main to prevent evolution from depriving them of those "weaker" beings who are so essential to their own strength. Lapsing for one last time into Spencerian jargon, we may say that the fit need the unfit, as a parasite needs its host, in order to survive. But the unfit do not really need the fit — not even as a source of alms — and can do without them very well.

FITNESS AND FASCISM

Since 1850, propagandists have played many variations upon the theme of biological inequality, against a counterpoint (similarly distorted) of Mendelian doctrine. In the 1920's, following World War I, there was an attempt to merge it with the nationalist passions which that conflict had generated, and thus to confound nation, race, and species in one indistinguishable mass. In a fairly popular book of those days — the sort of book which "informed persons" read — Dr. Samuel J. Holmes, a biologist, observed:

While there is no doubt that many of our immigrants are of excellent stock, it has been seriously doubted if the great mass of Greeks, southern Italians, Portuguese, Syrians, and Turks measure up to the general intellectual level of the peoples of Nordic stock.[15]

More lately, a man, though not a scientist, named Hitler held similar views concerning Mediterranean peoples.

But as the social crisis deepened in the mid-'thirties, it became possible to speak gloomily of the whole of humankind. The biological facts had not changed, but a desperate time made desperate conclusions seem more

[15] Samuel J. Holmes: *The Trend of the Race,* Harcourt, Brace & Co., New York, 1921, pp. 351–2.

convincing. And Dr. Alexis Carrel was on hand to provide them:

Most civilized men manifest only an elementary form of
consciousness. They are capable of the easy work, which
in modern society, insures the survival of the individual.
. . . They have engendered a vast herd of children whose
intelligence remains rudimentary.[16]

I have some difficulty with this passage, for the notion
of children as forming herds is not one to which I am
accustomed; yet I perceive that it is no longer Greeks
or Syrians or Turks who are unfit, but "civilized men"
generally. Dr. Carrel provided his readers with the
means of looking contemptuously upon anybody they
pleased.

To the twin scientists, Holmes and Carrel, goes
credit, also, for lighting the darkest corner of pseudo-
Darwinism. You remember that Spencer denounced
social reforms for slowing the weeding-out process. Well,
if it is wrong to slow the process, it is probably right
to speed it up. If the "unfit" are really a drag upon
progress, surely it is desirable to get rid of them as soon
as possible. Accordingly, Dr. Holmes proposed that

some means must be instituted for encouraging race suicide
among those to whom Nature has been grudging in her distribution of desirable endowments.[17]

And Dr. Carrel wrote that

An individual's survival was formerly wholly due to his
adaptive capacity. Modern civilization, with the help of

[16] Alexis Carrel: *Man, the Unknown*, Harper & Brothers, New York,
1939, p. 139.
[17] *Op. cit.*, p. 382.

hygiene, comfort, good food, soft living, hospitals, physicians, and nurses, has kept alive many human beings of poor quality. These weaklings and their descendants contribute, in a large measure, to the enfeeblement of the white races. We should perhaps renounce this artificial form of health and exclusively pursue natural health, which results from the excellence of the adaptive functions, and from inherent resistance to disease.[18]

"Perhaps," indeed! A cautious and a necessary "perhaps," for most of Dr. Carrel's readers would have started up in horror if they had glimpsed the consequences of such doctrines. It is part of the collaborationist mentality to abstain from the actual crimes, but to prepare the ideological path toward them. What Carrel preached the Nazis practiced: the planned destruction of entire populations, known under the hideous euphemism "genocide." At the Kharkov trials, a member of the German Secret Field Police named Retzlaff testified he had been taught that

the peoples of the U.S.S.R., and those of Russian nationality in particular, were inferior, that the vast number of them should be exterminated, while a small section should be utilized by the big German landowners in the capacity of slaves.[19]

In the days before the Nazis perfected their techniques of mass extermination, they went at the task like this:

After a round was fired from automatic rifles I saw several women stagger and throw their arms helplessly and,

---

[18] *Op. cit.*, pp. 211-2.
[19] Quoted in Sayers & Kahn: *The Plot against the Peace*, The Dial Press, New York, 1945, p. 121.

uttering heartrending shrieks, run towards the Germans standing about. The Germans shot them down with pistols . . . Mothers, driven out of their minds by fear and grief, ran shrieking about the glade, pressing their babies to their breasts, seeking safety. The Gestapo men tore the children out of their mothers' arms and, swinging them by their legs or arms, threw them into the pit. As the mothers ran after them, they were shot down.[20]

Is there any degeneracy so great as the slaughter of children? Surely not; and if one is to sink to it, one must first consider children as "herds." From Carrel to Retzlaff the distance is so small that hardly a *pfennig* could be set in between. Between pseudo-Darwinism and fascist theory you could not place a page of *Social Statics*.

It is now nearly a hundred years after 1848. The bright amplitude of early prospects may well seem lost in a bitter gloom. It will, indeed, seem so to all but those who have learned the secret of modern history, which is the forward march of common men. This movement of the peoples, now spread in growing unity throughout the world, repudiates alike the slanders of Greville, the dismal unscience of Nietzsche, and Spencer's fumbling conjectures. It has already swept aside its Nazi persecutors, and it prepares an even speedier oblivion for such tyrants as may yet appear. It is transforming struggle into triumph and jungle legend into civilized fact.

Man, the knowledged ape, is building a world.

[20] Testimony of an eyewitness, Alexander Bespalov. Quoted by Sayers & Kahn. *Op. cit.*, p. 122.

CHAPTER IV   THAT THERE ARE
            SUPERIOR AND
            INFERIOR RACES

Y ES, THEY get in everywhere," said my next neighbor, lifting a forkful of meat to his mouth. We
had arrived at the main course and the main topic of
conversation, for in higher circles food and talk run
parallel — or perhaps it would be truer to say that in
higher parallels food and talk run in circles.

The dinner had begun with soup and with lively concern over the safety of Iran. The roast having appeared,
a lady across the table, who bore some resemblance to
the animal we were eating, began to comment upon the
rarity of such meals and the sad emptiness of kitchens.

"They all want jobs in industry nowadays," she said
reproachfully. "They don't know their place any more."

"Who?" I asked. But she looked at me pityingly and
fell into talk with her hostess. It was then that my next
neighbor leaned over, as one having wisdom to com-
municate.

"Yes, they get in everywhere," he said. "Why, only

yesterday I had lunch at *Maxim's*. There was a whole tableful of them there."

"Who?" I asked.

"Why, Jews, of course. They get in everywhere."

"Is there any reason why they shouldn't get in?"

His mouth fell open so far that I could see a piece of the roast nestling against his lower teeth. Then he closed his mouth, and for the rest of dinner gave it over entirely to mastication.

* * *

There is a tradition in American politics which decrees that presidential campaigns shall be as much like circuses as possible. The tradition is pleasant so far as it indicates a certain gaiety of approach to problems, a gaiety which is perhaps our most endearing national trait. Yet elections are a serious matter, and one may reasonably lament a tradition which requires candidates, especially opposition candidates, to be successively acrobats, clowns, and medicine men.

The presidential campaign of 1944 differed somewhat from its predecessors. There was a wildness in the acrobatics, a malice in the clowning, a mendacity in the medicine-selling which surpassed anything ever seen before. In all the clamor attentive listeners could discern the strident sound of German politics just before Hitler.

Undoubtedly it was difficult to attack personally and in public a man who was both President of the United States and Commander in Chief of the Armed Forces. Moreover, before the judgment of citizens who had elected him three times to that office he was unlikely to be convicted of any great iniquity. The strategists of the opposition therefore selected as object of their main attack another man, who was by birth an alien, by profession a labor leader, and by cultural ties a Jew. The choice was shrewd, for the strategists thus hoped to achieve the greatest concentration of hatred from the greatest number of people. They came fairly close to success.

The victim of this strategy was Mr. Sidney Hillman, President of the Amalgamated Clothing Workers of America and Chairman of the CIO's Political Action Committee. There was nothing exceptional about his part in the campaign: he had chosen a candidate, and was actively helping to elect him. Mr. Hillman represented, however, that liberal-labor alliance to which reactionaries are extremely hostile. At the same time he was vulnerable to the favorite fascist attack: he was a Jew.

During the month of October, 1944, some three million Americans received postcards which had been mailed under the frank of a certain Busbey, congressman from Illinois. On the front of the card, where the recipient could not fail to see it, was a brief biography of Mr. Hillman, who — so the legend ran — was "born in Russia . . . married Bessie Abramowitz . . . formed the Communist CIO Political Action Committee." On the back of the card was a message reading, "This is your America. Do you want to turn it over to Sidney Hillman?"

Now, it is still one of the taboos of American political life that you cannot openly attack a man as a Jew. To this extent, at any rate, some decency prevails. The writer of the postcard had therefore to suggest the fact by innuendo, and he did so by using Mrs. Hillman's maiden name. Such is the effect of politics upon gallantry.

Lest the broth thus prepared be lacking in poison, the writer poured in also the contents of another Hitlerian vial, anti-Communism. Mr. Hillman was "born in Russia," and may be supposed to have imbibed the radicalism of that land. Why had he not had the grace to be born, let us say, in Britain, where he might have acquired a sense of the hierarchical fitness of things? Mr. Hillman heads the "Communist" CIO Political Action Committee. Can logic demand more?

Logic does demand more. And so did the voters.

*   *   *

Orators, columnists, and candidates have a sublime faith in the power of words. When certain selected words have been assembled in a certain selected order, they are supposed to achieve, by repetition, irresistible effects. Every phrasemonger and adman expects the walls of Jericho to tumble at the sound of his own trumpet. Sometimes it happens so, for the blasts are mighty. And sometimes the trumpeters merely crack their cheeks. It is perhaps the greatest service they could render mankind.

On page 7709 of the *Congressional Record* for September 12, 1944, will be found one of these attempts at bringing down the walls. Here, however, the clarion tone has been edged with anti-Semitism. I present the entire colloquy:

Mrs. Luce. Mr. Speaker, I ask unanimous consent to address the House for ten seconds.

THE SPEAKER. Is there objection to the request of the gentlewoman from Connecticut?

There was no objection.

MRS. LUCE. Mr. Speaker, clear everything with Sidney.

It was the shortest speech ever made in the House. It was also one of the most revealing.

On December 15, 1944, the gentlewoman from Connecticut had an audience with Pius XII. Her words have been conveyed to us in an AP dispatch, which clothed them in the chastity of indirect discourse:

Rep. Clare Boothe Luce (R. Conn.) said women always had less belief than men in peace by force and more in peace through understanding and charity.

All women?

*   *   *

In January, 1946, the Senate of the United States prepared to debate the Fair Employment Practices Bill. A motion was offered to bring the bill before the Senate, and upon this motion there developed a filibuster. Now, filibustering is, of course, a parliamentary device for preventing the passage of a bill which, if put to a vote, would be carried. A minority in opposition can prevent the enactment of legislation, provided the members of the minority are willing to undergo the physical rigors of talking indefinitely. As a matter of fact, the talking is never interminable, for after a time senators show a willingness to let the measure drop and to proceed with other business.

The filibuster on the FEPC Bill was led by Senator Bilbo of Mississippi. In the course of it, he revealed a good many of the political principles actuating his conduct. Among the most interesting was this:

Mr. JOHNSTON of South Carolina. I should like to ask the Senator from Mississippi a question. Does he not believe that if 60 or even 75 per cent of the laws which have been passed by the House and the Senate had been killed the nation would have been better off?

Mr. BILBO. I always thought there was more virtue in killing legislation than in passing it.[1]

More relevant to our purpose, however, were the Senator's social views and the Senate's response to them. We shall meet some of them again, later on. Just now I want to present, exactly as it appears in the *Congressional Record,* the first paragraph of a letter which Mr. Bilbo announced he had sent to a certain Dr. James A. Dombrowski:

Dear Dombrowski: [Laughter]
I have just received through a friend of mine in Jackson, Mississippi, two sheets that your un-American, Negro social equality, communistic, mongrel outfit is sending out throughout the country in your mad desire to build up a factual case against the right and prerogative of a United States Senator or Senators to filibuster any objectionable legislation that is proposed in this great body.[2]

The content of the paragraph is not so startling, in view of its source. What is startling is the introduction:

Dear Dombrowski: [Laughter]

1 *Congressional Record,* Vol. 92, No. 14, p. 648.
2 *Congressional Record,* Vol. 92, No. 13, p. 591.

In other words, at the mention of the name "Dombrowski" there was laughter in the Senate of the United States.

*   *   *

Near Maidanek, in Poland, the Nazis erected a vast community of destruction.[3] Scores of buildings stood within a circumference of barbed wire, but of them all two have especial interest. In one of these was found the store of clothes accumulated from the victims — a pathetic heap, which contained everything from men's suits to babies' shoes.

The other building had three rooms. In the first of these the prisoners were made to remove their clothing; in the second they were passed under a series of shower baths; and in the third they were packed so tightly that no one could possibly fall. Three pipes led into this room from the outside, and there was a fourth aperture through which a guard might watch the happenings within.

When the room had been filled with perhaps two hundred persons, there suddenly came a shower of crystals through the pipes. On contact with the air, these crystals generated deadly gases. Then the guard, through his aperture, had the duty, pleasant doubtless to him, of deciding at what moment all two hundred persons might be considered dead.

For a time the corpses were buried, layer upon layer,

[3] Sources for the information in this passage are AP and UP dispatches of September 1, 1944, and two bulletins of the Soviet Embassy in Washington (August 27 and September 1). The account in the two bulletins was written by the Russian dramatist, Konstantin Simonov.

in enormous trenches; but, as the tide of battle began to move westward, the Nazis sought to remove all traces of their crimes. For this purpose they built a crematory, a series of five ovens, each just large enough to hold a human body. The bodies were shoveled in on ladles of precisely the right shape and size. At first the cremations proceeded slowly, because the ovens were not hot enough. But then Nazi "science" worked the oven heat up to 1500 degrees Centigrade, and the furnaces began to consume as many as 2000 bodies a day. In this manner no less than 1,500,000 people perished at Maidanek.

One evening, when the furnaces were in full blast, a group of newly arrived prisoners came by. It was an error, for prisoners were not supposed to know of these events. By chance also the Nazi commandant was present at that moment. A woman among the prisoners, seeing thus suddenly the fate which awaited them all, shrieked aloud. The commandant ordered her to be silent, but hysteria had overcome her. Then, at a further command, two guards seized her and threw her alive into one of the furnaces. There was a flash of light as the hair caught fire, a last horrible cry. Then silence, silence, the silence of fascist death.

* * *

These episodes form a pattern, not of past history exactly, but of events as they may yet occur. There is a straight, direct line running from my friend at the dinner table, through the franked postcard, the insidious slogan, and the senatorial laughter, to the death factory at Maidanek. It is the path which Germany trod during the last twenty years. Other nations can tread it, too.

As journeys do not begin at their destinations, so not even the most wishful racist can build a death camp right away. He has to travel toward his goal, and he hopes, in the traveling, to take you with him. For, indeed, if you do not go with him, he will not get there at all.

Accordingly, he plays upon every sneer and whisper, upon idle talk and careless conversation, upon the newspaper practice of identifying Negroes while never identifying anybody else, upon the haunts of "restricted clientele," upon the quota systems of schools and colleges, upon the secret clauses in club and fraternity charters, upon the thousand spurious inequalities which feed his general campaign. He plays upon human vanity, upon the wish of abused and frustrated men to feel superior at least to something. And as if these things were not enough, our society implants the racial myths in children before they have any chance to be frustrated at all.

Thus the racists have set us a great and terrible problem. There is no other problem so large, except that of the entire reconstruction of society. We shall have to meet racism with every valid weapon: with the suffrage, to remove racists from public life; with legislation, to illegalize such practices; and with education, to protect all people against the corrupting myth. It is a matter of simple personal safety. For it always turns out that social inequality, from segregation to mass murder, consumes and devours everyone who is not willing to live and die a slave.

THE POSTULATES OF PREJUDICE

The concept of race, so far as it is useful scientifically at all, is useful as a device for classifying human beings according to their remoter origins. By this device an anthropologist, for example, can trace (conjecturally at least) the movements of peoples in the long ages before recorded history. By a comparison of skulls and the geological strata in which the skulls were found, he can also learn something about the evolution of Homo sapiens. But it would never occur to a reputable anthropologist to think of the Piltdown man as "sinister" or the Cro-Magnon man as "amiable."

Now, a classification is in part the recording of a fact — the fact, namely, that a number of individuals have one or more qualities in common. It is also an instrument, and its function as an instrument is to provide a point around which knowledge may be organized. Students of chemistry, of botany, of zoology, though doubtless harassed by the multitudinous groups and the formidable nomenclature, will recognize nevertheless that without those classifications the relevant knowledge could never be organized at all.

As instruments for the organization of knowledge, various classes have varying degrees of success. The fact that such and such a class exists or can be constructed is not in itself enough. A class gains in usefulness, and thus in scientific importance, in proportion as it permits a greater amount of knowledge to be organized about itself. One could construct a class of "yellow things," which would contain, *inter alia,* daffodils and sulphur. Such a class could be said to exist, but it would be poverty-stricken. So little can be inferred about the members of that class from the fact that they are members of it that hardly any knowledge can be assembled there. The class exists, but it is relatively — indeed, I think, totally — useless.

On the other hand, the grouping together of rats, squirrels, and beavers as "rodents" is very successful. Despite the fact that these animals differ considerably in their appearance, they have a common tooth-structure; and, as it happens, this tooth-structure will very largely explain their behavior and their mode of living. Thus a great part of what we know about rats, squirrels, and beavers can be assembled around that classification. The class exists and is a useful instrument.

You will have observed that it was the selection of tooth-structure as the basis of the classification which enabled us to organize so much knowledge around so small a point. Tooth-structure, in this example, illustrates what we mean when we speak of "essential qualities." Such qualities are decisive: they account, more than any others, for what the things are and what they do. By contrast, the quality "yellow" quite fails to explain the nature of daffodils and sulphur, which have in fact only a superficial resemblance. In their essential qualities they differ profoundly.[4]

When you want to organize knowledge, therefore,

[4] This discussion owes a great deal to S. H. Mellone: *An Introductory Textbook of Logic,* 18th Edition, William Blackwood & Sons, Edinburgh, Chapter V, Part III. The facts are familiar enough to any logician, but Dr. Mellone's book is the immediate source of my illustrative material as well as of my exposition.

you will be careful to base the classifications upon essential qualities. You will thus derive classes in which the members have the greatest amount of resemblance to one another and the greatest amount of difference from the members of other classes. But suppose that, instead of organizing knowledge, you set out to organize ignorance and prejudice. You will then have to do precisely the opposite. You will select unessential, rather than essential, qualities. You will entirely conceal the question how far the members of one group really resemble one another. You will keep the classification vague and flexible, so that it can be made to include just whatever individuals you choose.

These arrangements being made, you can now proceed to remove some members from the class, or to add others to it, as these maneuvers become tactically necessary. You can, like the Nazis, make "Aryans" out of the Japanese, or "Asiatics" out of the Russians. And if these classes cannot by any stretch of science be regarded as racial, what does it matter? You are organizing not knowledge, but prejudice; you are spreading not enlightenment, but hate. And, above all, you are completely debauching other people's minds by accustoming them to ignore science and to embrace myth.

When, therefore, a racist sets out on that brutal journey which is to end in the construction of death camps, he disencumbers himself of all science and all logic. He chooses as the basis of racial classifications, not any quality which is essential, but a quality which he thinks you can readily recognize and can be made to hate. Now, no quality is more obvious than the color of one's skin, and no facial feature is more plain than the shape of one's nose. We have only to open our eyes in order to perceive that some skins are yellow and others brown, that some noses are hooked and others flat. The amount of intelligence required to make these identifications is the amount required to see something directly before the eyes. Now, if you can be brought to hate yellow skins and black skins, hooked noses and flat noses, you can become at one bound an accomplished racist. And for this you will not need any intelligence at all.

It is thus obvious that racism and science have little more in common than the possession of a few identical terms, and even these terms the racists have so fearfully elaborated as to bury any reasonable meaning under a torrent of abuse. Indeed, the power of racism has grown so great, and its definitions have become so wild, that honest scientists are puzzled whether they should any longer employ the language. For, if the racists are fanatically persuaded that Jews constitute a race, the scientists, for their part, know very well that Jews constitute no such thing. And if many thousands of people accept the former meaning, what will it profit a scientist to use the term "race" in his own truer and quieter sense? He is bound to feel that a great deal could be gained if he simply used another word.

Such a view, however, would be mistaken. It would simply concede to the racists their right to abuse terms and prostitute meanings — a right which I think nobody has. On the contrary, the struggle must be joined; the vocabulary must be recaptured. Instead of supplying a new language to be learned, we must teach people to use scientifically the language they have got. If there are races, let us make it plain in what sense they exist.

If there are inherited characteristics, let us make it no less plain what those characteristics are. But especially let us understand the assumptions on which the entire racist position rests.

What is it that racism asserts? It asserts that there exist groups of human beings, identifiable by certain physical traits, who, by reason of their birth, constitute some sort of menace to the rest of mankind, and whom mankind is therefore justified in ostracizing, punishing, or, indeed, destroying. In order to establish this contention, the racists would have to demonstrate the following propositions:

(1) That certain groups of men are so unlike in nature to the rest of mankind that their behavior differs radically also.

(2) That these traits of behavior are hereditary, so that no member of these groups can avoid having them or can succeed in ridding himself of them.

(3) That some at least of these traits are "bad" and that the "bad" traits are dominant.

(4) That other groups whose members possess "good" traits are thereby entitled to domination over the groups whose members possess "bad" traits.

A little reflection will show that these are the propositions which the racist must hold. His wish to segregate minorities and to contrive various discriminations against them must be validated by some principle, and he therefore appeals to the moral superiority of his own group as against others. If he were to be granted this proposition, it might nevertheless be argued that the higher group ought to educate the lower group up to its level. But the racist does not want to educate; he wants to oppress. He therefore holds that the behavior traits of the lower group are ineradicable, because they are hereditary. Now, if they are hereditary, they must be bound up with the essential nature of that group; and that essential nature must be profoundly unlike the nature of other groups. This difference can be esteemed so highly that the members of "inferior" groups will appear to have the likeness, but not the reality, of men. A believing Nazi was fully persuaded that his victims were scarcely distinguishable from animals. The rest of the world came to have a comparable opinion of Nazis.

Such are the four postulates on which the racist view is erected. And, although they are men of turgid passion and dreary mind, the racists evince a dim awareness that this is what they mean. What they neither know nor want to know is that all four postulates, together with the conclusion, are false.

THE CRITIQUE OF RACISM

We have, thus, four statements whose truth is assumed, and a fifth statement which forms the basis of action. The relation between the four and the one is that of premises to conclusion. Ordinarily, if any premise in an argument is proved false, the conclusion becomes, not false, but merely doubtful. It might, that is to say, be true for other reasons. But in the argument before us there can be no other reasons. For, in discovering by analysis what the racist postulates are, we chose only the ones whose truth must be assumed if the conclusion is to be true. We were saying, "If E is to be considered true, then A and B and C and D must already be true." And from this we can infer that if A *or* B *or* C *or* D is false, then E is false. In other words, we need only show the falsity of *one* of these postulates in order to show the falsity of the conclusion. As a matter of fact, all four of the postulates are false. We have an embarrassment of riches.

I propose, then, that we take these postulates one by one in the order in which they are given, and subject them to analysis. The advantage of this procedure lies in the fact that it will fully reveal the inner absurdity of the racist view. For it does not suffice, I think, merely to assemble a quantity of facts on the opposing side. The argument becomes much more cogent when we show that racism is not only contrary to fact, but is by any rational criterion nonsense. Well, then, let us take the first postulate:

(1) That certain groups of men are so unlike in nature to the rest of mankind that their behavior differs radically also.

When any two groups differ radically from each other, they do so in respect of their appearance, their actions, and their relationships to the rest of the world. In such a circumstance the members of each class resemble one another far more than they resemble the members of other classes. Lions, for example, are unguiculates (clawed animals), and horses are ungulates (hoofed animals). Their appearance, their modes of life, and their relationships with the rest of the world differ accordingly. They cannot mate with each other; they cannot even associate, since the lion will regard the horse as a palatable meal, and the horse will regard the lion as a peril to be escaped. Evidently we have here two basically different animal types. If it could be shown (as it decidedly cannot) that racial differences are like those between the lion and the horse, racism could pretend to some scientific foundation.

Now suppose another example. If you were to compare a tiger with a leopard, you would immediately observe that the one has his stripes and the other his spots. You would notice, however, that the tiger and the leopard have very considerable resemblances. Both of them are unguiculates and both are felines. Moreover, they are the kind of felines that can roar, when others can only purr. If you weigh the importance of these various qualities, you will find that although the tiger's stripes and the leopard's spots provide a vivid means of distinguishing the two species, these qualities have rather less to do with their behavior. Their nature and their modes of life derive from the fact that they are feline. If it can be shown that racial differences are like those between the tiger and the leopard, then racism will be found to have no scientific basis at all.

In the opinion of the senatorial anthropologist, Mr. Bilbo, racial differences are like those of the horse and the lion:

I said that segregation was a law of nature. Segregation is perfectly natural in nature. It is natural in the animal world. We do not see horses out in the meadow land lining up with the cows. No; the cows go by themselves this way, and the horses by themselves the other way. Hogs and sheep keep apart. Hogs go by themselves and sheep by themselves. That general law also applies to the human race. People of the Mongolian races associate together. They intermarry and want to live together and do business together. The same is true of the Indians. The Negro race is the only one I know of which is ashamed of its race and which tries to obtain for itself social equality with the white race. Most of its leaders preach that segregation and mongrelization and intermarriage between the whites and blacks is the only solution for the race question in this country.[5]

Senator O'Daniel agrees, except on the question of how Negroes feel about their own group:

Texas is a wonderful state. I make that statement so that anything I say against FEPC will not be construed as an infringement of the rights of the colored race. In the South we like the colored folk and they like us. Each of us keeps his place. I do not know what we would do without them or they without us. We get along well, but we do not live together. We do not marry each other. The colored people in Texas are proud of their race. They are just as proud of their race as the white people are proud of their race.[6]

Senator Johnston passes through science into theology:

I notice, when I go to New York, that the colored people have congregated in Harlem. That is due to an inborn instinct. It will be found that the members of races con-

[5] *Congressional Record*, Vol. 92, No. 14, p. 649. The contradictory juxtaposition of "segregation," "mongrelization," and "intermarriage" is in the original text.

[6] *Congressional Record*, Vol. 92, No. 14, p. 670.

gregate together; they want to be together. They do not want other races to interfere with them. That is nothing but human nature. It has always been true in the past. By this bill (FEPC) there is an attempt to change something that God made. We did not make it. God made my face white and made some other face yellow and some other face black. I did not do it. Congress cannot change that state of affairs.[7]

Now, the qualities which scientists take as the basis of racial differences are primarily physical, and consist of height, head shape, color of skin, of eyes, and of hair, and the texture and quantity of hair. According to racism, which also makes some use of this basis, the most improved human being is perhaps six feet tall, long-headed, blond, and wavy-haired. Departures from this norm will, in their varying degrees, meet different intensities of disapproval.

Such are the assumed differences. From them the racists expect to be able to infer certain traits of behavior. They believe, for example, that a person who is curly of hair and negroid of skin will also be lazy; that a person whose hair is black, whose color is swarthy, and whose nose is aquiline will be usurious in his business dealings. They are full of examples, real and fancied, which are to be cited *ad infinitum* in substantiation of their beliefs. They employ, also, other examples, fewer and less spectacular, which are to be cited as "exceptions," so as to produce a gratifying display of fair-mindedness. But, scientifically, the effort is vain. No rule is proved by the first set of examples, and there-

[7] *Congressional Record*, Vol. 92, No. 13, p. 579.

fore no rule exists to which the second set can be exceptions.

What connection can there possibly be between the way people "look" and the way they behave? What could one possibly predict about behavior, basing oneself on the mere evidence of skin color, hair texture, and height? It is quite obvious that one could predict nothing. If men who are tall and blond — "Nordics," as they used to be called; "Aryans," as they are called now — are by that fact virtuous and intelligent, then virtue in our day has become singularly easy. If men who are short and black are therefore vicious, then vice is for them unavoidable. They can incur no blame, as their self-styled betters can incur no praise.

Finding it difficult to establish a relation between skin color and character, some racists have put their faith in the shape and size of the head. A large skull will house a large brain, and a large brain, it might seem, would give one more to think with. But, alas for such hopes! The largest brain thus far found is that of an imbecile, whilst several men of great intelligence have had rather small brains. The size of the human brain and the shape of the human head have nothing whatever to do with intelligence.

Thus it is quite impossible to join the physical attributes which distinguish races with any behavior which could be called good or bad. Still more perplexing, however, is the fact that no groups can be found which exclusively possess even the designated physical attributes. Height varies *within* groups: The Shilluk Negroes, who live at the sources of the Nile, are six feet two, whereas the neighboring brown pigmies are only four feet eight. Tall and short people are found together all over the world.[8] Head shape varies *within* groups: both long heads and round heads will be found among the American Indians, for example, or the peoples of Asia Minor — even, indeed, among close relatives.

As for skin color, the facts are perhaps most remarkable of all. Speaking geographically, you can say that the darkest skins will be found in West Africa, the lightest in Northwest Europe, and the yellowest in Southeast Asia. But it turns out that these are extremes rather than norms, for most skins in the world are of intermediate shades. In all probability these intermediate shades represent the common original, and the extremes represent a later development. Any racial classification rigorously based on skin color would therefore have its evolutionary data exactly reversed.

It is now known, moreover, that skin color is determined by two chemicals, one of which (carotene) produces the yellow tint, and the other (melanin) the brown. It is known, also, that every one of us has these chemicals in his skin, though in varying proportions. These variations, together with the color provided by the blood vessels underneath the skin, will account for every difference observable.

I think it is very striking how the unity of mankind is proclaimed in the very attributes which are thought to divide us. We may be black or white or yellow, but we have all got melanin and carotene. We are brothers

[8] These facts, and others in the present passage, are taken from *The Races of Mankind*, by Ruth Benedict and Gene Weltfish, Public Affairs Pamphlets, No. 85. This is the pamphlet which the House Military Affairs Committee refused to permit to be distributed throughout the Army in April, 1944. "The stone which the builders rejected. . . ."

in the skin, as well as under it. And, without laboring too much the platitudes of old Kipling, now safely laid away with the lore of empire, we may add that East (which, as we know, is East) and West (which is West) now meet daily and forever upon the surface of the human body.

It is therefore but a feeble logic which invests the categories of the racists. In every group the members are such that they share with the members of other groups even the qualities which are supposed to be peculiarly their own. In every group the basis is such that nothing whatever can be inferred about the behavior of the members. The classifications, therefore, fail to organize knowledge, and fail to divide people in any significant way. In short, they are precisely the sort of classifications we have said would be useful for the organizing of ignorance. In such devices what possible source can there be of rational self-esteem?

The failure of racial classifications is due, of course, to the fact that men live, not by skin color or head shape or quantity of hair, but by the qualities which make them men. Divide men as you will and upon whatever basis you choose, they will always resemble one another more, by virtue of being men, than they can be made to differ by the qualities you select. They have a common anatomy, a common physiology, a common psychology. They have the same basic economic needs, the same desire for companionship and play. None of them is exempt from conditioning by environment, and for all of them there exists the possibility of improvement or deterioration. This is what Shakespeare had in mind when he made Shylock say:

"Hath not a Jew eyes? hath not a Jew hands, organs, dimensions, senses, affections, passions? fed with the same food, hurt with the same weapons, subject to the same diseases, healed by the same means, warmed and cooled by the same winter and summer, as a Christian is? If you prick us, do we not bleed? if you tickle us, do we not laugh? if you poison us, do we not die? and if you wrong us, shall we not revenge? If we are like you in the rest, we will resemble you in that." [9]

The last sentence is a profound addition: "If we are like you in the rest, we will resemble you in that." For human behavior is influenced, regardless of race, not only by anatomy and physiology, but by society — that is to say, by other people's behavior.

In view of the vast community of human characteristics, it is wholly incredible that racial differences are in any way fundamental. If they were so, we should have to suppose that nature went to the trouble of producing the same anatomy, the same physiology, the same psychology over and over again in slightly different ways, starting anew after each effort. Obviously no such thing occurred. Obviously the various human groups have a common origin. Obviously the differences are not primordial, but are of rather recent development in evolutionary time. And as if this were not enough, nature has so mingled the various "stocks" by intermarriage over some fifty millennia that not a single representative of any imaginable pure race can possibly be found.

[9] *The Merchant of Venice*, Act. III, Scene I, ll. 50–58. It is interesting to observe that in the passage Shakespeare shows himself aware that Jews are not a race, but more nearly a nation.

We therefore dismiss the first of the racists' assertions: that certain groups of men are so unlike in nature to the rest of mankind that their behavior differs radically also. In the largest sense, the nature and behavior of men are similar. And if, as racists sometimes say, it is proper for each to stick to his kind, it will follow that the supreme duty of men is to stick to one another. Logic vindicates, not fascism, but democracy. I suppose this is why fascists prefer to think with their blood.

THE MYTHOLOGY OF BLOOD

We take next the second of the racist postulates:

(2) That these traits of behavior are hereditary, so that no member of these groups can avoid having them or can succeed in ridding himself of them.

Of all the mysticisms which have plagued mankind for innumerable years, the mysticism of blood is perhaps the most fanatical. Now, blood is a genial fluid, without which none of us can survive. It is therefore precious. Blood lies close to our physical existence and is therefore intimate. It runs beneath the skin and is therefore hidden. Something precious, something intimate, something hidden — this is all that any mysticism can require.

Blood, moreover, has had a long career as poetic metaphor, during which it has been made to symbolize both life and the sacrifice of life, both redemption and damnation, both the incidence of things new and the survival of things old. An image which thus suggests so many contraries will admirably suit the needs of men who desire it to mean anything they please. By concealing the difference between metaphor and fact, they can pass the concept off as a description of the real world. And they can find believers.

In feudal society, where nobles had the problem of keeping their estates in the family, it was useful to suppose that property could move from father to son along with "the blood." With colorful garments of this sort, apologists of the system were able to clothe the bare economic fact that each aristocratic family was the center of a large property holding. Under capitalism, where wealth derives from control of factory systems and from access to large markets, the concept (or image) of blood has necessarily been extended to include whole peoples. This extension was achieved in the nineteenth century by a union of the concepts "blood" and "nation." The Comte de Gobineau, more flatteringly known as a writer of detective stories, erected his theory of social superiority upon national divisions. It remained for the twentieth century to disclose the ingenuities of combining "blood" with "race."

The concept of racial blood ties has served two chief purposes: it has provided nations with an excuse for foreign conquest, and it has enabled them to divide their own populations at home. Since, for example, German nationals and their descendants are scattered all over the world, it has been very useful for Nazis to be able to say that Germany exists wherever there is German "blood." Each time the territory of the Reich expanded, the Germans thus newly brought back into the Fatherland could be said to have been "rescued" from the oppression of an alien and inferior people. The *Wehrmacht* undoubtedly hoped to move on until all persons of German stock had been thus rescued. From these saviors the world has had to save itself.

At the same time, the Nazis consolidated their rule at home by creating a spurious division within their own people. Availing themselves of a prejudice already widely and fanatically held, they caused the Jews to be deemed responsible for the evils they had themselves intensified or ordained. The brutalization of a whole people followed by swift, yet subtle, stages, until those of them who were not actual murderers were willing at least to adorn themselves with the clothes of the victims.

If a study of the social uses of blood-myths does not suffice to display their falsity, a few scientific facts ought to be conclusive. For one thing, blood is divisible into types, but these types bear no relation whatever to racial groupings. They will be found, in fact, among the members of every conceivable race. Men of democratic mind should derive some pleasure from knowing that they share the blood types of Australian bushmen and American aborigines. And to set a seal upon the unity of mankind, one may observe that the part of the blood most needed for transfusion is the plasma, which is altogether the same in everybody.

In the second place, blood is not the bearer of hereditary traits, which are in fact carried by biological units called "genes." The evidence of genetics appears, like all the other evidence, to point toward mankind as a community rather than a hierarchy of races. Since men presumably have a common origin, and since human groupings have intermarried throughout history, the possession of any particular gene for any particular physical characteristic will now be found in various peoples all over the world. If, therefore, you were to mark off a "race" on the basis of certain qualities, you would find that individuals who might be included because they have one of the qualities would have to be excluded for lacking the others.

In the third place, racism attempts to pass off, as hereditary, behavior traits which are not hereditary at all. Deaf-mutism and hemophilia are determined by genes, but there is no evidence to indicate that political and social behavior is so determined. If, for instance, we were to suppose the existence of a gene for profit-making in the capitalist sense, we should have to suppose that the feudal lords and the ancient slaveowners were motivated by yet other genes, which have ceased to be dominant. We should have to say that the genes for capitalist behavior were either recessive in feudal times or came into existence by mutation. Thus a frank historical account of social change would give way to an obscure and mythical application of genetics.

Within the extremely broad limits of an inherited anatomy and physiology, human behavior is determined by environmental influences. The greatest of these is society itself. Capitalists exist not because of any special hereditary equipment, but because of a particular social mode of producing and distributing goods. The same social mode determines the existence and the nature of industrial workers. There is no genetic reason why either group is what it is, or why any supposed racial group should be attached to one or the other.

Even the reigning folklore admits this fact, when it advertises the possibility of ascent from the one class to the other.

Thus there is only a social, and never a biological, reason why Negroes are "last to be hired, first to be fired," why they have access mainly to menial jobs. There is only a social, and never a biological, reason why Jews are to be found chiefly in a few particular trades and professions. And the social reasons reflect little credit upon the rulers of society, for the Negroes owe their plight to their having been kept as a huge reservoir of the cheapest possible labor, and the Jews owe theirs to the desire of "Aryan" businessmen for the elimination of astute competitors.

Well, if the Nazis provided us with the myth that human behavior is predetermined by a "racial soul," it must be confessed that they also provided us with the completest refutation of that doctrine. For, when they came to the problem of consolidating their regime and of organizing the German people for conquests abroad, they trusted not at all to any sublime Teutonic personality nor to any primeval forest whispers. On the contrary, they seized the press, the radio, the schools, the universities, the various cultural media, and bent them to their purposes. They utilized, that is to say, every conceivable means of *conditioning* their people into the desired modes of behavior.

Whatever fascist theory may say, fascist practice clearly admits that social behavior is the result of conditioning. If it is so, then we may reasonably expect that conditioning will change it. Accordingly, if we find in some people behavior traits which we deem to be undesirable, our duty will lie not in segregating or exterminating the people, but in removing the environmental causes. If research should reveal an occasional lazy Negro, our duty would not lie in increasing his poverty and therefore his laziness. We have only to give him adequate food, and the laziness will disappear.

ARE THERE "BAD" RACES?

Let us take the last two postulates together, for both of them have to do with ethics:

(3) That some at least of these traits are "bad" and that the "bad" traits are dominant.

(4) That other groups whose members possess "good" traits are thereby entitled to domination over the groups whose members possess "bad" traits.

These blanket moralizings are extremely unpersuasive, for they conceal what we most need to know — the behavior of individual people. They show every sign of a wish to condemn in advance or to justify in advance, before actual behavior has been studied at all. Moreover, if it is impossible to generalize very accurately upon the physical characteristics of races, there is not likely to be any greater success in generalizing upon moral characteristics. We shall have trouble enough deciding what "good" means and what "bad" means, without applying the term to whole groups of people and disposing of their destinies in accordance with the application. We shall have trouble enough determining the content of moral principles, without imposing upon multitudes all the torments which bigotry can devise. It is not so much a common sinfulness as a lack of understanding which impedes the execution of moral judgments. It is one's *eye* that the beam is in, when one objects to the mote in another's.

But I think the question can be settled more simply and without recourse to metaphysical refinements. Suppose we compare the behavior of allegedly inferior races with that of the allegedly superior races. The results are as plain as they are devastating. It was not a Negro or a Jew who sat next me at that dinner. It was not a Negro or a Jew who franked the slanderous postcard, or invented the insidious slogan. It was not Negroes or Jews who built the death camp at Maidanek. No, all these people were (God save the mark) "Aryan." In the whole of history, no Negroes or Jews, no members indeed of any "inferior" races, have inflicted upon mankind sufferings which remotely compare with those inflicted by the self-styled "superior" races.

The moral balance is thus precisely the reverse of what racists affirm it to be. If to possess every conceivable vice is to be virtuous, then racists are virtuous. If to contrive every manner of injustice is to be just, then racists are just. If to bathe in abominable impurities is to be pure, then racists are pure. But to these "Aryans" and all their insufferable kin more rightfully belongs the famous judgment of Jonathan Swift: they are "the most pernicious race of little odious vermin, that Nature ever suffered to crawl upon the surface of the earth."

If groups of men are to submit to moral judgment, the savagery of recent years makes it very plain where the proper attributions lie. But let us entertain one final supposition, the wildest of all. Let us suppose that these "Aryans," with all their equipment of whips, gas chambers, and portable gallows, with all their sneers, exclusions, and segregations, are nevertheless morally superior to other groups. Would this superiority entitle them to dominate the others, governing and oppressing at pleasure? How could so monstrous a thing be true? Oppression is a forcible and often violent exploitation by a small group of men. Superiority in power will achieve and sustain it; but no superiority, physical or moral, can justify it. A democratic ethics must abhor it and seek its universal destruction.

*   *   *

Thus, even if a racist could show (as he cannot) that human groups differ profoundly, even if he could show (as he cannot) that such differences are transmitted as hereditary traits of behavior, and even if he could show (as he cannot) that the traits of some groups are good and of others bad, he still could not show that the group with the good traits is justified in dominating the others. On his four statements he has a perfect score, which is zero. One shudders to think how close such men have come to achieving control over the entire world.

One shudders, but then one resolves to act. And act we must. By patient education and by effective political control we must bring it to pass that the public life of nations will exhibit no more Maidaneks, no more Hitlers, no more Quislings, no more congressional racists, and no more anti-Semitic slogans. When this has happened, it may be possible to break one's bread in friendliness, and to eat it without a chattering accompaniment of hate.

There is no reason why we should not succeed. The Master Race produced its greater masters, and it found them in us, the democratic peoples of the world. We have the necessary knowledge; we have the necessary power; we have the necessary union of knowledge and power to effectuate the victory. The myths of race, however fortified with violence and hate, will not in the end prevail against us.

CHAPTER V   THAT THERE ARE
TWO SIDES TO
EVERY QUESTION

IN AUGUST 1933 the *Living Age,* an old but scarcely
venerable periodical, published a trilogy of articles
under the confident heading *Forward with Hitler.* By
that time the fraud of the Reichstag fire, the brutal
antics of storm troopers, and the reactionary lusts of
the new regime were perfectly evident. One contributor,
however, Dr. Alice Hamilton, managed to view the
scene with calm. She took a larger view, she tried to see
the Nazi side, and this is what she wrote:

It is easy to condemn such men wholesale, as madmen or
cowards, but that is too simple. After all, it must be remembered that this is war-time in Germany, and surely we
have not forgotten the strange change that came over some
of our own idealists during the Great War. In spite of all
the cruelty, bigotry, and ugly personal vindictiveness, one
feels that there is something coming out of this movement
in Germany that the German people have been hungering
for, and however exaggerated, even hysterical, the outpour-
ings of its devotees may seem to detached Anglo-Saxons,

they are not wholly absurd; there is something here that calls for thought on our part.[1]

Now, the author of this passage was in no way sympathetic with Nazi ideology. The very judiciousness of the tone is proof of that. There is in the passage a kind of implacable fairness, which refuses to be moved by the sight of a few incidental crimes. Yet, equally, there can be no doubt that the effect of the passage was favorable to the Nazis and to the "something coming out of this movement." At a time when decisive action by the peoples of the world might yet have overthrown Hitler and thus have spared mankind the consequent disasters, the author asks us to pause and consider.

She appeals, furthermore, to a similar trait in ourselves, to the fact that we are "detached Anglo-Saxons." We are to distrust simple and obvious explanations; we are to remember that "it is easy to condemn"; and we are to be sympathetic with what the German people have been "hungering for." Modern journalistic literature is full of marvels, but I doubt if it exhibits elsewhere so remarkable a misapplication of fair-mindedness.

The detached Anglo-Saxon! It is not a bad name to bestow upon the political animal for whom this chapter is written. I shall, however, use the name symbolically and purged of racial overtones, for it is very sure that the animal so denominated flourishes in all climes and among all peoples. His greatest talent is acquired by learning and not by inheritance. It is the difficult art of sitting still.

[1] The *Living Age*, Vol. 344, p. 484.

At first sight, such an art may seem unreasonably simple. We have only to relax our muscles, and the desired effect will follow. Yet action is so often imperative, both as a biological need and as a social demand, that we seem to require reasons for doing nothing. The superstitions discussed in Chapters II and III recommend inaction because of the alleged futility of action. If human nature never changes, or if the evils of social inequality are set by evolutionary mandate, then clearly there is no use bothering our heads (or our feet) about them.

Such reasons for inaction, however, appeal chiefly to people of not very acute moral perceptions, people whose satisfaction with their own lot leaves them merely puzzled by others' misery. This is understandable enough, for it has long been recognized as one of the numbing effects of private prosperity. There exists, however, a considerable group of people who have comfort and even affluence, and who retain also a feeling for their fellow men. They are aware of suffering; they protest injustice. It would be quite natural for them to carry these ideas into action; in fact, they are always on the point of doing so. They live their lives balanced, it seems, upon a wire: one slight movement, and they would be plunged fully, deeply, irretrievably into an act.

The problem of men who want to prevent such action is, therefore, how to keep these people balanced upon the wire. It is a delicate maneuver, and failure will mean the plunge. Well, if the maneuver is delicate, it is also beautifully simple. Ask yourself what it is possible to do when balanced upon a wire. There is only one thing you can do, and that is *talk*. And what will you talk about? You will talk about the relative merits of falling off on the right side or the left.

There is yet another group which may be added to this category. These are people who enjoy the feeling of activity and of intimacy with events, but who do not wish to commit themselves to any particular current. They desire some acquaintance with action and (as they call it) an inside knowledge of what goes on, such as a tightrope artist cannot acquire. Yet at the same time, they wish to retain what they regard as their impartiality and their integrity. Impartiality will then consist in being at home in all currents, and integrity will consist in never making up one's mind.

Beside the balancer, then, we may set the wobbler. Now wobbling, it must be said, is not a form of gymnastic. The purpose of gymnastic is to train the muscles so extensively that they will readily control the movements of the body and, through that, the surrounding world. In a word, gymnastic is discipline. But wobbling, though it may appear very athletic and even acrobatic, reveals not discipline but the absence of it. Its most astonishing feats result simply from the play of contradictory forces, over which the wobbler exerts no influence at all. Tossed like a cork upon conflicting waves, he follows the wave that is stronger, riding, as it seems to him, sagely and majestically, with the familiar sky above and the familiar flood beneath. He enjoys direct acquaintance with the waters which bear him, and he reflects with satisfaction upon his own inner constancy — the true, the pure, and unsubmersive cork.

The world so vast and liquid, so buoyant and changeful, thus presents itself as an immortal ebb and flow. Surge meets surge and eddy meets eddy, with a kind of mechanical authority. The cork floats up one side of the monstrous wave, to glimpse at the apex a multitude of similar heights, and to glide swooningly down the other. There are, so it seems, two slopes to every wave. There are two waves to every trough. There are two sides to every question.

Perhaps we shall do well to admit at once that there is a strict, logical sense in which two sides do exist for every question. It is always possible to find for any statement another statement which is its exact contradictory. The second statement will be one which contains just what is necessary, and only what is necessary, to deny the first. Thus, for example, if I say that it rained here yesterday, my assertion will be denied by the statement that it did not rain here yesterday.[2]

This is the only sense in which we can be sure that there really are two sides to every question. But, unluckily for those who wish to avoid conclusions, this is also a sense in which one of the statements must be false. It is perfectly obvious that the two statements, "It rained here yesterday" and "It did not rain here yesterday," cannot both be true. It is equally obvious that one of those statements must be true and the other false. Even persons of the most inveterate detachment must see that the two "sides" are altogether unequal with respect to truth. For this reason it is very important that in all debates the central issue be carefully ex-

---

[2] *I.e.* assuming that the terms "here" and "yesterday" refer to one and the same place and time in the two statements.

pressed in terms of logical contradictories. It is the only means we have of being wholly sure what the argument is about.

By the same token, if two equally valid alternatives do on occasion exist, the alternatives will not be contradictories; and if they are not contradictories, their number is not necessarily limited to two. There is no definite limit which can be placed upon the number of statements which are capable of being consistent with one another. The wobbler and the balancer, therefore, face this dilemma: if the alternatives are contradictories, their number will be precisely two, but one of them will be false; and if the alternatives are not contradictories, they may be consistent with one another, but their number will not necessarily be two. Either the number or the validity is open to question.

It is probable that neither the wobbler nor the balancer will be much irked by this dilemma. For one thing, they were not thinking rigorously in terms of logical contradictories, but were loosely and urbanely aware that contestants seem to gather ultimately into two parties. Still less would they be alarmed at a possible multiplicity of sides. The greater the number of sides, the larger the area to be discussed. The larger the area to be discussed, the greater the indecision. The greater the indecision, the longer the postponement of action. I am afraid that my dilemma will only confirm the wobbler in his wickedness.

Let us try another approach. When people say that there are two sides to every question, they are not primarily thinking of determining scientific truth. They are thinking, rather, of political and social issues. They are aware of various programs competing for their support. They are rightfully suspicious of the ardor of zealots and the guile of propagandists, and the belief that "there is much to be said upon both sides" offers them a refuge in their perplexity.

Now it is the fate of principles to lose their content in proportion as they become mere devices of argument. So used, a principle begins to appear in so many different contexts that any strictness of original meaning is relaxed, and a multitude of meanings, corresponding to the multitude of contexts, takes its place. The resulting ambiguity is fatal to accurate thought. The principle becomes simply a counter which is moved about in an effort to forestall defeat.

The doctrine that there are two sides to every question suffers from a multiplicity of meanings more than any other of the myths discussed in this book. We have just now observed that its strict, logical meaning is one which nobody ever intends. Since, therefore, the doctrine is cut loose at the very start from its logical meaning, we may justly expect a good deal of variety and of whimsical choice among the meanings actually employed. These cannot be deduced from any logical content in the original assertion, but must be inferred from the various occasions on which the assertion is made. It may be that my list of the meanings is incomplete; or, on the contrary, it may be that I have overextended it. (I begin to sound like a wobbler myself!) At any rate, I can only appeal to the reader's personal experience to decide how accurate I have been.

In the statement that there are two sides to every question I find no less than seven possible meanings.

I shall state them at once, and then go on to discuss each in turn. The seven meanings are these:

(1) That major social issues divide mankind into two groups, each of which presents a certain amount of valid argument and exhibits a certain amount of self-interest.

(2) That in any given situation there is a plurality of equally good choices.

(3) That all theories contain a certain amount of truth and a certain amount of error, and that therefore one ought to select the truth from each.

(4) That taking sides destroys scientific impartiality.

(5) That the more you understand opposing theories, the more you are led to sympathize with the men who hold them.

(6) That all parties to a controversy have a right to be heard.

(7) That you should never come to a decision until you have thoroughly studied the issues.

The first, second, and third meanings, I should say, are characteristic of the wobbler. The fourth, fifth, and sixth are characteristic of the balancer. The seventh, which is plainly true, may be assigned to anybody.

SIX SUPERSTITIOUS MEANINGS

(1) The first possible meaning seems to be that, while there may not be two sides to *every* question, there are two sides to most major questions; and that on each of the two sides will be found a certain amount of valid

argument and a certain amount of self-interest. Major questions, that is to say, produce a polarization of forces. Because they tend to involve entire populations, there will be fewer and fewer people not entering one camp or the other. Their choice of camps will be based upon their interests; that is to say, people will choose what they think to be the camp of friends rather than the camp of enemies. Both camps, while the struggle is on, will make the best possible case for themselves; and since both camps will possess leaders of talent in propaganda, the two programs will appear about equally cogent. Being opposed yet equally cogent, the two programs seem to cancel each other out. Being motivated by self-interest, the two programs seem equally suspicious. The cork finds the swimming much the same on either side.

Equal cogency, then, and equal suspicion. The former puzzles, and the latter paralyzes. Now, the puzzling results from a concealed act of abstraction. The two programs are "weighed" against each other; that is to say, they are compared on the basis of their inner consistency and their outward persuasiveness, as if they had no relevance to a definite historical situation. This relevance, however, is precisely what they have, and is precisely what decides their merits. Abstracted from the immediate social context, the programs may appear convincingly equal; plunged into that context, they will manifest a decisive inequality. The choice which lay silent in its vacuum now cries aloud to be made. The reluctant chooser, to whom all such voices are siren, can now escape only by closing his ears.

The paralysis, on the other hand, results from supposing that the presence of self-interest on both sides corrupts them equally. It may seem astonishing, but there really are people who decline participation in human affairs because every social institution and every political movement is in this manner impure. Dazzled by the exceptional radiance of self-sacrifice, such people sit waiting for a movement and a program which will procure no advantage to its sponsors. They will wait a long time, for a social movement the members of which were consciously engaged in procuring disadvantages for themselves would be a very odd social movement indeed. Thus, to announce that both sides of a controversy exhibit self-interest is approximately as illuminating as for the cork to announce that there is water on both sides of the wave.

Now, it is perfectly true, of course, that self-interest can corrupt arguments. It does so whenever self-interest requires the deception of other people. But self-interest does not always (and, for most of us, not often) require the deception of others. On the contrary, self-interest is quite consistent with honesty — to such a degree, indeed, that Mr. Franklin, in a burst of optimism, affirmed honesty to be the best policy. Now where there is no deception, there is no willful corruption of argument. From the existence of self-interest in a group, then, we cannot infer that its program is necessarily specious. If a man helps me to put out the fire in my house in order to protect his own, it would be idiotic for me to say that his action is mistaken. And it would be less than gracious, if, for the same reason, I refrained from thanking him on the ground that he had intended me no service.

The concealed hypothesis which underlies such arguments is the proposition that a policy which favors oneself is automatically a policy which contributes nothing to the welfare of others. This proposition, in turn, rests upon the view that each man's personal interest is at least independent of, and probably opposed to, the interest of everybody else. The *bellum omnium contra omnes* — the war of all against all — is assumed as a basic fact. This assumption, as we observed in Chapter III, is sheer fiction. Even the animal kingdom exhibits as much co-operation as it does conflict. The falsity of the assumption is the ground of all our hopes for a decent world.

The fact that a given program displays the self-interest of a group, therefore, does not suffice to show that the program is either fraudulent or bad. The fraud and the evil can be inferred from the program's actual effects, and from these alone. But to judge these accurately, we must attempt to see all issues and programs in an entire historical perspective. So viewed, the question whether this group or that group is acting from self-interest becomes a very petty question indeed. The question which above all must be answered is this: what part does the given group play in social progress? If it is so placed as to have a progressive role, its self-interest is not a handicap but a boon to mankind.

This condition exists specifically for the labor movement. The laborers are so placed in our society that their struggles for self-improvement are also struggles against the inequalities and the tyrannies, small and great, which harass and imperil everybody else. Some sections of society (notably the lower middle class) have shown from time to time a susceptibility to fascism; but labor, by reason of its very position, has to be fascism's irreconcilable foe. Some sections of society can afford (or think they can afford) the gross pleasures of anti-Semitism, discrimination against Negroes, and the deportation of "undesirable" aliens; but the labor movement simply cannot survive if it tolerates such divisive activities within its ranks. Some sections of society can indulge without too great hardship a host of myths and superstitions such as are discussed in this volume. To the labor movement all such myths are fatal, and, as soon as they are discovered, they are destroyed.

Thus, just as the capitalists were the bearers of physical science in the days of their revolutionary triumphs, so the labor movement is the bearer of social science in our own day. It is not a question of the amount of knowledge possessed. It is simply that, just as the success of capitalists was incompatible with alchemy and astrology, so the success of labor is incompatible with the absurdities of Manchester economics and the grosser lies of *Mein Kampf*.

Some people, then, are peculiarly fortunate in the historical place they occupy. For many of us virtue is at worst a struggle and at best a chore. How must we envy those multitudes who cannot afford mysticism, ignorance, and brutality, and who therefore cease to be mystical or ignorant or brutal! They are with ease what we can be only with difficulty. Their self-interest is magically attuned to the interest of all. Let wobblers embrace this easeful virtue, forsaking the risks of endless doubt.

*   *   *

(2) From the peak of his wave the cork, we said, glimpses many similar peaks. He is likely, therefore, to be much impressed with the number of possible alternatives. Accordingly, when he asserts that there are two sides to every question, he sometimes means that in any given situation there is a plurality of equally good choices. In part, this view results from extending into important social issues the casual attention we bestow upon commonplace problems. If, for example, I am planning a vacation, there are perhaps half a dozen things I can do, all of which are about equally attractive and equally recreative. Or, if I decide to spend a few hours in reading, there are doubtless several books which can be read with equal pleasure and profit. A man whose life is full of varied interests and many satisfactions will be likely to feel that all occasions offer the plurality of choices to which he has grown accustomed.

It was Aristotle, however, who first worked out the notion that every occasion has just one act which is adequately suited to it. This act he called the mean, and all departures from it he regarded as extremes, since they will be acts which offer less than the occasion requires or more than it will bear. If a company of soldiers is holding a position which it is feasible to defend, the "mean" or courageous act consists in their remaining in that position. If they retreat from it, they display cowardice (the extreme of deficiency) ; and if they move forward, exposing themselves and risking the position, they display rashness (the extreme of excess). The suitable act, moreover, changes with changing circumstances. Thus, if the position becomes untenable and the soldiers nevertheless still occupy it, they display rashness instead of courage; whilst, if an attack becomes feasible and they remain in the position, they display not courage but cowardice.

This theory, which is one of Aristotle's most important contributions to human thought, really states the essence of all good planning. We have first the analysis of the objective situation, then the determination of a policy exactly suited to it, then the carrying out of the policy in action. The situation thus serves as a standard by which all proposals can be tested, and the fact that the situation is objectively real ensures protection from wishful thinking. To act upon decisions thus reached is indeed to act, as Aristotle would say, like "a man of practical wisdom."

I suppose that departures from the norm will sometimes be very slight, and on such occasions it may seem that there are several equally good choices. Yet even here the notion of a single policy which is the best possible will serve as an ideal to enforce rigor in our analysis. We can persuade ourselves of its existence, even though our best efforts fail to find it. Then we shall content ourselves with an approximation, and *act*.

But it is in collective action that the multiple-choice theory shows its most dangerous effects. If large numbers of men are to achieve certain goals by acting together, it is clear that they must be agreed upon the program they intend to carry out. They cannot act in concert if some of them accept one program, some a second program, and others yet a third. They could not do so, even if we were to grant that the three programs are equally good, as probably they are not. The men would nevertheless be carrying out three programs instead of one. Their energies would be divided. Instead of uniting their efforts to push one boulder up the hill, they would strive mightly to push three boulders, all of which remain stubbornly at the bottom. It is imperative that all of them get behind the "right" boulder (*i.e.* the one that really can be pushed to the top), and concentrate every effort there.

So true is this fact that the denial of it has become a time-honored means of sedition. Under such cover, traitors and renegades are able to profess the same purposes as their fellows and yet do all they can to render achievement impossible. They "agree," for instance, that fascism must be destroyed; but they urge that fascists should be personally reformed instead of being combated. In this manner, they say, we shall vanquish fascism without injuring anybody. A debate thereupon ensues, which may be made to last indefinitely. Meanwhile the fascists themselves arrive with tanks and artillery, at which moment the question of who reforms whom becomes fairly academic.

Tactics of this sort are familiar in all organized groups. The device of the glittering alternative exists to prevent action while seeming to propose it. And the alternative can be glittering indeed. It can be made to contain every sort of attractive trait — kindness, honor, feasibility. In the absence of the supreme test, whether the program actually suits the circumstances, the glitter will remain without tarnish; and the group itself, like Buridan's ass, will die of starvation between two equidistant bales of hay.

* * *

(3) Let us suppose, next, that we have a wobbler home from the sea and slightly regenerate. The long alternation of rise and fall has deprived him of all sense of novelty, but he has grown aware of dangers lurking in the various waves. It strikes him that one respect in which sides are very similar is that each contains a certain amount of error. Would it not be possible to purge the sides of error and draw them into a unity? If there is much to be said on both sides, why not isolate that "much" and compose it into a single theory, a single program? The wobbler turns eclectic.

Now the supposition that no theory has all of the truth, but that every theory has some part of it, is a view both cautious and amiable. It hurts nobody's feelings, since everyone is credited with some sense; and it runs no risks, since everyone is said to fall short of complete accuracy. There is in the notion, moreover, an element of time-saving: we spare ourselves the effort of discovering, analyzing, and systematizing truth, and we simply rely upon a judicious selection from the results of other people's labor. Our product may resemble a stew; but the stew, so we are told, is nourishing.

Well, in the first place, I think it is obviously not true that every theory contains some valid assertions. Some theories, though perhaps few in number, are monumental in error, and can sprawl to an astonishing length without once bringing themselves into contact with truth. I should wonder, for example, what assertions our eclectic philosopher would care to choose from astrology or numerology, with which to furnish his view of the world. What statements would he select from the racist doctrines of Dr. Goebbels?

In the second place, we cannot really make selections from various theories unless we already have a fair idea of what the facts are. If we are to select, we must do so on the basis of some criterion which will enable us to separate the true from the false. Otherwise we choose indiscriminately, and our composite result will be a mixture of truth and error such as we presumably did not intend. But if, in order to choose wisely, we must already be in possession of some of the truth, then we cannot have got this portion by eclectic means. The uses of eclecticism, therefore, depend upon a process of truth-finding which is not eclectic. The man of liberal mind, in search of truth on various sides, will first have to discover what the truth is before he can discover how much of it the various sides contain.

When he has done this, he will further find that the sides manifest a grave imbalance with respect to truth. It happens that the assertions which make up a total theory are by no means of equal importance to the theory itself. Some of them are vital to it; others are a good deal less than vital. There are theories which are correct in their basic assertions and wrong in some details, and there are theories which are wrong in their basic assertions but accidentally right in some details. Still others, as I have suggested, are wrong — and often deliberately wrong — throughout. It would be a curious exercise of impartiality to regard all these theories as equally interesting and equally valuable, with an equal amount of error interspersed among the various excellences.

The great danger of eclecticism, therefore, lies in its talent for putting personal (and in all likelihood, whim-

sical) choice in the place of scientific inquiry. There is
a subjectivity about it, a sense that facts matter less than
the way one thinks about them, which, if it were reso-
lutely pursued to the end, would annihilate all science
and all wisdom. It represents the kind of open-mind-
edness in which the mind is so open that everything falls
through. There remains a dead and silent, though
doubtless not an aching, void.

*   *   *

(4) So much for the wobbler. The balancer, for his
part, appears in three aspects, all of which display aloofness if not intellectual acumen. He presents himself respectively as the scientist, the humanitarian, and the
man of justice. They are three extremely potent roles.

In the first of these, the balancer tells us that to choose
one program as against others destroys the impartiality
which a scientific point of view requires. This is what
he means when he says that there are two sides to every
question. It is a point of view generally and, as I think,
somewhat slanderously regarded as academic. For the
most part, men of the learned world are as active in
effectuating their ideals as is consistent with the retain-
ing of their posts. Nevertheless, there are among them
scholars who really do believe that, once decision is
followed by action, the free play of thought and judgment is forever impaired.

We may find this view, for example, in many sociologists. These gentlemen are prone to say that their studies
are descriptive and not normative, by which portly ter-
minology they mean that, as they look about society,
they simply describe what they find, and they make no

recommendations for improvement. They do not even assert that any particular social situation is good or bad, for such assertions would mean that they had taken sides.

Now, *scientific* impartiality means the acceptance of knowledge of things as they are, without any distortion or prejudice. If, therefore, any form of social action is to be regarded as destroying impartiality, it would have to be a form which prevents or corrupts the knowledge of things as they are. And if it is held that all forms of social action destroy impartiality, then it must follow that all forms of social action prevent or corrupt a knowledge of things as they are. In other words, scientific impartiality would imply political neutrality.

Well, it does nothing of the sort. Negatively stated, scientific impartiality means that you do not start with desired conclusions and then invent reasons for them. It means that you do not accept statements as true simply because you want them to be true, even though to doubt them may seem to rob life of any value. It means, lastly, that you do not ignore or distort facts in order to maintain the program of any party or of any group whatsoever.

Does it follow from such a concept of impartiality that we must be neutral on all social issues? Or, to put it another way, if we decide in favor of a certain program, does it follow that we no longer accurately understand the content of the programs we decided against? Obviously it does not follow. In the first place, our knowledge of the other programs contributed to our choice of the one we favor. In the second place, it remains relevant during action. Without such knowledge we should never understand what groups we are fighting or what groups constitute our possible allies. Once action is under way, all this knowledge becomes even more important than it was before, and its accuracy has a yet higher value. Thus it is not true that decision necessarily stultifies knowledge. Exactly the opposite can be true. With action, our understanding is clarified and deepened; with inaction, it fusts unused.

Let us return to a previous example. It is a fact that fascism persecutes racial and national minorities. It is a fact that fascism destroys popular government and civil rights. It is a fact that fascism abolishes independent labor unions and enormously increases the exploitation of labor. It is a fact that fascism has one and only one foreign policy: world conquest. These facts are determined in the way all facts are determined, namely, by observation of the actual data. In no way are they conclusions for which reasons have been invented, or beliefs accepted out of wish, or partisan distortions of fact. They are asserted with full scientific impartiality.

Now, then: can it really be said that I cease to be scientifically impartial if I fight fascism? Do I change, modify, or ignore those assertions in any way if I denounce fascism as an evil to be removed as soon as possible? On the contrary, it is precisely because fascism does those things that I propose to fight it. It is precisely upon those facts that my stand is taken. My decision cannot distort the facts *because it follows from them*. I am not politically neutral, but I remain scientifically impartial. And, in general, how much of a scientist would I be, if I did not fight the great enemy of all science and all culture?

There is a second assumption which we must examine; namely, that taking sides introduces an ethical element into science. Rigorously held, this belief would mean that a scientist could hold no moral opinions at all — at least not upon those subjects in which he is a scientist.

There is a good historical reason for the existence of this belief. When modern science emerged from the mists of medievalism, one of the things it had to get rid of was the use of ethical reasons to prove natural facts. Thus, for example, Aristotle had "proved" the sphericity of the moon on the ground that the sphere is the best shape and that God would create only the best. The conclusion of the argument happens to be true, but it is obvious that the reasons are no reasons at all.

In the long struggle against this sort of proof, scientists tended finally to the other extreme. They came to believe that there is no connection whatever between fact and value, between ethics and natural science; indeed, they have sometimes appeared to think that the two disciplines are mutually contradictory and repellent. Let us look at this belief.

We grant it true that facts cannot be proved on the basis of moral reasoning. Does it follow from this that, once the facts have been scientifically demonstrated, there can be no moral reasoning about them? Clearly it does not follow. A prohibition upon the use of ethics in the demonstration of facts is not a prohibition upon the use of ethics in the *evaluation* of those facts. Though you may not assign moral reasons for the things existing around you, you are certainly entitled to use such reasons in making choices. Science decides the context in which action occurs and the means which action employs, but ethics decides which of the various programs is right and ought to be followed. A scientist, then, who eschews ethics completely may remain to some degree a scientist, but he will be only half a man. He will, perhaps, have knowledge, but he will not act. He will confess himself informed, but useless.

Lastly, I think we should observe that on great issues neutrality is an illusion. Once the battle is joined — once, that is to say, there really are two sides to the question — everything done, or left undone, assists one side or the other. The diffident gentlemen who in these times have not come to the aid of democracy must be considered to have helped fascism. Their "scientific" inaction is one of the things Hitler most relied upon, and not without success.

We arrive, therefore, at a conclusion which completely upsets the original contention; for we find that where there are two, and only two, sides to a question, it is in fact impossible not to take one or the other, no matter how one tries. Aloofness, so fondly nursed in theory, is nullified in fact.

*   *   *

(5) When the balancer turns his eye inward to examine, not the dubious aspects of an outer world, but the cordial intimacies of his own soul, he discovers that he is a very humane man. He is able, he finds, to sympathize with both the warring parties. He reflects that he is a man even as they are men, with an inclination to contentiousness which he, however, has overcome. The issue itself, he feels, is dwarfed by the presence of human beings on both sides of the question.

This agreeable point of view, which, in itself, exhibits more than a little vanity, often matches that vanity with a quite appropriate illusion. Generally speaking, it will be humane to sympathize with the various contestants, provided the contestants are themselves humane. But if one of the parties turns out to be engaged in practices harmful to mankind, that would be an odd humanity indeed which finds itself in sympathetic accord with it. There is a maxim to the effect that we should "hate the sin and love the sinner." The practice of this maxim I leave to those who are capable of such athletics.

It seems time to place strict limits upon the ancient platitude, *tout comprendre, c'est tout pardonner*. There is evidence enough, for example, that fascism can be perfectly well understood both in its social and psychological origins, without our being obliged to treat it with sympathy or shower it with forgiving tears. In their social actions fascists are men in whom every humane impulse, every prompting of kindness or affection, has been carefully suppressed and, if possible, extirpated. In the place of all such normal feelings is set a devouring hate, a restless, insatiable craving to destroy all that other men have cherished and admired. The Third Reich was decorated with the trophies of slaughtered cultures (including the German), like a cannibal's hut hung with skulls. The revival of medieval horrors, such as the headsman and his ax, gave way to the awful efficiency of mass extermination. Surely the men who have been able to look upon such practices with a sympathetic eye manifest a strange humanity indeed. And the sooner such men are forcibly restrained from their sympathy, the better it will be for mankind.

I conclude, therefore, that, although we are doubtless required to understand all the things we pass judgment upon, we are not required to approve all the things which we understand. If the knowledge of evil does not move us to detest it and fight it, we shall have surrendered man's noblest attribute — the power to triumph over invading wrongs. I know of no ethical principle which requires us to sit in sodden, sympathetic inaction, while our best hopes go drowning in an unfathomable glue of good will.

To be humane is to love mankind. To love mankind, I rather think, is to destroy its enemies.

*   *   *

(6) The balancer is, lastly, a man of justice; and when he tells us that there are two sides to every question, he often means that all parties to a controversy have a right to be heard. Nothing can seem more just and liberal than such a doctrine, especially so long as it is divorced from social fact. Plunged into the real world, however, it has a perverse habit not only of changing its moral complexion, but even of negating itself.

The main justification for supposing that all parties have a right to be heard is the desire that no truths shall be suppressed and no valid claims ignored. It is assumed, further, that even though the parties are mistaken in their assertions or their claims, they honestly thought they had a case to make for themselves. To say that they "honestly thought" they had a case means, essentially, that they did not concoct their arguments for deception and malicious propaganda. The man who sincerely argues a mistaken view is altogether different from the man who turns every opportunity for public utterance into the calculated dissemination of lies. Everyone will grant that men of truth deserve to be heard. Most of us would grant that the man of honest mistakes deserves to be heard. But, other than the liars themselves, who would care to maintain that liars deserve a hearing?

I think that, merely as an abstract principle, it could very well be asserted that conscious mendacity has no right to express itself. But the cogency of this principle is overwhelming when we turn to concrete examples. In Germany, in the days before Hitler's ascendancy, the leaders of the Social Democratic Party were obsessed with the notion that the principle of free speech meant free speech for Nazis. Now in order to seize power, the Nazis had to establish a mass base in the German population. The establishment of such a base required free opportunity to circulate its mendacious doctrines (anti-Semitism, for example) by pamphlets, books, and oratory. The granting of that free opportunity to Nazis ended in the loss of freedom for everyone else. It ended, also, in persecutions, murders, and war — that is to say, in the death of millions of the world's people. Thus abused, the right of free speech negated not only itself but all the other rights fostered and cherished by progressive mankind.

It must be so always and everywhere. Whenever there exists a group of people bent upon oppression, it will, unless checked, consume and annihilate all other groups. The fate of men who cannot formulate their own views will be to have their views made for them and taught

with whips and castor oil. Tolerance can endure everything but intolerance. Freedom can reach to everyone,
except to those who make men slaves.

*   *   *

(7) Having now opposed the balancer and the wobbler on six separate assertions, we owe them the kindness of granting them a view for which some case can
be made. Accordingly, let us interpret the statement,
"there are two sides to every question," to mean that
one should never come to a decision until the issue has
been carefully studied. This view seems altogether un-
exceptionable. I think, indeed, that it is so, provided
the limits of carefulness are not so far extended as to
procure an indefinite postponement of action. The balancer and the wobbler may contrive to look very studious. They may perpetually say, "Wait a moment, wait a
moment, I have not yet finished my examination of the
evidence." Events, however, do not so readily wait as
people do. The problem under study finds some resolu-
tion in the course of events, and the studious examiners
are left balancing and wobbling as before.

The practical purpose of all study is to exert some
influence upon changing environment. To exert that
influence in accordance with our wishes requires a pretty
accurate knowledge of events in the physical and social
world. There is no doubt that, ideally at least, we ought
to know all possibilities and all programs before making
up our minds, for otherwise our decision may well defeat
itself through ignorance.

This is one limit upon our planning. There is, as I
have suggested, another. All plans are made for a certain

moment in history; they are relevant to that moment, and to that alone. When the moment passes, it will be succeeded by another moment to which the original plan no longer relates. The plan, however ingenious in concept and detail, is then left with nothing to do, nothing to influence in the intended way. This is the moral, the philosophy, of that famous happy-unhappy phrase, "Too little and too late."

Human beings, therefore, in their attempts to control the world around them, are locked within two limits. They must, on the one hand, not act before knowledge is acquired; but, on the other hand, they must act before opportunity vanishes. These limits are at all times narrow, and sometimes desperately so. Man's transcending of these limits to exert an ever-increasing mastery over the world constitutes, I think, the most laureate of all his triumphs.

WHY WOBBLERS WOBBLE

We are now in a position to see how ambiguous is the belief we have been discussing, and how unsatisfactory the various meanings we have disentangled. None of the meanings is true without qualification, and most contain in ample volume all the deceptiveness required for deliberate darkening of counsel.

It will not suffice, however, simply to explain, by an analysis of their contents, how thoroughly misleading these notions are. We need, in addition, some account of how it comes to pass that certain people are especially susceptible to these particular illusions. At this point, it would be tempting, and might even be enlightening, to pursue a psychological inquiry into the nature of special temperaments. For my part, however, I have not these hieratic gifts; and, in any event, it seems much more profitable to set both the illusions and the susceptible temperaments in their historical place.

We start with the fact that some people either cannot or will not make up their minds on social and political issues. Or, again, on a series of issues they waver so remarkably as to reveal an absence of any consistent, over-all program. Why is it so?

Indecision upon social issues arises from contradictions among basic beliefs. Any social theory, whether consciously or unconsciously held, contains a number of assertions. It is possible — indeed, it is only too likely — that when these assertions are applied to a specific problem, they will begin to contradict one another. Suppose we have a man who believes in the institutions of political democracy, but dislikes labor unions, Jews, Negroes, aliens, and whatever other items you care to add to this melancholy list. Now suppose that labor unions begin to utilize the institutions of political democracy in order to enact wage-and-hour legislation, unemployment insurance, old age pensions, and so forth. Our friend (who, alas, is not imaginary) is now torn between his belief in democracy and his dislike of unionism. If he continues his support of political democracy, he has to accept the steady advance of labor; if he continues his dislike of labor, he has to yield, equally steadily, his belief in democratic institutions.

There now ensues a period of wavering. Sometimes

our friend supports the democratic measure, sometimes the antilabor restriction. Sometimes he won't make any decision at all. He gives it up: the world has become too perplexing, too full of selfishness and conflict. The old clarities, the old self-sacrifice are gone. He doffs the role of wobbler; he becomes a balancer and an Olympian.

Though now above the battle, he still smarts from the frustration he has received. Filled with sorrow and with somewhat angry ideals, he scolds his contemporaries for their worldliness. He denounces even the leaders whom he once followed and whom, perhaps, he yet regards as the best of a bad lot. Every tactical concession which they make in the course of battle he attacks as a surrender of the whole cause. Why will they not listen? Why will they not see the things he sees from his height? *"O tempora, O mores,"* he sighs — it is all the Cicero he can remember.

Our friend, as I describe him, is a composite image; but he is no fiction. He represents, indeed, a whole movement of thought which stretches from the seventeenth century into the twentieth. It is what we call the liberal tradition.

Now, this tradition arose in justification of capitalist society as against feudalism. It worked out in detail the jurisprudence of individual property rights. It also evolved the doctrines of political democracy and civil liberties, which were the great weapons against the feudal lords. After 1688, Locke added to the body of the theory the further doctrine of general tolerance, of live and let live. For the merchants had discovered that, if they were to spread commerce all over the globe, or even to conduct it amicably in Europe, they could not afford to be too intolerant of other people's opinions. As Josiah Tucker observed in 1750, religious liberty is a good thing, regarded "merely in a commercial point of view."

Private property, political democracy, and tolerance — these are the three main elements in the liberal tradition. The tradition itself has been perhaps the most powerful of modern times. Most of us in the western world have grown up in it, and our political thinking arises from it as from a system of self-evident truths.

In the past twenty years, however, the three principles of liberalism have not dwelt together so serenely. The section of Italian and German capitalists who embraced fascism in order to maintain (their own) private property, evidently sacrificed the other two principles of liberalism. Their influence upon recent history has been so great as to make it appear that the three principles would never again be reconciled. Whether they are in fact reconcilable remains to be established by contemporary events.

I am not prophet enough to know what the immediate issue of these events will be. It seems safe to say, however, that if the present system of private property shows itself reasonably compatible with improved living standards at home and with increasing freedom for colonial peoples abroad, then a reconciliation of the principles will occur. But if the system of private property defends itself by driving down the standard of living and by continuing the enslavement of colonial peoples, then no reconciliation of the principles will be possible. In the face of these alternatives, liberals must undertake either to recover their liberalism on a higher plane or to transform it into another theory which will be more representative of social advance.

At all events, it is clear that men can no longer afford to withdraw from social action or to postpone it indefinitely. Even as a mere matter of knowing the world, it is true that, where decision is absent, all else is mistiness and futility. Patience, tolerance, impartiality, and all kindred excellences are really aids to decision, not hindrances upon it; and we should never pursue them so exclusively as to miss the goals they were appointed to achieve.

CHAPTER VI

THAT THINKING
MAKES IT SO

THEY PASS quickly, the blue patches and the red. An inverted triangle of white is cut by a width of blue. There is a dome shape of scarlet with yellow fluttering away from it. Underneath, everything is hardness. Sounds intersperse the patches. The streaks of revolving gray associate themselves with a quiet whir. There are squeaking sounds as the black quadrilateral stops next a red circle. A sweet and pungent taste steals in upon the sounds and patches. There is the pleasure of a solid that yields to touch, an intimate sense of continuing, victorious effort.

This is the way a certain portion of the world would look to a solipsist out for an afternoon stroll. He is walking along a city street, observing other people as he goes. He notices a man wearing a white shirt and blue tie, a woman wearing a scarlet hat with yellow feathers. He hears the whir of automobile tires on the paved street, the squeak of brakes as a truck stops before a red light. His mouth enjoys a sweet taste, for he is chewing candy. Every motion of the jaws sustains in him a thriving sense of accomplishment.

But, you will think, what a way to describe perfectly commonplace events! I agree that it is strange. The way, however, is not mine, for I merely repeat a language which contemporary philosophy has made fashionable. The mode now is to talk about "color-patches" rather than about "objects," and the reason is that the former term clearly assumes less than the latter and therefore seems to avoid more problems. The theory, indeed, is born of an infinite caution. The philosopher who seeks to be both precise and empirical knows (or thinks he knows) that he indubitably has a red patch in his consciousness, though he can never be sure whether there is any object to excite the patch. And he feels that what one cannot be sure of, it is safer not to assume.

"Solipsism" is, of all words, one of the most faithful to its etymology. It was compounded, by deliberate act rather than by unconscious growth, of two Latin words, of which the first means "alone" and the second "oneself." The term thus becomes admirably expressive of the view that everyone is immediately aware only of his own existence and of the sensations which fill his consciousness. If it is believed, further, that such immediate awareness is the only guarantee authenticating our knowledge of what exists, the conclusion will follow that the existence of oneself and the existence of one's sensations are the only things abiding sure.

The step from doubt to denial is brief and easy. If I know *only* my own existence and that of my sensations, then I do not know the existence of anything or anybody else. And if I do not know the existence of anything or anybody else, what is the use of supposing their existence? What, in general, is the use of assuming what

I can never know? The conviction grows upon me that there probably isn't anything in the world except the conscious Me. In the course of time, the "probably" disappears. My cautious agnosticism vanishes before a warm belief that I alone exist. Stars, suns, and planets shrink to become the furniture of a little room which is my consciousness, and there in the midst of marvels I sit, a lonely and patient perceiver, the archetype of all being, the eternal and indestructible Self.

What does the Self do in its seclusion? It thinks. It entertains feelings, desires, ideas. In the lucidity of simple awareness it sustains, like an unwearying Atlas, the fabric of innumerable worlds. Is there food to be eaten, and a body to be fed by it? Yes, so far as my consciousness presents them. Are there chairs to be sat on and people to be talked with? Yes, so far as I have "bundles of sensations" answerable to these names. Are some things good and others evil? Yes, so far as they suit or contradict my feelings and desires. The things exist because I think them. The values exist because I think them. It is thinking that makes it so.

Now, of course, not very many people are willing to confess themselves complete solipsists. Everything they *do* is based upon quite the opposite hypothesis. When they arise in the morning, it is from a bed which they take to be more than sensations in their minds. They move about in a world presumed to be independent of themselves. And to that suspended consciousness which is sleep they return at night, wholly convinced that the physical universe loses none of its existence during the hours when they know it not.

Thus the man-in-the-street, that mythical being upon

whom are fathered all the absurdities which philosophers love to refute, is on the whole a common-sense
realist. It never occurs to him to suppose that the world
exists merely in his own mind. The sophisticated abstractions which produce a Bishop Berkeley are not for him.
Only the plain and level world, with its obvious other-
ness, its obstinate differentiation from himself. And the
man-in-the-street is wise beyond his reputation. As Mr.
Bertrand Russell once remarked, when you begin to
philosophize, you must make up your mind whether
you are going to be logical or going to be sane. Philosophers are often logical. The common man is mostly
sane.

There are other paths to solipsism beside the doubt
whether objects exist behind our sensations. It is possible to think, for example, that the world around us is
not so firm and rigorous a system as to preclude the free
play of thought and fancy. Thus Mr. Lewis Mumford
writes:

Often man's imagination has led him into error and his
search for light has plunged him into deeper darkness, even
as his will-to-perfection has sometimes made him inhuman,
cruel, life-denying. It was easier for myth and religion to
personify subjects than for science to objectify objects. But
the final outcome of these efforts has been a deeper insight
into his condition and destiny than his practical activities
by themselves could ever have called forth. For it is by
means of his ideal fabrications that man circumvents his
animal fate: his idolum and his super-ego help him to tran-
scend the narrow pragmatic limits of human society.[1]

[1] Lewis Mumford: *The Condition of Man*, Harcourt, Brace & Co.,
New York, 1944, p. 11.

We perceive from this passage that myth and science are thought to play co-ordinate roles in human life. Science works with difficulty, myth with ease; but myth, though sometimes deceptive, is altogether more profound. We get beyond our "animal fate," whatever that may be, not by increasing our scientific knowledge of the world, but by "ideal fabrications," by setting up an "idolum" which shall express the substance of our wish.

Now, an idolum is a complex of ideals which dominate the thinking of any epoch, and it therefore reflects, so to say, the majority opinion as to what is most desirable. According to Mr. Mumford's theory and practice, the test of an idolum is not its correspondence with fact. The test is the adequacy with which the idolum represents the essential needs of man. The test is therefore applied subjectively to the human self rather than objectively to physical or social conditions. The self may be revealed in myth and dream, but science is tied down to literal statements which shall be as mathematically precise as possible. By a kind of poetic inspiration, then, an idolum gets deeper into human realities than science does.

One may doubt that it gets deeper. It does, however, get muddier; and, in conceptual thinking generally, muddiness is often mistaken for depth. At all events, the view is certainly solipsistic. For if science, with all its careful techniques, succeeds in presenting only a secondary reality, the primary one escaping it altogether, then our insight into fundamental truths is necessarily restricted to nonscientific and nonrational processes. Each of us finds himself back in that little room, the castle of the Self, where the only questions are whether the space is tidy, the floor swept, the furniture dusted, and a semblance of order reigning over all. We shall wear our opinions as we wear our clothes, for the sake of comeliness or charm, and for the avoidance of mere nakedness.

What used to be regarded as a special vice of philosophers has thus become the firm practice of men who supply the public with its ideas. In men like these we find a general belief that the world's ultimate secrets lie buried in scarcely fathomable mines of the Self. We find, also, a belief that by no means all selves contain this hidden gold. Members of the intellectual elite are pleasantly convinced that they themselves possess it; yet, at the same time, they are less pleasantly convinced that the great multitude of selves possess no gold at all. There develops an ingenious co-operative enterprise by which men who are rich in thought, uniting with men who are rich in money, scatter their own largesse freely, and compensate by their own prodigality for the more reluctant charity of their allies.

In recent years these solipsists, in whom are locked the secrets of existence, have appeared before the public as political and military experts. A knowledge of politics and of military affairs, in the sense of acquaintance with objective reality, does not appear to be a universal, or even a common, attribute of this status. For among the assertions which these experts have made will be found the following: that the Munich Conference established peace in our time, that Czechoslovakia was actually more secure without her fortifications, that Germany and Russia would never fight, and that neither Germany nor Japan would ever attack America.

The German invasion of Russia, which was believed to have upset nobody but the world's Communists, produced the following set of expert predictions:

In my judgment, Hitler will be in control of Russia within 30 days.[2]

Despite all conflicting reports from the Russian front, U. S. experts have not wavered in their belief, arrived at regretfully, that in the end Russia cannot stem the tide of Nazi mechanized force.[3]

One thing, however, may be assumed with reasonable assurance; that we are witnessing the violent and ignominious end of the Caucasian brigand-chief Dzugashvili, known to history as Joseph Stalin.[4]

One thing seems to me certain: the Soviet State of the last quarter-century is finished. It will either be conquered, or split into several pieces, or reorganized on new non-communist lines.[5]

Mr. Snow in his innocence may imagine that the (Soviet) government will extend "full political support" to Soviet guerrillas and give them "the authority to lead mass resistance among the millions." Anyone who has known Russia under Stalin is aware that his government would never dare to allow armed forces to operate in Russia outside the control of its police power.[6]

The last of these predictions is perhaps the most pathetic, for it obviously has been deduced *a priori* from

[2] Martin Dies, as quoted in the *New York Times*, June 24, 1941, p. 3.

[3] Drew Pearson and Robert S. Allen: *Washington Merry-Go-Round*, July 18, 1941.

[4] Eugene Lyons: "The End of Joseph Stalin," *American Mercury*, August, 1941, Vol. 53, p. 136.

[5] Freda Utley: "The Limits of Russian Resistance," *American Mercury*, September, 1941, Vol. 53, p. 300.

[6] *Ibid.*, p. 298.

the author's belief that the Soviet government was a tyranny seated upon a discontented people. The fact that Russian guerrillas were already armed and trained and that their liaison with the regular army was already worked out was known at the time Miss Utley wrote.

Between the statements of such experts and the actual course of events no remarkable correspondence appears, and indeed the two sequences seem to have moved in opposite directions. Yet one seldom hears of a commentator's being dismissed because his assertions fail to correspond to reality. The military experts who pronounced the German army invincible or who insisted that air-power by itself could win the war are still at their jobs analyzing the news. The political experts who have predicted everything from the imminence of famine [7] to the arrival of Communism in America (an event especially conjectured in election years) are still predicting, and with very similar success.

CAN YOU KEEP YOUR WITS ABOUT YOU?

How are such things possible? It might be said, of course, that the experts are not experts but propagandists, that they seek not to explain events but to influence action. Let us, however, set aside uncharitable

[7] *E.g.* Louis Bromfield: "We Aren't Going to Have Enough to Eat," *Reader's Digest*, August, 1943, p. 111: "Though ours is the richest agricultural nation, our people are not going to have enough food. . . . The situation will grow worse this fall, and reach its most desperate stage this winter, especially from February on. . . . If it were possible, I would rather not think about next February. By then most of our people will be living on a diet well below the nutrition level." Quite a contribution to war time morale!

imputations. What concerns us here is the fact that an expert's credibility apparently does not lie in any relation between his statements and a world independent of him. Well, if his credibility does not lie there, it must lie somewhere else. It must lie in a persuasive arrangement of his own ideas — their inner logic, their esthetic appeal, or (the possibility exists) their moral fervor. It is his thinking that makes it so.

Or, to dally for a moment with the derogatory hypothesis, suppose that the expert is writing tendentiously in order to make us do what he wishes. He must believe — must he not? — that our acceptance of his views will help bring the event itself to pass, or that, if the event fails, we shall go on crediting its existence nevertheless. In the first circumstance he would be a William James; in the second, a Mussolini.[8] Let us examine these two notions more closely.

Out of sheer good will and impatience with delaying fortune, James produced a theory of truth by which men's eagerest desires might find the fruition immediately available. "Faith in a fact can help create the fact"; your will to believe in your assertions can swiftly make them true. And so the old romanticist mused:

How many women's hearts are vanquished by the mere sanguine insistence of some man that they *must* love him! he will not consent to the hypothesis that they cannot. The desire for a certain kind of truth here brings about that

[8] There is a good historical reason for juxtaposing these two names. Mussolini, who always had a flair for literacy, acknowledged James's pragmatism as one of the sources of his thought. Politically, James was the opposite of a fascist. Peace to his shade! he was a democrat beguiled by boundless curiosity.

special truth's existence; and so it is in innumerable cases of other sorts. Who gains promotions, boons, appointments, but the man in whose life they are seen to play the part of live hypotheses, who discounts them, sacrifices other things for their sake before they have come, and takes risks for them in advance? His faith acts on the powers above him as a claim, and creates its own verification.[9]

I cannot report upon the aptness of this theory for successful courtship, since, before I had knowledge of the passage, I had rendered its use unnecessary. My acquaintance with promotions, boons, and appointments is, though a little distant, such as to suggest that the getting of them evidently requires a greater intensity of wish than I have been able to summon. Promotions, boons, and appointments do seem to depend on other causes than myself, upon causes over which I exert either little influence or none at all. There is not, I find, much comfort in the view that thinking, if thought be passionate enough, will make these things so.

Nevertheless, the effort required to make things true by thinking them true can fan the mind to a terrible heat. Our thoughts begin to burn with scarcely extinguishable fire, and the conflagration will continue so long as there is fuel. This fuel it is the task of experts to supply. When they cannot supply it from the actual realization of our wishes, they have to supply it from ideas and fancies which we like. They ransack our tastes and our aversions, our crumbs of knowledge and our loaves of ignorance, our doubts, hopes, fears, admira-

---

[9] William James: *The Will To Believe,* Longmans, Green & Co., New York, 1899, p. 24. James's italics.

tions, and regrets. Once they have gained upon us sensibly, they insinuate the belief that the mind's inner life is more important than its outer awareness, and that of the mind's inner life the innermost sanctuary is passion. Thought triumphs over experience, and emotion triumphs over thought. Let us listen to the masters:

It is true that Fascism is, above all, action and sentiment and that such it must continue to be. . . . Only because it is feeling and sentiment, only because it is the unconscious reawakening of our profound racial instinct, has it the force to stir the soul of the people, and to set free an irresistible current of national will.[10]

Misery came over mankind . . . because it neglected to follow its instincts in this respect and by indulging in half-baked intellectual education. . . . The outside world still has not grasped the spiritual foundation of the National Socialist revolution and is still debating about democracy versus dictatorship, while the German revolution is democracy in the highest sense of the word. . . . I am also one of the people and not a foreign intellectual or apostle of international revolution.[11]

Every great political transformation, if it is really great, is never a matter of exterior events but always arises from a philosophic conception.[12]

We no longer believe that reason controls life. We have realized that life controls reason. Life has no goal. Mankind has no goal. We witness the sublime aimlessness of a

[10] Alfredo Rocco: "The Political Doctrine of Fascism," in D. O. Wagner's *Social Reformers*, Macmillan, New York, p. 644.

[11] Adolf Hitler: Speech to the Reichstag, January 30, 1937; *Vital Speeches*, Vol. 3, p. 265.

[12] Alfred Rosenberg: "For Culture and the Spirit," in the *Living Age*, March, 1935, p. 33 (Translated from the *Völkischer Beobachter*).

great performance. Ideas act irrationally through the blood. Consciousness is a matter of indifference. Life is the alpha and omega, and Life is devoid of all system, all progress, all reason. It exists simply for its own sake.[13]

The basic pattern of human existence is not the understanding of things and a mutual understanding between men; it is the growth and struggle of vital energies in their anthropological manifestations.[14]

The Germans are merely following the course which the nineteenth-century German thinkers mapped out for them. The history of the past hundred years is a good illustration of the fact that in social evolution nothing is inevitable but thinking makes it so.[15]

An interesting collection! Of these six quotations, the first five are direct from prominent fascists — although the word "prominent" seems a little feeble when applied to Hitler. The sixth, which is not (so far as I know) the remark of a fascist, is an apt comment upon its predecessors. The purpose and effect of their common doctrines will best be observed, if we first make plain the two great principles of rational scientific method. Those principles are (1) to test all statements by comparing them with observable events in a world independent of the thinker, and (2) to compose statements into a system which is internally consistent — that is to say, into a system in which the statements do not contradict one another.

[13] Oswald Spengler, quoted in Leonard Barnes: *Empire or Democracy?*, Gollancz, London, 1939, p. 226.
[14] Ludwig Klages, quoted in Leonard Barnes: *op. cit.*, p. 225.
[15] Gladstone Murray, Public Relations Counsel, formerly General Manager of the Canadian Broadcasting Corporation: "Is the Profit Motive Anti-Social?", in *Vital Speeches*, Vol. 11, p. 149.

Now, these principles are extremely rigorous. The first of them ties us down to a world which simply is what it is, a world in which we cannot change things to suit our fancy, unless we manipulate them according to our knowledge — and not always then. The second ties us down to the requirements of logic, so that we cannot assemble just whatever statements we please, but only those that will actually go together.

The *leaders* of fascism know all this very well, and they never consciously endanger their own program by practicing the epistemological nonsense which they preach. But when you set out to enslave whole populations, including your own, it is absolutely necessary that you (1) prevent men from seeing the world as it actually is, and (2) that you prevent them from critically examining the contents of your ideology. Now, the statements composing your ideology are chosen each for its own propagandist purpose; and thus the total assemblage contains statements which cannot by the wildest extension of logic be made to fit together. For example, you cannot in the same system have the statement "Aryans are blond and blue-eyed" and the statement "Japanese are Aryans" — or, for that matter, the statement "Hitler is an Aryan."

Well, then, what do you do? You corrupt the first rational principle by a series of doctrines running something like this: "The social sciences cannot be sciences," "Science distorts reality," "Science is not enough; we must have faith," "The deepest realities cannot be reached by intellectual effort." You thereupon cap this sequence with the doctrine that "we live only in the spirit."

Next, you corrupt the second rational principle as follows: "Logic is a strait jacket." "It doesn't matter how you think but how you feel," "Emotion is the path to truth," "None of this half-baked intellectual education!" "I am not a foreign intellectual" (he's telling us!), "Ideas act irrationally through the blood," "Life exists simply for its own sake." And this sequence you cap with the now celebrated dictum, "Think with the blood!"

When men have undergone this double process — the mental equivalent of castor-oil dosings — they will be completely in the fascists' power. They will have abandoned all interest in, or concept of, objective reality: and they will have lost all awareness of consistency among ideas. They can then listen, not only without laughter, but with credence, to remarks like these:

Fascism has its own ethics, and we intend to adhere thereto in any circumstances, and these ethics of ours oblige us always to be frank and outspoken with everybody, and, once we have made real friends with anyone, to remain faithful to him to the last.[16]

Thus the fascist loves in actual fact his neighbor, but this "neighbor" is not merely a vague and undefined concept, this love for one's neighbor puts no obstacle in the way of necessary educational severity [!], and still less to differentiation of status and to physical distance.[17]

What moves us the most at this moment is the deep-

[16] Benito Mussolini: "Germany and Italy: The Greatest and Soundest Democracies," a speech made in Berlin, September 28, 1937. *Vital Speeches*, Vol. IV, p. 17.

[17] Benito Mussolini: "The Principles of Fascism," in the *Living Age*, Vol. 345, p. 238.

rooted joy to see in our midst a guest [Premier Benito Mussolini of Italy] who is one of the lonely men in history who are not put to trial by historic events but who determine the history of their country themselves.[18]

It is sobering, though hardly consoling, to reflect that this same illusion exists in non-fascist countries, and can be utilized for the same purposes. The destruction of the myth by philosophical criticism is therefore part of the general struggle for democracy throughout the world. And, as a prelude to criticism, perhaps it will be well to set down here some examples of the myth as it has actually been employed. The following quotations are attempts to pass the Great Depression off as a "mental" phenomenon.

I believe that general business conditions for this year [1930] will, as a whole, compare favorably with those of 1928. The year 1929 was abnormal and the inflated peak situation prevailing during that year should not be considered sound for comparison. I believe that the agitation caused by a natural return to conservative and economic progress is misjudged for general depression.[19]

If the people of America could have been made to understand that this little affair down in Wall Street was just between a few rich men trying to get richer and that it need not affect them and their daily lives we would not

---

[18] Adolf Hitler: Speech of September 28, 1937, on the same occasion as Mussolini's (supra). Vital Speeches, Vol. IV, p. 18. These words are wildly amusing, coming as they do from the mouth that was about to swallow the oyster.

[19] William H. Crocker, President of the First National Bank of San Francisco (named by James W. Gerard as one of America's 64 rulers), in the New York Times, August 31, 1930.

have any depression. If the workman had gone about buy-
ing his automobiles and radios and the clothes his family
wanted and the merchant had gone on as usual there would
have been no depression. But instead the big bankers
called in the big merchants and manufacturers and told
them that hard times were coming, that now is the time to
gird your loins for the struggle. . . .[20]

Business depressions are caused by dissipation, dishonesty,
disobedience to God's will — a general collapse of moral
character. Statistics show this plainly. With equal precision, they show how business depressions are cured. They
are cured by moral awakening, spiritual revival, and the
rehabilitation of character. The American Bankers' Association can provide capital. The American Statistical Association can measure results. But the Association which
goes to the real root of the matter is the Young Men's
Christian Association. This latter has far greater possibilities than the others combined. To bring back prosperity
people must be conditioned in the right ways of working
and living on all sides of the triangle — physical, mental,
and spiritual values.[21]

In the first of these passages, the Great Depression is
dismissed as a statistical error in the minds of analysts.
In the second, it has become a rumor insidiously propagated by the "big bankers" (there is more than a hint
of Hitler in this phrase). In the third, which is for its
own part an astonishing example of painting upon
vacuity, the depression is attributed to a lack of "spiritu-

[20] Gilbert T. Hodges, President of the Advertising Federation of
America, *New York Times,* October 19, 1930.
[21] Roger Babson: Message to the National Committee of the YMCA,
New York Times, September 13, 1930.

ality." Had Americans possessed the "right" ideals, there had been no economic disaster.

It is obvious, of course, that all these passages are attempts to avoid saying that the depression issued out of the nature of capitalism — a system in which Crocker the banker, and Hodges the advertiser, and Babson the statistician had each a formidable stake. Nothing is easier than to suggest that the depression is something "mental," with all the overtones of wavering reality, speedy recovery, and moral concern which that word possesses. If the disaster is mental, the cure will also be mental. We shall not have to deal with the actual sequence of economic events, but can content ourselves with reinterpreting statistics, launching contrary rumors, or joining the YMCA.

Now is it possible for such "explanations" to take hold, or even to be uttered without peril of mirth? It may be, of course, that the authors of these remarks were so swathed in the fatuity of their own thinking as to be unable to judge how their words might be received. Nevertheless, it is unfortunately true that there exists among our people a disposition, encouraged by press and pulpit and radio, to resolve all problems into mere questions of the mind. In its grosser form, this practice appears in consultations with astrologers and mediums. In its higher form, if higher form there be, it appears in various organized and unorganized efforts at rectifying the maladjusted psyche, environment and all its potent influences being forgotten. The world's perplexities, however, are not so readily drowned beneath a trickle of gladsome thoughts.

It would be easy, and not wholly untrue, to call this

disposition escapism — a word which is, if possible, uglier than the practice it connotes. But escape from reality follows paths familiar to the escapist, who obviously will not journey to a place as rigorous as the one he flees. If, therefore, multitudes of people, when confronted by a hostile reality, take refuge in their own minds, it is because a long tradition has sanctified that asylum. The tradition itself must be many-sided, for it must invite in the required direction men of intellect and men of action, men of science and men of sentiment, the faint of heart and the faint of hope, the sceptics, cynics, believers, waverers, and men of vague opinion. In point of fact, the tradition exists and lies at the heart of modern philosophy.

THE HISTORY OF A REFUGE

The Greeks, even in their long and melancholy twilight, exhibit no special bent toward solipsism. The medievals, for all their confusion of fact and fiction, do not exhibit it either, except among the mystics. But of the great philosophers of the seventeenth and eighteenth centuries, Spinoza is the only one who is entirely free from it. Solipsism exists, in seed or in flower, in Descartes, Leibniz, Locke, Berkeley, Hume, and Kant.

This fact is the more remarkable because philosophy in those days was divided into two apparently conflicting schools of thought. The rationalists, who called Descartes father, sought basic truth in some ultimate proposition which, being self-evident, must be unchallengeable. The empiricists, who descend from Locke, sought basic truth in the immediate deliverances of sensation. The conflict lay in the fact that the rationalists regarded sensation as confused and deceptive, whereas the empiricists regarded "self-evident" truths as having no basis in observable events. The conflict was not in fact irreconcilable, and I ought to observe in passing that the two principles of scientific method which I earlier set down were drawn from the empiricists and the rationalists respectively.

For our present purpose it is important to see that the two schools fell, with the same certainty but for opposite reasons, into solipsism. Descartes, pursuing his search after the one indubitable truth, tried the experiment of doubting every statement he could think of. He seemed then to find that all statements except one could be doubted without inconsistency. The one statement which to doubt is to contradict oneself is the statement "I exist." For if I doubt that I exist, I have to exist in order to do the doubting. My doubting therefore presupposes my existence, and by a neat turn of argument places my existence beyond further doubt.

This is, of course, the *cogito ergo sum* principle — perhaps the most famous of all philosophical theories. Let us now see what Descartes has obtained by his argument (which, incidentally, is fallacious). He has obtained a fundamental principle which reads, "I exist." This statement, however, is singularly barren of results. For how, from the mere fact that I exist, can I infer the existence of anything else? Clearly I cannot, since I would have to combine with the statement "I exist" certain other statements which, according to

Descartes's own theory, are not self-evidently true. From the very start of the argument I am plunged into the solipsist dungeon. I have locked the door and thrown away the key.

The result is no better if we take the empiricist approach. This theory holds that the real is what is given us in sense experience: "If I myself see a man walking on the ice," says Locke, "it is past probability, it is knowledge." [22] Now the immediate data of sense experience are colors, sounds, tastes, textures, and odors. Locke supposed that they have their *source* in independently real objects, but that the place of their existence is human consciousness itself. Thus arises the following situation: the mind has immediately before it only its sensations; the objects which presumably excited the sensations are never directly perceived. Now, if it is true that the real is what is immediately perceived, it follows that, while the sensations are certainly real, the existence of objects is doubtful.

This result led Bishop Berkeley to formulate what has become the most famous of all the versions of solipsism. The existence of objects, he said, lies in their being perceived; and from this the conclusion is inescapable that when objects are not perceived, they don't exist. Thus, if we suppose a door closed upon a room and all its contents, and no consciousness at hand to maintain them in existence, they will simply cease to be. This theory, which spectacularly frustrates common sense, moved Berkeley (I think by its very difficulty) to affirm in a passage of magnificent prose:

[22] John Locke: *Essay on the Human Understanding*, Book IV, Chapter XV, ¶ 5.

that all the choir of heaven and furniture of the earth, in a word all those bodies which compose the mighty frame of the world, have not any subsistence without a mind, that their *being* (*esse*) is to be perceived or known; that consequently so long as they are not actually perceived by me, or do not exist in my mind or that of any other *created spirits,* they must either have no existence at all, *or else subsist in the mind of some eternal spirit. . . .*[23]

Thus empiricism, by accepting as certainly real only the sensations immediately present in consciousness, immured the mind within those sensations and rendered it wholly unable to find passage into a world existing apart from itself. The final working out of Locke's hypothesis is, indeed, even more devastating than anything in rationalism. For it happens that the human self (or "soul") is not given immediately in sense experience either, and must therefore be dismissed as of very doubtful existence. This part of the amputation was performed by Hume, whose remorseless analysis left nothing whatever except a flow of sensations, with no objects to excite them and no mind to receive them.

Berkeley's theory, I suppose, is commonly regarded as exemplifying the sort of oddity which philosophers delight to invent. I must insist, however, that the theory is very widely held, although its holders are not always aware that they hold it. Strong traces of it exist, for example, in the philosophies of Sir James Jeans and Sir Arthur Eddington, two physicists who are rather less celebrated for their physics than for their unexpected

[23] George Berkeley: *The Principles of Human Knowledge,* Part I, Sec. VI. Berkeley's italics.

services to theology. The only genuinely odd thing about Berkeley is that he set the theory down with perfect precision and faced its implications with the most complacent fortitude. Why should we pour laughter upon the good Bishop (as Kant called him), whose chiefest sin was clarity, while we crown with praises men whose sins are hidden deep in the obscurity of their own thought?

Thus a study of *The Principles of Human Knowledge* will prove, in itself, an excellent antidote for empty idealism. *There* will be found the true essence of the theory, without any rococo ornaments of transcendentalism or elaborate machinery of World-Souls, Cosmic Consciousnesses, and Absolute Ideas. *There* the theory stands naked and unashamed, and in its nakedness it has indeed a kind of beauty. For we see there, as nowhere else, the plain doctrine, plainly stated, that consciousness is prior to nature, and that consciousness alone makes possible the existence of the world.

Let us now ask ourselves another and, as I think, more searching question. What accounts for the popularity of a view which contradicts the most obvious inferences of common sense? What induces people to believe that the universe cannot exist as an independent system, but must exist in their consciousness, or in somebody's consciousness, or in God's? It cannot be Berkeley's arguments, for these, though they are as good as any, fall far short of the conclusion sought after. Moreover, the viability of philosophical theories does not depend entirely (or even greatly) upon the proofs assembled on their behalf. Viability — that attribute which makes a theory thrive in *many* minds — depends upon the relevance of the theory to life as it is being lived in a given social context.

Let us put the case more simply. Everybody philosophizes somewhat — that is to say, everybody constructs some generalizations based upon his experience of the world. The generalizations may be few and fatuous; nevertheless, they are there. Now, the experience which sustains them is, of course, the life history of each generalizer, a series of interactions between him and the physical world, between him and the society he inhabits. If a philosophical theory is to win wide acceptance, it must corroborate, or at the very least not contradict, the generalizations which a majority of people have been making. Herbert Spencer's theory of automatic social progress was excellently viable during prosperous Victorian times, but it never survived the First World War. In those years and the years following, people discovered that social progress, so far from being automatic, has to be fought for, and may even then not occur. And so it is true, as Santayana shrewdly observes, that philosophies are not disproved, but are simply abandoned.

We have observed that modern philosophy, whether rationalist or empiricist, carries solipsism at its heart. The implications of this statement are considerable. We are talking, not of a single theory, but of the *main course* of modern thought; and we find it afflicted with solipsism as with a congenital disease. The reason for this will be found in a single, dominant point of view which has its source deep in modern society. It is the point of view which I think may be accurately named Individualism.

Now, Individualism has been nothing less than a complete world-view, in terms of which every area of study was successively interpreted. Its nature, and its importance too, are best got at by an examination of the world-view which it destroyed — the one, namely, which purported to describe, and unquestionably did defend, the medieval form of social organization. Feudalism was a vertical, hierarchical system based upon the ownership of land. At the bottom of this social column was the serf, who was bound to the land he tilled and who owed allegiance to a lord, the owner of that land. The lord in turn owed allegiance to a king, the king to the Holy Roman Emperor (or so the Emperor believed), the Emperor to the Pope (or so the Pope believed). The Pope derived his sovereignty from Saint Peter, who was not available to have his right contested. Saint Peter had it from very nearly the highest authority — the Second Person of the Trinity — who had held it upon the highest authority of all. There ran, therefore, an unbroken line from the serf of the field to that Being whom Bishop Butler called "the Lord and Proprietor of the Universe." Society was thus erected upon the calm, majestic principle of subordination. It was hoped that where subordination existed, submission would gently follow.

The hierarchical fact, thus transformed into a principle, was fortified by a judicious application of Pauline sociology. "We are all members one of another," the great missionary had said. Human society resembles the human organism: each member is appointed to a special function. The lungs cannot perform the office of the heart, nor the heart of the head. In the medieval manner, this analogy was developed in detail. There was some question whether the Pope or the Emperor was the head, for, as the legalists sagely observed, a body could not reasonably have two. But the judiciary was established (rather well, I think) in the liver, and the populace was identified as the toes. When the people grew rebellious, the body politic was said to have gout.[24]

Unfortunately for these idylls, medieval society needed commodities, and therefore needed a class of people who should produce them — a class which was not slow to discover that, as a general thing, the more goods you make and sell, the greater the wealth you acquire. Moreover, the feudal lords revealed a pressing need for money: landowners are notoriously borrowers. Moneylenders then appeared as part of the commercial class, and their practice, though denounced by the Church (itself a landowner) as usurious, grew and prospered upon the needs of rulers themselves.

As things turned out, the interest of the commercial class was in direct conflict with that of the feudal aristocracy. The intricate system of rules which governed medieval relationships became just so many obstacles to growth in the production of commodities. Medieval society then met the fate of all societies which do not permit themselves to produce as much as they can: it cracked open. The handsome vertical column was discovered to be made of wood and to be infested with termites which had eaten out its heart.

[24] It may seem incredible that such ideas were ever seriously entertained. I must indicate, therefore, that the evidence for their being so is to be found in Giercke: *Political Theories of the Middle Ages*, Macmillan, New York, 1900, Ch. IV *passim*, notes 76–79.

These termites (the word is not a favorite of mine, but it has a certain ironic appropriateness) were, of course, precisely those merchants, bankers, and tradesmen we have referred to, the historical ancestors of modern capitalists. For the past four hundred years, history has been largely the record of their exploits, and philosophy has been largely the record of their notions. It is particularly instructive to observe what the growth of commerce did to medieval social theory.

From the very first the effect was remarkable. It was all very well for medieval thought to say that everyone has his appointed place in society, that the aristocrat had his special function and the man of commerce his, and that neither should usurp the other's. The fact was that a merchant could not be a "good" merchant (*i.e.* a profit-maker) without clashing directly with the aristocracy. And, equally, the aristocrat could not be a "good" aristocrat (*i.e.* a prosperous landowner) without limiting the actions of the merchant. The theory therefore had a tendency to stand on its head, for the more adequately these classes performed their functions, the greater was the conflict between them. Instead of enjoining peaceful subordination, the theory, when applied to fact, actually justified discord.

Aware of this nonsensical result, the theorists who defended commerce (radicals I regret to say they were) prepared to do away with the doctrine altogether. In its place they substituted the precisely opposite view. They denied that a man's worth was definable in terms of his discharge of any social function; and they asserted, rather that his worth was definable in terms of what he could achieve for himself. For the notion of society as an organism they substituted the notion of society as a congeries of individuals. These social atoms had each a motivating core of self-interest and a skin impenetrably thickened with natural rights. They were conceived as entering into temporary relations with one another, held together by the satisfaction of reciprocal interests and by the beneficent, if rigorous, law of contract. But as for influence upon one another, these individuals had perhaps as much as marbles in a heap.

The recovery of emphasis upon the individual, his talents and his powers, was a tremendous gain for human thought. The disappearance of the concept of social function was equally, however, a tremendous loss. For the butcher could no longer appeal to society's need of food as a justification of his existence. He had simply to say that butchering was one among other ways of earning a living. He would be a "good" butcher, not because he supplied a great deal of meat to a great many people, but because he had achieved an income remarkably large for a butcher.[25] The passage of thought was therefore from a static, organic theory to a dynamic, atomistic theory. These opposites (if I may be allowed a play of dialectics) await reconciliation in a dynamic, organic theory, which bears our future hope. The other alternative, a static, atomistic theory, which is the sub-

---

[25] These remarks refer, of course, to Adam Smith's wonderful epitomizing of the whole theory: "It is not from the benevolence of the butcher, the brewer, or the baker, that we expect our dinner, but from their regard to their own interest. We address ourselves, not to their humanity, but to their self-love; and we never talk to them of our own necessities, but of their advantages." *The Wealth of Nations*, Book I, Ch. II.

stance (though not the face) of fascism, waits now to be finally destroyed.[26]

The notion of society as a collection of atomic individuals conditions the entire thought of the seventeenth, eighteenth, and nineteenth centuries. It receives its *reductio ad absurdum* philosophically in Leibniz's theory of the "windowless monads," economically in the Manchester Man, historically in Carlyle's doctrine of The Hero, and ethically in Bentham's definition of social happiness as the "sum" of the happinesses of the members. Throughout the whole modern epoch, psychology has been mainly the study of the *individual* man: social psychology is an appendage, an afterthought. Ethics has been mainly the study of what the *individual* man ought to find desirable: social ethics is likewise an afterthought. Political science has been preoccupied with the abstract and artificial question of The Individual *vs.* The State: the real question, Whose State Is It? remains an afterthought. There is not a single discipline or area of study left untouched by the dominant, the ineluctable *I*. It is as if the whole of modern history had been a brief transaction among billiard balls.

Such being the general intellectual atmosphere, one can readily perceive why solipsism has flourished. So long as the objective world seems comfortless, while the Self seems cozy, there will remain an obstinate belief that thinking makes things so. Americans, who have

[26] The reader may, if he wishes, work out this dialectic according to the following definitions: *static* means rigidly hierarchical in form, *dynamic* means fluid in form and allowing for democratic opportunity, *organic* means filled with the sense of social responsibility, *atomistic* means dominated by self-interest and lacking in the sense of social responsibility.

been exhorted to this faith by the relentless imperatives of Emerson and the shining prophecies of William James, may find the habit exceptionally difficult to shed. But shed it they must, if they wish to prosper. He who lives in his own thoughts will never live in the world. He who listens to his own voice will never learn the music of the spheres.

ASYLUM IGNORANTIAE

We have now surveyed the historical reasons why people are likely to believe the doctrine that thinking makes things so. We have also examined the fascist consequences to which such a belief tends. These facts serve to warn us of danger, but they do not in themselves show that the belief is false. For that purpose further argument is required.

To say that thinking makes it so is to say that things are what they are because we so regard them, or, to state it more accurately, that the existence and the nature of things are determined by our own consciousness. Without our consciousness, according to this theory, things would not exist or have any nature at all.

Consciousness is therefore the primordial fact. On it everything else must depend. It must therefore have existed as long as the universe has existed, and possibly longer. This, of course, cannot possibly be true of the individual consciousness of any single one of us. Well, if it cannot be any one man's consciousness which has sustained the universe, perhaps that has been done by the consciousness of men generation by generation.

This hypothesis will fare no better. The age of the earth, as geology reckons it, must be placed in the billions of years, whereas the human race has existed for only about 500,000. As for the universe itself — well, did it ever begin? Clearly, then, it cannot have been human consciousness which has kept the earth and the universe in existence. There were incalculable eons of time when human consciousness was not, and the stars moved in their courses indifferent to any astronomers.

A last possibility remains: that the universe has existed in a cosmic consciousness or world-soul. This notion, however, bears every mark of a device employed to resolve a difficulty. You have no reason to assume the existence of a cosmic consciousness unless you are already convinced that thinking makes things so, and wish to render your conviction fully tenable. The hypothesis has no other use. Astronomy records the history of the stars, geology that of earth, and anthropology that of man, without in the least having to invoke a cosmic consciousness as a means of explanation. Thus, although we cannot know for certain that there is not a cosmic consciousness, we do know that for all scientific purposes the hypothesis is unnecessary.

Or let us take the problem as it is stated by Berkeley, where the assertion simply is that it is meaningless to regard objects as existing independently of our consciousness. Now Berkeley agrees, and everyone agrees, that our sensations have some other source than ourselves. Sensations are obstinate; they neither arise at our pleasure nor take their content from our wish. A man, opening his eyes upon the world, will see just what he has to see under the given circumstances. But if sensations have a source other than ourselves, surely the most reasonable hypothesis will be that they come from objects. Their "obstinacy" will then testify to the independence of that source from us and will constitute proof that there really is an objective world.

Again there is an alternative, and it will have to be the one Berkeley himself chose. Let the external source be, as he said, God. Then it turns out that this hypothesis suffers precisely the same disabilities, as a means of philosophical explanation, which were suffered by the doctrine of a cosmic consciousness. It is clearly a device which is not required for an explanation of the facts. Even if we accept the testimony of religious experience as valid, we shall find little in it to suggest that Deity is an immediate source of physical sensation. The God who exerted his omnipotence to create earth and the firmament was not engaged in providing mere content for his creatures' minds.

Finally, it seems probable that the whole error arises from a mistaken view of human experience; namely, from the view that experience is primarily contemplative. The mind receives sensations, and, so to say, looks them over. If this "looking" were in fact all it did, the mind might not unreasonably begin to wonder whether objects do lie behind the sensory veil. But human experience is not mere contemplation. It is — and indeed it is far more — an active manipulation of the world. We receive sensations, it is true, but we also mold environment. And surely we have long known that this manipulation, this molding, if they are to be successful, require us to regard the world as an independent

system which can be dealt with only so far as we understand its nature. The supreme achievement of science
lies precisely in this, that, with the aid of mathematics
and by laboratory analysis, it is able to give an account
of the way objects behave when we do not perceive
them. And to this achievement our growing control of
the physical universe bears constant witness.

The general truth seems then to be that consciousness, so far from being prior to nature, is secondary to
nature. Since nature produces, among its manifold
riches, the human beings in whom consciousness resides,
since, further, it shapes that consciousness by a potent
and uninterrupted influence, we should be standing the
universe exactly on its head, were we seriously to believe
that thinking makes things so. From such an error can
come only greater error. The brief and transitory
pleasure of substituting thoughts for things is far overmatched by the real removal of real evils in an objective
world.

To this latter business, which surely is our main concern, all seasons, of crisis or of ease, invite us; to it the
energies of rational men are necessarily bent. It may
seem curious, but it is true and it is just, that only men
of rational mind and of social purpose can in the end
achieve that peace of spirit which the various mysticisms
so falsely promise. For they persuade us to escape the
world. Reason, however, persuades us to change it.

CHAPTER VII THAT YOU CAN—
NOT MIX ART
AND POLITICS

ONE OF the minor prizes turned up early in our oc-
cupation of Germany was Leni Riefenstahl, once
reputed to be Hitler's favorite cinema actress. "Baby,"
said the soldier who questioned her, "I've been going to
the movies a long time and I never heard of you."
Doubtless he had not, for, despite a visit to Hollywood,
Leni never became an American film celebrity. She had
fame enough, however, in Europe; and, as it seems,
she had also an esthetic theory. The AP dispatch describes it thus:

The producer-actress said she thought Hitler pretty wonderful, but she had stood aloof from the Nazi party because
"I am zee arteest, I cannot take part een politics," talking
just like that. Also, because "some of my best friends are
Jews."

"I cannot take part in politics." The words reminded
me at once of a painter I had met some years ago under
the double heat of conversation and whisky. "I am an

artist," he said, asserting perhaps more than was true, "and I think it enough if I save a few flowers to hand over to posterity." At that time Spain was going under, the long shadow was deepening over Europe, and it did seem that an artist might do more than gather flowers. For a successful defense of the Spanish Republic would have saved the lives of millions since dead, the anguish of yet other millions, and the captivity of peoples. To assert that all these things are "politics," with which art has nothing to do, is to assert that art does not concern itself with humanity.

Who should profit from such illusions? Not my friend the painter, for, in ignoring Spain, he ignored the cause of human freedom, with all the vast fertility which such a theme can give to art. Not you and I, for we needed to be stirred out of the deadly quiet of those years. Not the people of Europe, who faced enemies abroad and collaborators at home. Only the fascists could profit; only the would-be conquerors, who thus gained a self-imposed silence upon the part of their natural foes. The assassin steals close, the dagger is lifted; but the victim murmurs, "I am an artist: I have no comment to make."

Thus the belief that art and politics are incompatible has its social uses. The primary purpose is to silence and disarm. Everyone knows that ideas, when transmitted in the excitement of esthetic experience, have a powerful effect upon the mind. Not only are they then more readily accepted, but they are more readily acted upon. The flame lit in contemplation becomes a holocaust. If you have an *Uncle Tom's Cabin*, you may have a Civil War. Reactionaries therefore take no chances.

So far as they can manage it, there will not be any novels or plays or paintings expressive of human suffering and the means of remedy.

While democracy persists, it is difficult to prevent such works by the use of governmental machinery. Suppression must be subtler. There can be no suppression more subtle and at the same time more effective than to persuade novelists, playwrights, and painters that their true vocation lies elsewhere. Once social themes are abandoned by the very men who could most passionately treat them, little need to be feared from the imperfect performers who remain.

The primary use is thus preventive. A secondary, though valuable, use is as a weapon of attack against those works which, despite all cajolery and enticement, continue to plead the hopes of mankind. To say that these are "propaganda but not art" is to say that the creator either has no knowledge of his craft or has sacrificed it to purposes beyond his legitimate reach. In this manner the novel is made to lose its readers, the play its audiences, and the painting its spectators. The superstition achieves all this without once hinting that the real object of attack was not the work itself but the social ideas it contained.

If, lastly, the superstition, having fully concealed its origin and purpose, sets up as an independent esthetic theory, it will have an almost limitless capacity for harm. Creative genius, the mightiest of human faculties, must then confess itself a shorn Samson and humbly put its body to the wheel. Betrayed by a faithless Delilah and blinded by shrewd Philistines, it will have neither the thought nor the wish to pull down temples.

IS IT POSSIBLE TO SAY NOTHING?

There must be some irony in the spectacle of artists striving to avoid politics on behalf of a doctrine whose purpose is political. Yet sincere artists are sincere craftsmen. Their various skills are as painfully acquired as they are brilliant when achieved. It is perfectly natural for writers and musicians and painters to be somewhat more concerned with the means to an effect than they are with the effect itself. And we, for whom their creations are made, come also to prize technique as the ultimate manifestation of their talents. The mark of connoisseurship lies, we begin to think, in observing not what has been done, but how it was done.

This separation of form from content, of technique from result, arises simply from our being interested rather more in the one than in the other. The preference itself is one which has not always existed and doubtless will not always exist. All thought of such a separation vanishes when we inquire how far an artist can detach himself and his works from the life around him. To attain complete detachment, what would he have to do?

Well, take a writer, for example. His medium is words. Now, words have meanings and, with those meanings, emotional associations. Despite all cynical doubts, it is very difficult for a writer not to say something whenever he assembles words, and he likewise cannot avoid stirring in some measure the emotions of his readers. But so far as he does these things, he is intimately bound to life and to the world about him. He could be completely detached only if he treated words as sounds which have no sense, and this he would have to do in such a way as not to suggest any meaning through the very absence of it. This technique has been attempted by some writers, notably by Miss Gertrude Stein, but it cannot be said to have caught on.

The painter has a wider area in which to practice detachment. He does not have to represent on canvas the forms and movements of ordinary life. He may, if he likes, paint "non-objectively"; that is to say, he can assemble colors into patterns of his own choosing without any resemblance to objects as they are seen. There can be no objection to this procedure so long as it remains one among many possible choices for painters to make: we do not require literal representation upon rugs or drapery, and there seems to be no reason why we should specifically require it of painting. Yet even here, if complete detachment were to be attained, the painter would have to annul any possible suggestion which might lie in the painting's emotional appeal. Kandinsky, for example, copies nothing; but the magnificence of his composition suggests harmony and movement, which in turn can suggest other concepts to the very boundary of an observer's thought.

The composer seems, at first sight, more detached from life than any other artist. Unlike the writer, he actually does deal with sounds that have no fixed meanings. Yet he is bound to life by emotional association fully as much as writers are. No one can take Tchaikovsky to have been an optimist; no one can imagine Beethoven to have been a man of small ideas. For his part, the old giant maintained that in every work he expressed some portion of his philosophy. The apparent meaninglessness of musical composition is in fact an invitation to listeners to supply it with meanings as their minds roam free. Probably the only way to cancel all possible meanings would be to make the work so dull as to be no invitation.

It seems unlikely, then, that there can be many works of art which have no reference to life and the problems of living. For most artists it must remain insuperably difficult to negate the very humanity which is the source of their own skills. Try as one may to empty art of content, there will remain some hint, some whisper, which shall set in motion the minds of other men. I recall how often, during the rise of fascism, I used to repeat to myself the lines of MacLeish's lovely poem "You, Andrew Marvell":

> And Spain go under and the shore
> Of Africa the gilded sand
> And evening vanish and no more
> The low pale light across that land
>
> Nor now the long light on the sea —
>
> And here face downward in the sun
> To feel how swift how secretly
> The shadow of the night comes on . . .

The poet intended no more than a description of approaching night, but his lines became irresistibly symbolic.

These things being true, one may look with justifiable

doubt upon works of art which expressly assert their detachment from life. We shall certainly feel that the artist is likely to be mistaken about this, and we may feel, in addition, that he is being disingenuous. For if, as is probable, the work does have a reference to life, though he says it has none, this condition may be due to his having missed the reference or to his having concealed it. There are thus two possibilities: an illusory detachment in which the work contains unconscious comment, and a hypocritical detachment in which there is comment deliberately hidden.

It may be difficult to tell into which of these categories a given work will fall, but the membership of both is surely large. Lately, for example, a kind of neo-Victorianism has begun to set in. Art exhibits now display new versions of the old farms, water mills, and Mississippi steamboats which one used to see on the ancestral wall. Mr. Eliot has edited the poems of Kipling, and Mr. Auden those of Tennyson. I am not sure why two of the most abstruse poets should turn toward two of the most plain-spoken, but I don't suppose they turn thither in order to recapture the morality of Galahad. Wittingly or unwittingly, they are commenting upon our present world — and commenting, I think, unfavorably.

But these are limited examples, and we need a larger view. It seems to be a fact that the more a work of art is directed to mass audiences, the greater the amount of surreptitious comment it contains. Best-selling novels present themselves as pure narratives, that is to say, as chronicles of speedy and exciting events, without the least commentary. Yet the sufferings of Scarlett O'Hara would almost persuade us to love those wayward and exquisite slaveowners who refused to pass peacefully out of power. And if we love the owners of human flesh, how shall we learn to love the men whose flesh was owned? Even for reactionaries, grief over a lost tyranny is a waste of tears.

A more humble art form is the comic strip, but the public which it reaches is now so enormous that one can exclude oneself from it only by a violent exercise of will. In my boyhood, comic strips contained one joke per day, with no attempt at continuity. Even then, however, *Bringing Up Father* was a spirited expression of democratic revolt against parvenus and aristocrats. I do not know whether Mr. McManus drew all this consciously, but I acknowledge that I am in his debt.

Beneath the extravagant narratives of contemporary strips one can discern all sorts of ideologies, among which the antilabor philosophy of *Little Orphan Annie* can hardly be unintentional. Superman, who (as we are told) is not a bird or a plane, clearly compensates by his incredible powers for the impotence of common man. We readers, thwarted on every side by a social system which we do not control, find pleasure in the imaginary existence of a man whose powers are limitless and whose purposes are sublime. Unfortunately, he acts as a substitute, not an inspiration. He leads us to rely on intervention from outside us and to forget how massive our strength can be, if we but organize it. *Superman*, I am afraid, is founded upon a retrograde social theory. At any rate, it is certainly not mere narrative.

The greatest of all mass arts is the cinema, and nowhere else does the belief more ardently prevail that entertainment is the goal, not propaganda. "Entertainment" has acquired the power of a shibboleth. It appears to mean, primarily, escape from tedium or anxiety, from ugliness or defeat. It means, also, the sublimation of frustrated desire, as when the screen exhibits rooms we would like to live in and cannot, men or women we would like to love and cannot. It means, perhaps, the mere holding of attention, by which a few moments can be made to slip by.

Does the cinema "teach?" Obviously — one may say, notoriously — it does. No protestations about "entertainment" can long conceal the fact that movie audiences over a period of years have been absorbing an entire philosophy. They have been learning that no woman over twenty-five can be handsome or attractive, though men can be both to a fairly ancient age; that the feminine landscape should be as visible as possible without being actually seen; that the most interesting people are those who are well-dressed, well-loved, and acquainted with cabarets. Above all, they have been learning that there is nothing fundamentally wrong with our society.

The existence of censorship puts the fact beyond doubt, for all censorship is indoctrination. The fate which overtook Donald Ogden Stewart's script for *Keeper of the Flame* will show what kind of censorship we have. This movie had to do with a woman who discovered that her husband was plotting to become the American *Führer*. She permitted him to be killed in an automobile accident, by failing to telephone him that a certain bridge had been washed away. After his death, the fascist plot was discovered and destroyed.

Mr. Stewart had intended to close the story with Miss Hepburn and Mr. Tracy where we like to see them, in one another's arms. But at this point censorship intervened. The wife had been guilty of a mortal sin in the accident which befell her husband. The penalty of mortal sin is death. Therefore Miss Hepburn had to die, while Mr. Tracy, an engaging newspaperman, lived on to the partial satisfaction of the audience.

We need not discuss the moral casuistry which is able to rate the struggle against fascism lower than the prescriptions of a special code. It suffices to perceive that movie-goers were being told (1) that things ought to happen in a certain way, and (2) more remarkable yet, that they do happen that way. In this particular case, I think the lessons were lost on the audience. Generally, however, the lessons strike home. One can only guess to what extent American racism is sustained by film stereotypes of the amusing, lazy Negro and the insidious Oriental, the latter of which completely frustrates any clear understanding of Japanese fascism.

Cinema comment is plainly the kind which enforces a certain set of values, and therefore influences action. It is, consciously or unconsciously, propaganda in any reasonable sense of the term. Movie-goers may think they are being merely entertained, but actually they are being instructed. And not always well.

HOW THE IDEA STARTED

When, therefore, we survey the entire realm of art, we cannot fail to observe how rare and how difficult is genuine detachment from life. Try as he may, an artist will seldom contrive to be absolutely speechless. He is almost certain to say something about something. When he does this, he comments; and when he comments, it will take an analytical genius to decide whether or not he has committed propaganda.

This being the case, we can hardly help wondering how so many artists have got the idea that they can avoid comment and that they ought to. For, in their eyes, this practice is not only possible, but is the overruling ideal. Although with some it may be an excuse for evasion, with many it is a concept passionately believed. We cannot dismiss it as a merely chance illusion.

The idea is significantly recent. You cannot imagine Fra Angelico declining to do a Madonna on the ground that it would be propaganda tending to confirm the worshiper in his faith. You cannot imagine Michelangelo, despite all his combats with Julius II, refusing to do the Sistine Murals because of a wish to avoid pictorial narrative. You cannot imagine Bunyan abandoning *Pilgrim's Progress* because it contained a religious point of view which had political implications. These men, I fancy, would hardly conceive what it might mean to say that an artist must avoid comment. They uttered, quite simply and very grandly, what was nearest their hearts.

The idea is recent because it has its roots in modern society; indeed, it belongs to that stage which is contemporary with us. Its very denial of content suggests that it regards the world as something to be shunned rather than delighted in, and that it belongs to an epoch of crisis and decline. Its sources are partly economic and partly ideological.

One of the characteristics of modern society is the fact that painters and musicians and men of letters have never been able to determine just what part they were to play in it. They have lacked, as their feudal predecessors did not lack, an obvious function. It is plain enough what employers and laborers do in the production of commodities, and it is plain enough that scientists are a group which employers cannot possibly do without. But artists are not connected with the essential economic arrangements of society; they are perhaps the only "free" producers, marketing a commodity called beauty. Their market, also, is by far the most uncertain. In it the buyers exert a dreadful power, intolerably limiting the producers' wishes. Shoe-manufacturers and shoe-buyers may readily agree as to what constitutes a good pair of shoes; but where are the makers and buyers of paintings, books, music, who shall agree as to what constitutes a good painting, a good book, a good symphony? The artist finds himself producing not what he thinks beautiful, but what his prospective purchasers think beautiful. He no longer says the things he wants to say, designs the forms he wants to design. His inspiration dries up. He sees before him the horrible future of a hack.

As if this were not enough, the wealthier buyers used to distinguish themselves by that attribute which Matthew Arnold called Philistinism. For many decades they were not in the least interested in fostering new talent. When they expended their wealth upon painting, for example, it was with the intent, so admirably described by Veblen, of showing how much money they had available. For this reason they collected old masters. You cannot exhibit wealth by spending one thousand dollars for a contemporary painting, but you can exhibit it by spending fifty thousand for a Rembrandt.

These conditions affected painters rather more than other artists. Nevertheless, the general effect was to institute in all the arts a tradition of rebellion and experiment. The invention of photography ended the last documentary uses of painting, and the old art forms were evaporating in academic sterility. Thus at the very moment when slavery seemed bitterest there appeared a new and unexpected release. Painters could paint the world for the sake of design, or, equally for the sake of design, might not paint the world at all. Musicians might explore the whole-tone scale or atonality. Poets, leaping back to Cowley, might find a novel power in learned and obscure conceits.

In art, practice begets theory; a new technique soon finds itself the parent of a new esthetics. The early nineteenth-century romantics had tried to earn a place in society by offering their wounded spirits as a sacrifice for mankind. By the end of the century, artists have reversed the program: they have renounced the world around them, have passed (with the help of Nietzsche) beyond morality, and are inviting mankind to suffer for them. It seems a little heartless, but then these men were proud and independent and of splendid powers. You cannot expect such people to love their chains.

The new epoch was inaugurated by a sort of Emancipation Proclamation from Benedetto Croce, the Italian philosopher. Croce undertook to show that art has nothing to do with rules or standards, nothing to do with ethics, nothing to do with utility. It is, he said, simply expression. You utter in words or paint or musical sounds what is, so to say, on your mind. No theory ever arrived more opportunely, and it was greeted with raptures worthy of a better cause. For the trouble with academic rules was not that they were rules, but that they were academic; and the trouble with Victorian morality was not that it was morality, but that it was Victorian. The Croceans made the same mistake as their opponents by taking the then existing taste and the then existing morals as absolutes in their kind.

The proclamation, however, did not emancipate as much as had been hoped. If all art is expression, what of those artists who want to say something about the world? What if they want to utter social comment in general or revolutionary comment in particular? No Crocean can possibly object to this. His theory does not forbid the expression of social comment; it only forbids any obligation to express it. There is no principle in Croce which can require or enforce complete detachment from life.

This lack was finally supplied, during the 1910's, by two Englishmen, Clive Bell and Roger Fry. Asserting that form is the sole object of esthetic pleasure, they were able to dismiss as irrelevant all meanings, all resemblances to life, and especially all intimate personal suggestions which a work might have for us. Color and design are thus the *only* values in painting; thematic material and development are the *only* values in music. The delighted spectator, beholding these impersonal transactions, is lifted at once above the common life and the common man. Otherwise, says Bell:

I have tumbled from the superb peaks of esthetic exaltation to the snug foothills of warm humanity. It is a jolly country. No one need be ashamed of enjoying himself there. Only no one who has ever been on the heights can help feeling a little crestfallen in the cosy valleys. And let no one imagine, because he has made merry in the warm tilth and quaint nooks of romance, that he can even guess at the austere and thrilling raptures of those who have climbed the cold, white peaks of art.[1]

Looking back after thirty years, we do not find the peaks so cold or the raptures so austere. But in those days, when imagist poets carved jade and painters discovered the cube, it was enthusiastically believed that space had at last shut out the heavens and that geometry had canceled the stars. By that curious power which enables an abstract principle to satisfy opposite concrete needs, this belief led truly creative artists to embark on voyages of marvelous discovery, while at the same time it provided a permanent haven for snobs. On the one hand, you have Picasso redeeming new worlds from the unknown; and on the other, you have Bell himself indulging an observation like this: "However wicked it may be to try to shock the public, it is not so wicked as trying to please it."[2]

The preoccupation with design, so brilliantly shown in French painting, has been enormously fruitful. Re-

[1] Clive Bell: *Art,* The Frederick A. Stokes Co., New York, 1914, pp. 32-3.
[2] *Ibid.,* p. 163.

actionaries, however, were not slow to see how the corresponding esthetic theory could be put to other uses, how, as a dogmatic and exclusive principle, it could silence undesirable voices. It is not the first time, I suppose, that the labors of liberty have been distorted in the direction of bondage. At any rate, the valuable content in the theory can now be rescued only by an artistic practice which shall unite pattern and comment so intimately as to require the exclusion of neither.

BEAUTY, CONTENT, AND UTILITY

Let us see what fortifications a man might erect who, for fear of comment obnoxious to himself, wished to defend the view that art should have no social comment at all. The word "should" is, of course, somewhat ambiguous. In all probability, our antagonist would not mean anything ethical by it; that is to say, he wouldn't mean that such a work of art is immoral. He would probably mean that such a work is esthetically unsuccessful, that its beauty has been impaired by the comment or removed altogether. How could he defend this view?

First, he could wall in the entire area, after the manner of Bell and Fry, by saying that form alone is the source of esthetic merit, content being a distracting irrelevance. Apart from the great difficulty of deciding what, in any work of art, is form and what is content, this argument must assume that form and content are in fact separable. And they must be separable to such an extent that either (1) there can be works of art which have form but no content whatever, or (2) in works which have both, but are nevertheless esthetically successful, attention can be restricted to the form (the source of excellence) without any influence from the content.

Now, as for assumption (1), we have already observed how rare such achievements must be. For, in order to do this, an artist must be at pains not only to say nothing overtly, but also to make sure that his saying nothing overtly does not itself suggest some genuine comment. For if a man says nothing, when everybody is expecting him to say something, then his silence (or, at any rate, his meaninglessness) will be bound to seem significant. I do not know how many modern painters have done their abstracts with the intent of avoiding comment; but it seems clear to me that they have been teaching us new ways in which to look at the physical world, and have thus been commenting all the time. In some of them, like Léger and Picasso, the comment has been perfectly conscious and extremely persuasive, so that it is now part of the natural life of men in the western world. It is one of the things you would think of, if you undertook to answer the question, "What does life, as we now live it, signify?"

Assumption (2) covers certainly most of the works of painting, sculpture, literature, and music as men have produced these in the past, before there arose any conviction that comment should be avoided. The effect of the assumption seems to be to take the soliloquies out of Shakespeare, the Franciscan narratives out of Giotto, the chorales out of Bach. For in these works the commentary which forms their content is an essential part of their esthetic effect. Otherwise, you would have to suppose that Hamlet merely utters lovely syllables, whose meaning is accidental and irrelevant. You would have to suppose that Giotto's admiration for St. Francis had no effect upon the frescoes and found no expression in them. In general, you would have to suppose that ideas as such have no esthetic appeal. This view is so fantastic, so contradicted by the great works of the past, that one is led to suspect in the men who hold it some special and curious hostility to thought. It must be that they are misologists, "haters of reason," such as Plato used to denounce.

Having thus breached the outer wall, we should find that our antagonist had built an inner defense. He would by this time concede that works of art may have thought content without being spoiled by it; but he would perhaps say that, if the thought content is intended to influence our action later on, then the work of art had a utilitarian purpose in addition to that of merely being beautiful. He would say, dimly remembering Emerson, that "Beauty is its own excuse for being," and that beautiful things lose their beauty as soon as they are put to some use. In short, the beautiful and the useful are incompatible with each other.

Such a view is far easier to disprove than to support. If it were true that nothing utilitarian can be a work of art, then architecture would disappear immediately as a source of esthetic experience. One can think of hardly any building which has been erected for no useful purpose but for the sake of its beauty alone. All the architectural marvels which spring to mind are

tombs or temples or churches or houses or office buildings, all of which bear the obvious mark of utility. It is
an interesting commentary upon the influence of economics on art that even the most conspicuous spend-
thrifts decline to lavish money upon buildings that
have no purpose at all.

Furthermore, the beautiful is so far from being incompatible with the useful that some products clearly
gain in beauty in proportion as their form reveals the
uses they are to serve. According to the Functionalists,
who have certainly demonstrated their theory by convincing practice, the architecture of a home, for example, ought plainly to show that the building is intended to be lived in; it ought not to conceal the fact
behind Spanish, Dutch, or English Tudor façades.
Hence the new style of the modern home, which gets rid
of irrelevancies, and makes the form expressive of the
use.

Evidently it cannot be maintained that utility necessarily corrupts beauty. There remains, however, the
chance that a work of art which is useful in the sense
of influencing later action will be damaged on that account. If, for example, the work of art were a play
which describes some social injustice and calls for action against it, one might hold that the "message"
(*i.e.* the call to action) was an intrusion which destroyed the esthetic effect. People do in fact hold this
view, and it is precisely what they mean when they
say that you cannot mix art and politics. They like to
point out that Shakespeare (an excellent dramatist) dis-
cusses many problems, but seems never to advocate anything. In saying this, they have certainly forgotten the

patriotic fervor of the Histories. And they have forgotten Ibsen altogether.

To understand the error of this view, we shall have to remember that esthetic experience is spread out in time. It begins, it continues, and it ends. The *esthetic* success of the experience relates to that extent of time which is encompassed by the beginning and the ending. The *utilitarian* success of the experience, however, relates to a period of time after the experience has ceased. There is no apparent reason why these two kinds of success should conflict with each other, as they might conceivably do if they related to the same period of time. For all one knows, an object which is beautiful to us *within* esthetic experience may, without damage to its beauty, have effects upon our actions later on.

Everyone can test this by his own experience. During the long crisis of the last fifteen years, when mankind has lived in exceptional torment, I have returned more and more frequently to the reading of Milton's *Lycidas*. When my blood seems turned to water and my bones to jelly, I find in *Lycidas* that vertebrate strength which enables men to walk erect and lay hands upon the future. Evidently in all this I have been putting the poem to use. Strength in the midst of adversity is a practical aim, and poetry has long been recognized as one of the means to it. What is the effect of such a purpose upon the beauty of *Lycidas?*

Well, I cannot find that the beauty is in any way impaired. A pleasure which even repetition will not dull is likely to be proof against irrelevancies. But I learn this fact also: *Lycidas* is not beautiful because it gives me strength; on the contrary, *Lycidas* gives me strength because it is beautiful. One could pick up a score of volumes entitled "Poems of Inspiration" or "Cantos of Courage" with the desperate foreknowledge that they will contain nothing which can encourage or inspire. True beauty, however, has precisely this power. It is what Shelley meant when he said, rather extravagantly, that "poets are the unacknowledged legislators of the world." The conclusion is, then, that to decide the beauty of a work of art is one thing, and to decide what effects it will have, because it is beautiful, is quite another. Social comment can be art, provided it is *art*. If it remains merely comment, it will not be art certainly, and probably not successful persuasion either.

This, too, can be verified from personal experience. I, for one, can testify that a conviction of truth is not enough. My first realization, some years ago, of what was really wrong with the world touched off in me an explosion of versifying. "I lisped in numbers, for the numbers came." As they came, they seemed good; at any rate, they were remarkable in quantity. A kindly editor to whom I sent them replied that their good stuff had to be "quarried out, more or less." He was perfectly right, and I am by now accustomed to the despair of being no poet. Yet it troubles me that I (having of course the right ideas) can never be a poet, while T. S. Eliot (having of course the wrong ideas) indubitably is. Facts are facts, nonetheless.

Except for reservations like these, social comment is fully capable of appearing in art. When the comment is obviously biased, or paid for, or altogether mendacious, there will be much greater difficulty. At the best it will appear an attempt to "put something over," and at the worst it will arouse such distaste for lying as to kill any esthetic experience in decent people. But artists should have the benefit of every doubt. For our part, we ought never to let a fear of being propagandized prevent us from learning the minds of other men.

The best refutation, however, is one which I cannot give, for it remains to be given by artists themselves. Arguments like mine may prove whatever they prove; but the superstition will die, when it does die, under the skill with which artists treat the problems of their day. A contemporary Milton might (and would) be traduced as a subversive influence, but even the Hearst press would hardly venture to call him an incompetent poet. I can imagine a time, not perhaps far distant, when the belief that you cannot mix art and politics will crumble before a battery of works too powerful for resistance and too magnificent for reproach.

When such expectations have been fulfilled, let the content of these pages be laid, unremembered, by. There will then be no need to persuade artists that they are full of speech, and that their speech can have fair meaning for mankind. As there is no creator who is not in some degree a man, so there is no man who is not in some degree a creator. Without surrendering any of the admiration we feel for the insuperable achievements of genius, we may nevertheless hope for a narrowing of the distance between ourselves and them, for the awakening of a universal interest in art *and* in life. When artists have fully recovered their humanity, humanity at last will have recovered art.

CHAPTER VIII   THAT YOU HAVE
TO LOOK OUT
FOR YOURSELF

DOUBTLESS, in a sense, you do. If you were to impose entirely upon others the task of satisfying your needs, while contributing no efforts of your own, your life would be purely parasitic. You would be acting like any leisured, coupon-clipping gentleman, whose wants are met by a sort of tax levied upon other people's labor. Or, if we supposed a society in which no one did anything for himself but everything for others, we should have that fabulous community in which people earned their livelihood by doing one another's laundry.

Neither of these alternatives, however, is what the maxim ordinarily means. The ordinary meaning is rather this: that life is a violent and mortal struggle, in which everyone must seek his own advantage or perish. One's own advantage thus becomes the sole discernible good, defeat and death the sole discernible evil. Any act which helps achieve the former and avoid the latter is justified simply because it does so. The bricks which are to build my happiness I take from the wreckage which was yours.

Whatever may be said about this notion — and for the past twenty-five centuries a great deal has been said — it is frank, and because it is frank, it is supposed to be disarming. Its apostles, we are led to think, are certainly hiding nothing. They assert with great candor that they are "on the make." They give us fair warning. It is our folly if we do not take care.

Perhaps it is for this reason that the notion exists, as I have discovered, in some extremely innocent and guileless minds. During several years of teaching Ethics, I have had many students who stoutly defended the theory, defended it indeed with such resolute consistency that they were willing to blacken their own characters, though they were always careful not to blacken mine. I remember one fellow, a room clerk in his spare hours, who contended that only fear of the police prevented him from burgling the hotel safe. Possibly that was true, but, for my part, I would have put a lot of faith in his genial capacity for dissent. Without exception, these young protagonists of selfishness were both kind and reliable, and I surmise that they proved better citizens than their occasionally unctuous classmates.

If the cult of aggressive success exists among the youth, who are, I think, remarkably untouched by it as a rule, it will be found elsewhere than in those who openly profess it. In my college days, for example, senior classes used to vote on a number of questions, among them whether "education" or "contacts" had been the most valuable gain of the past four years. "Contacts" always won. This meant that a majority of seniors thought less highly of knowledge and of insight than of acquiring those relationships which would enable them to sell bonds and propagate insurance. The wisdom of ages failed before the simple fact that a present friend is a future customer. I do not recall that anybody inquired whether a present customer is a future friend.

Guileless or not, the candor of the theory is somewhat deceptive. It puts us off our guard by the very act of warning us to be on our guard. Duplicity, we think, would never announce itself so plainly. Instead of suspicion, we develop faith in the sincerity of one who has just told us that it is the secret of his ethics to be insincere. And insincere such a man must be, if he is to be consistent. For sincerity is a virtue only so far as it guarantees to other people a certain constancy of behavior. It is, therefore, a social virtue. But all social virtues are canceled under the ethics of selfishness. A man who shall be true to that ethics will have to lament the presence in his character of every such trait, and strive to rid himself of it as quickly as possible.

The theory before us, therefore, is set in the midst of remarkable contradictions. The innocent, to whom it is wholly unsuited, will nevertheless sometimes profess it, as a safe outlet for youthful revolt. The not so innocent will even act upon it, imitating in their elders those practices which were thought concealed. The theory itself cannot acknowledge any virtue in its own frankness, and thus cannot decide whether or not to admit that it means what it says. One perceives in the theory a state of desperation, a final paroxysm of justifying the unjustifiable, and beyond that the void which swallows dead ideas.

And that is precisely the fact. Suppose that you are a person whose income is derived from profits made upon the products of other people's labor. There are many people contributing to your income, and your income is large because theirs per capita is small. At the same time, you are aware that some thousands of people get their income exactly as you do. You discover, if you did not know it to begin with, that you have competitors in exploitation, and that unless you defend your portion of the total yield, it will pass into other hands and leave you bankrupt. You must maintain the *source* of your income and your *access* to that source. You must keep people working for you, and you must keep anybody else from taking your place.

Under such circumstances the world will seem to you to be full of enemies. The government, the trade unions, the monopolies, other businessmen great and small, will seem to be plotting your ruin. You struggle with every weapon at your command, and, curious as it may seem, among these weapons is ethical theory. Ethics is an instrument of power, because it is an instrument of justification and persuasion. Accordingly, you may try to suggest that in all your actions you are simply helping nature to weed out the "unfit," or that there are certain people "inferior" by nature and therefore deserving of the treatment you give them, or that you are acting out the inevitable patterns of human behavior.

But suppose, now, that these and other justifications fail. Suppose the veils of flattering ideology to be stripped away, with your station and behavior left naked in the glare of economic fact. You will have no further recourse except to justify your nakedness, and you may as well be frank about it. When all means of concealment are gone, there is nothing left but to be candid. You will say, therefore: this is the way people really are; this (as one sees) is the way I am; let each make what he can out of it. Thus, when jungle behavior can no longer be convincingly portrayed as exhilarating, or natural, or beneficial, or just, or inevitable, there remains only a sort of final sigh, as who should say, "Oh well, hang it all, I'll go ahead with it anyway." To perform this office is the task of the ethics of selfishness. It is not clear whether the office is that of physician or gravedigger.

Such is the social use of the theory. Precisely because it is a last resort, however, it raises the most basic of all moral questions. Since it asserts that no one need be concerned with anybody else's welfare, it forces us to inquire whether such a concern has any justification at all. We are all, of course, taught that other people's welfare should be our primary concern. We are taught to admire virtues like courage, self-control, and loyalty, which involve self-sacrifice and self-denial. Even in acquisitive and competitive societies these virtues are extolled, if only because the rulers benefit by discouraging acquisitiveness and competition among the mass. But when we come face to face with a theory which asserts that these virtues have no value, that they are foolish and dangerous, then we must examine the whole of our ethics down to the very bottom. We must try to discover whether there *are* any reasons why social-mindedness is to be preferred above selfishness.

Well, then, shall I seek my own good, forgetting others; or others' good, forgetting myself; or, since the two are by no means incompatible, shall I seek both goods at once? This question is probably the most important we ever have to decide. If we follow where the answer leads, we shall pass through politics, economics, and sociology into the smallest details of personal life. The answer will strongly influence our choice of parties, our support of legislative measures, our views on industrial relationships, and even minor decisions like whether or not to be prompt in fulfilling an engagement. The best way to put the question, the way which embraces all the various implications, is this: Are you for people or against them?

FOR AND AGAINST MANKIND

The answer "I'm against them" has, besides its frankness, the merit of simplicity. It does not require that the mind be stretched to encompass the whole of humanity. It turns no careful and discerning eye toward the systems under which men live. It sees at best one interstice of the web, one corner of the hive, where pauses for a moment the well-beloved self. To secure the comfort of that moment and ease of passage into the next is all that can be heeded. I have known businessmen who were so bemused by the problems of their little private worlds as to be convinced that there exists no economic *system* at all. "What are you worried about?" said one of these to me. "There's no such thing as capitalism."

Compared to this sublime simplicity, the other answer will seem intolerably complex. For here we add to the woes, already great, of maintaining our existence in the world further anxieties over the lot of our fellows. To place oneself on the people's side is to care whether they have enough food and shelter and clothing. It is to feel, not indeed with the immediacy of direct suffering, but keenly nevertheless, each hurt and loss which can befall them. Nor is it possible to set shrewd limits to the range of sympathy. The true democrat and people's partisan finds his sympathy increasing as he passes down the social scale, so that the more oppressed and despoiled people are, the more lively and eager is his love. His emotions are governed not by the dreadful and corrosive calculus of "what is each man worth?" but by awareness of the social forces which have condemned men to their present destiny.

Complication does not end here. Men who choose the people's side do not merely increase the range and intensity of their emotional lives. They act. They undertake campaigns. They ring doorbells, hand out circulars, interview celebrities, and remind legislators (when such is necessary) of the rights of man. They conduct meetings on street corners and in halls. They assault the press with correspondence, and for a few days the letter columns are filled with community sense instead of neighborhood idiocies. They form committees to combat this and establish that. They fill apartments, homes, and hired auditoriums with smoke and debate and a never-flagging hope. Society, like a sober elephant, shudders bulkily and moves on, often in the right direction.

How there is time for all these giddy motions no democrat ever knows. The day retains its immutable extent of hours; the clock turns at no slower rate. Yet time exists — time borrowed from lunch and dinner, from recreation, and, alas, from sleep. The borrower develops perhaps an exaggerated sense of crisis; he lives "as ever in my great Taskmaster's eye." Surely his life is full, with much labor spent and a little lost, with achievements to be rejoiced in and failures to be endured, with sunlight and shadow drifting across the surface of the world.

I do not suggest that all socially-minded people agitate quite so violently the waters around them. While agitation may well be a sign of concern, this latter can exist with much less outward manifestation. There is a quiet affection for mankind which shows itself more gently, and accomplishes often with a touch what intenser spirits cannot do with blows. Yet the calm affection has depth, and in those depths some anguish, as hating to see others balked of benefits which it itself enjoys.

Measured in the thought, the feeling, or the doing, social-mindedness is altogether the more difficult creed. How much easier as well as safer it must seem to narrow one's gaze to the ego and his own, to calculate his comfort and plot his prosperity, to lard his flesh and exalt his spirit as if the universe were a garden for no other appetites than his, and at last to mourn over six feet of earth as the end and dissolution of a world. Easier, certainly; safer, perhaps. But it will be our task to show that, whatever its attractions, the ethics of selfishness is false.

THRASYMACHUS

Let us now set forth the theory with all its arguments and exhortations. We shall not meet it with any appeals to law as such, whether human or divine, nor with any mystical pleadings, nor with hopes of reward and threats of punishment in another world. We must confront it on its own ground, there to fight and overcome it. If we cannot do this, we shall have to confess that, despite all its difficulties, the theory cannot be completely demolished.

The ethics of selfishness has had, I should say, two classical expositions in the history of human thought. One of these belongs to the ancient world, and the other to the Renaissance. They are, respectively, the speech which Plato attributes to Thrasymachus in Book I of the *Republic,* and that famous treatise on government, *The Prince,* written by Machiavelli in 1513. Both expositions are brilliant; indeed it is a considerable tribute to Plato's fairness of mind that he was willing to write down so eloquently a view which he abhorred. He wrote it, in fact, so well that he came very near not refuting it in the course of the remaining nine books.

Perhaps, now, we may imagine ourselves at a sort of house party at the Piraeus during a festival in honor of the goddess Bendis. The Greeks were stupendous talkers, especially the gentlemen among them, who, as it seems, had little else to do. The ripest fruit of their loquacity was Greek philosophy itself, and I, for one, am willing to concede that leisure so spent was justified.

On this occasion the talk has fallen upon the concept of Justice, two definitions of which are demolished by Socrates almost as soon as they are uttered. There is in the company, however, a young man, bright and restless and bellicose, who finds Socrates's remarks intolerably sententious. This youngster, Thrasymachus by name, is a portrait Plato loved to draw; he is perhaps the prototype of all the "practical" men who have in various ages made history a turmoil. He breaks in with a view to blowing away the ethical cobwebs and returning the discussion to those facts which are hard and those tacks which are brass. Justice, he cries, is simply "the interest of the stronger," or, to put it another way, "the interest of the established government."

Attacking this view, Socrates undertakes to show that government exists to take care of the citizens, as a shepherd exists to take care of the sheep. No analogy was ever more luckless. For, as Thrasymachus is not slow to point out, a shepherd cares for his sheep in order (1) to fleece them, and (2) to eat them. This was the very point Thrasymachus originally made, and Socrates's rebuttal turns out to be an argument *pro* instead of an argument *con*.

Encouraged by this preliminary victory, Thrasymachus sets out upon a full exposition, which, since it is the finest and compactest statement of the theory, deserves to be given entire:

You may see by the following considerations, my most simple Socrates, that a just man everywhere has the worst of it, compared with an unjust man. In the first place, in their mutual dealings, wherever a just man enters into partnership with an unjust man, you will find that at the dissolution of the partnership the just man never has more than the unjust man, but always less. Then again in their dealings with the state, when there is a property tax to pay, the just man will pay more and the unjust less, on the same amount of property; and when there is anything to receive, the one gets nothing, while the other makes great gains.

All this perhaps twenty-three centuries before people discovered how to incorporate their families and yachts as a means of avoiding taxation.

And whenever either of them holds any office of authority, if the just man suffers no other loss, at least his private affairs fall into disorder through want of attention to them, while his principles forbid his deriving any benefit from the public money; and besides this, it is his fate to offend his friends and acquaintances every time that he refuses to serve them at the expense of justice.

Where, indeed, would local politicos be, if they could not exempt their "friends and acquaintances" from the consequences of a parking ticket?

But with the unjust man everything is reversed. I am speaking — says Thrasymachus — of the case I mentioned just now, of an unjust man who has the power to grasp on an extensive scale. To him you must direct your attention, if you wish to judge how much more profitable it is to a man's own self to be unjust than to be just. And you will learn this truth with the greatest ease, if you turn your attention to the most consummate form of injustice, which, while it makes the wrongdoer most happy, makes those who are wronged, and will not retaliate, most miserable. This form is a despotism, which proceeds not by small degrees, but by wholesale, in its open or fraudulent appropriation of the property of others, whether it be sacred or profane, public or private; — perpetrating offences, which if a person commits in detail and is found out, he becomes liable to a penalty and incurs deep disgrace; for partial offenders in this class of crimes are called sacrilegious, men-stealers, burglars, thieves, and robbers. But when a man not only seizes the property of his fellow-citizens but captures and enslaves their persons also, instead of those dishonorable titles he is called happy and highly favored, not only by the men of his own city, but also by all others who hear of the comprehensive injustice which he has wrought. For when people abuse injustice, they do so because they are afraid, not of committing it, but of suffering it. Thus it is, Socrates, that injustice, realized on an adequate scale, is a stronger, a more liberal, and a more lordly thing than justice; and as I said at first, justice is the interest of the stronger; injustice, a thing profitable and advantageous to oneself.[1]

In surveying this splendid defense of evil, it may be desirable to emphasize the major theses: (1) that what passes for social justice is in fact a collection of laws and customs maintained by the ruling class for its own advantage; (2) that justice, as a *moral* principle, is purely an illusion invoked by the weak to protect themselves against the strong, whom otherwise they would be only too happy to imitate; (3) that injustice (*i.e.* selfish behavior) is the one sure source of personal gain; (4) that only one condition attaches to injustice, namely, that

[1] Plato: *Republic*, Bk. I, 343d–344c. Davies and Vaughn translation.

it must be "comprehensive," that it must be practiced on "an adequate scale." Small-scale injustice is far too risky; punishment and disgrace lie so near at hand as to make it almost certainly self-defeating.

This last proviso renders the ethics of selfishness completely unworkable for 99 per cent of the world's population. They have not "the power to grasp on an extensive scale." When they appropriate the property of others, or seize their persons by kidnaping, they face prison terms, if caught, and if not caught, a life of danger and insecurity. It is reserved to a few (whom we need not call favored) to fatten upon the lives and property of others, not only without fear of prison, but with an ever more secure respectability. A tiny group of men, sitting in an island kingdom, sweats wealth from a nation of no less than three hundred and fifty million people, thousands of miles away, keeping them ninety-five per cent illiterate, and maintaining in one of the world's richest regions an average life span of twenty-three years! Thrasymachus has some facts on his side. It almost seems that the greater the gains of injustice, the greater the safety of committing it.

MACHIAVELLI

As is plain from the title, *The Prince* recognizes that the ethics of selfishness is workable only for a few. What Machiavelli did in this book was to generalize very brilliantly upon the political practices of his time, the high Italian Renaissance, which abounded in masterpieces of art and villainy. Of those ecclesiastical and secular rulers, of popes, princes, and dukes, it suffices to say that there was no vice left unpracticed by them, nothing cruel or abominable or unspeakable which they did not do. This statement has no exaggeration but is literally true. If you catalogue the vices of Alexander VI, you will find everything there, from tyranny to murder to incest.[2]

It is not exactly fair to Machiavelli that his name has come to stand for the ethical theory (if one can call it that) which defends selfishness. He nowhere asserts that it is a good thing for princes to rule in this way; he only asserts that this is the way princes must rule, if they are to acquire and retain power. Moreover, his thinking exhibits some unquestionably progressive elements, such as his plea for the unification of Italy, his attack upon mercenary armies, and a curious but genuine democratic feeling.[3] In view of this, it would be interesting to know whether *The Prince* was placed or the Index because of its anti-Christian ethics or because of its anti-feudal doctrines.

Be this as it may, Machiavelli did his work so well and contrived his generalizations so aptly that since his time knowledgeable tyrants have followed his advice, unaware that possibly he was kidding them all. The late Signor Mussolini, for example, openly announced himself as Machiavelli's disciple, and took enough time

[2] An excellent account of his, and others', iniquities will be found in John Addington Symonds: *The Renaissance in Italy*, Part I, Chapters III, VII, and VIII.

[3] This is most apparent in his admiring description of the prince whose rule is founded in the love of his subjects — *The Prince*, Chapter IX.

from his labors as dictator to write at least the introduction to a doctoral dissertation upon his master. The University of Bologna thereupon bestowed upon him the appropriate degree.[4] We shall do well to bear in mind this little historical episode, for the Duce's career sheds a great deal of light on the nature and profitability of Machiavellian principles.

Beginning, now, not where Machiavelli begins, but with the logical basis of the theory, we may observe that there are two ways of conducting political contests: one is by law, the other by force. Machiavelli says, revealing for a moment what are perhaps his true sentiments, that "the first method is proper to men, the second to beasts."[5] But the first method is demonstrably insufficient, so that the prince must learn how to make use of both. Adopting the beast, then, he ought to choose the lion and the fox. "It is necessary to be a fox to discover the snares and a lion to terrify the wolves."[6] In short, the prince has two chief weapons: craft and force.

Of these two the first is far more satisfactory so long as it will work, for it makes no enemies and it conceals its actual purpose. Of all the deceptions which a prince should attempt, the most important is to pass himself off as a man of spectacular virtue. There is a difficulty in this, for he dare not really possess the virtues he pretends to have: they will be weights which must drown him in the end. Thus:

[4] Cf. Melvin Rader: *No Compromise*, Macmillan, New York, 1939, Chapter V, Part 2.
[5] Machiavelli, *The Prince*, Chapter XVIII, p. 141 in the Everyman edition.
[6] *Ibid.*, p. 142.

. . . it is unnecessary for a prince to have all the good qualities which I have enumerated, but it is very necessary to
appear to have them; . . . to appear merciful, faithful, humane, religious, upright, and to be so, but with a mind so
framed that should you require not to be so, you may be
able and know how to change to the opposite. . . . Everyone sees what you appear to be, few really know what you
are, and those few dare not oppose themselves to the opinion of the many, who have the majesty of the state to defend them.[7]

By way of example, one might mention an allusion
of Machiavelli's, Messer Ramiro d'Orco, into whose
hands Cesare Borgia gave the pacification of the Ro-
magna. Ramiro's cruelties speedily rendered him odious.
When this reputation began to touch Cesare himself,
who abundantly deserved it, he had Ramiro executed,
thus assuming the role of avenging justice and minister-
ing angel to the people. But in the twentieth century,
villains like Cesare will seem to be small fry indeed.
Following Machiavelli's own taste for contemporary illustration, let us cite him who was, in our day, the
father of guile and the Moloch of human sacrifice,
Adolf Hitler. This man let it be known, across the
breath of organized rumor, that he had been appointed
and sent by God to be the savior, not indeed of the world
at large, but of the fairest portion thereof, Germany, a
nation in which the Deity for some decades past was
known to have been peculiarly interested. The divine
appointee was recognized, not without some dissent, by
the people he had come to save and even by some *in*

[7] *Ibid.*, pp. 143–4.

partibus infidelium, as I have heard with my own ears.

Now, nothing can guarantee virtue like an apotheosis, a sudden incorporation, however managed, of the human with the divine. The Roman emperors, themselves not unacquainted with crime, understood the technique admirably; and the recent (but only the recent) emperors of Japan have imitated them with an accuracy somewhat less successful. A being created by the ordinary fertilization of an ovum and locked in the frailties of parental genes is transfigured into an emanation descending from clouds, or from the sun, or, as the apter Teutonic myths have it, from primeval trees. *Bonum est quid Deus vult:* What God wills is good. Such a being can do no wrong, not even when he murders millions of "inferior" peoples.

Along with the magnificent attributes of divinity, however, these armed apostles manifest, or have manifested for them, certain more homely virtues. Hitler's chastity was widely and, as it now seems, inaccurately advertised. Hitler's sobriety was equally famous, and this virtue, if it be a virtue, he may very well have had: it is useful to statesmen when they are conducting negotiations. Hitler's passion, we were told, brooded over Greater Germany, into which ardent and omniterrestrial love he sublimated those appetites which Freud described and that racial unconscious which Jung obediently invented.

One can hear also a weaker voice, but it is that of Machiavelli's disciple. In a passage like the following it is hard to say which are more appallingly trivial, the virtues which are claimed or the vices which are denied:

I love all sports; I drive a motor car with confidence; I
have done tours at great speed, amazing not only to my
friends, but also to old and experienced drivers. I love the
airplane; I have flown countless times. . . . I ask of my
violin nothing more than serene hours of music. Of the
great poets, such as Dante, of the supreme philosophers,
such as Plato, I often ask hours of poetry, hours of medi-
tation.

No other amusement interests me. I do not drink, I do
not smoke, and I am not interested in cards or games.[8]

I am very much afraid that the great Machiavelli's disciple, the doctor of philosophy from the University of
Bologna, the leader and chief of the New Roman Empire, was in many ways an ass.

But while there is considerable mirth in hearing
Mussolini announce that "my inmost moral fibre is invincible," [9] I hardly know what emotion or compound
of emotions may rise at the words of another contemporary figure, executed for the most odious of crimes, to
which his name had already been given as a synonym in
our language. "Not many," said Vidkun Quisling, "have
done so much for humanity as I." [10] The bravado of
this utterance must eclipse the fame of all previous trea-
sons. *The Prince* itself affords no comparable example

---

[8] Benito Mussolini: *My Autobiography*, Scribner's, New York, 1928,
pp. 204–5. This is the book of which two reviewers wrote as follows:
(1) "For all his egocentricity, his bombast, Mussolini's native sincerity
is obvious." (R. E. Larson, *The Bookman*, 68:703) ; (2) "This volume
is delightful. There is not, as its ambassador-editor says, an insincere
line in it." (Arthur Livingston, *New York Herald Tribune Weekly
Book Review*, Oct. 28, 1928, p. 4.)

[9] *Ibid.*, p. 96.

[10] UP dispatch from Oslo, August 22, 1945.

— benignly virtuous in the seeming, invincibly wicked in the being, to the very last.

Yet craft is never enough, though fortified with propaganda techniques and the much overvalued cult of the Great Lie. Says Machiavelli:

. . . all the armed prophets have conquered, and the unarmed ones have been destroyed. Besides the reasons mentioned, the nature of the people is variable, and whilst it is easy to persuade them, it is difficult to fix them in that persuasion. And thus it is necessary to take such measures that, when they believe no longer, it may be possible to make them believe by force.[11]

Machiavelli admits, very plainly, the proposition which Mr. Lincoln made famous in America: "you cannot fool all the people all the time." For if "the nature of the people is variable," this is not because they are congenitally fickle, but because they inevitably discover what the rulers are up to. Machiavelli would have served his disciples better by making this point clear, for they always overlook it. A ruling elite has many blindnesses, but the most dangerous is its belief that people never learn. People do learn, not only without books and education, but with books which lie and education which stultifies. The schooling of disease and the instruction of a hungry belly are proof against even the most cunning deception.

When craft fails, then, says our teacher, violence must be used; but the violence must be administered with craft. The ruler is not to use violence, so to say, artlessly, but with precision and speed.

[11] Machiavelli, *op. cit.*, pp. 48–49 (Chapter VI).

. . . injuries ought to be done all at one time, so that, being tasted less, they offend less; benefits ought to be given little by little so that the flavor of them may last longer.[12]

Swift violence shatters the opposition and destroys its organizational scheme. By the time recovery can begin violence has ceased, craft has resumed its sway, and counter-violence lacks an immediate pretext for exercise. We are told that Hitler used to say, "I bide my time, and then I strike like lightning." It is a faithful copy of the master's principle. Within certain limits it had the predicted success.

Having now got hold of the essential doctrines, we need not further explore the wisdom of *The Prince*, although a thorough knowledge of that book will benefit whoever studies it. It so completely reveals the inner machinery of power that it is a priceless guide to the behavior of potentates, whether economic or political. But our present purpose is rather more limited, for we are not to search out the particular secrets of particular rulers, but only to decide the merits of a life lived according to such principles. What, in short, are we to think of a man, or a group of men, whose single purpose is self-aggrandizement, to be achieved by every means that craft and violence can devise? And again, shall we want to adopt, each for himself, similar purposes and similar methods?

[12] *Ibid.*, p. 73 (Chapter VIII).

IS SELFISHNESS SUCCESSFUL?

There is a sense in which everybody lives two lives, one in a smaller, one in a larger, circle. The smaller circle contains the people with whom we are in more or less daily contact: our family, our friends, our acquaintances, our associates. The larger one is the whole national society in which we happen to live. The two are joined and yet distinct, and we behave rather differently in each. We cannot regard society as a whole with quite the same intimacy and familiarity we feel for our family and friends, though we may regard it with approval and even with love. When we think about what is good for society, we think in general economic and political terms; when we think about what is good for our friends and family, we think, less generally and more concretely, in terms of individual human beings.

I have no wish to press this distinction beyond proper limits, for certainly our life in each of these circles is modified by our life in the other. Taking sides on a great social issue, for example, may very well shatter friendships and families. But the distinction will be useful in forming some opinion of the ethics of selfishness. For this ethics asserts not merely that it is realistic and practicable, but that it is the only ethics which is so. All else, say the Machiavellians, is illusion and romance. The claim is ambitious and worthy of first attention.

Let me say at once that I do not intend to argue that the ethics of selfishness will *never* work. History shows very clearly that it sometimes does. Quite a few Machiavellians have died in bed and even in the odor of sanctity. But history shows, no less clearly, that it sometimes doesn't work. Quite a few Machiavellians have destroyed themselves with their own armament. When this happens, the Machiavellians always try to absolve their ethical theory from blame and to attribute failure to a personal mistake. This may on occasion be true, but it is much more probable that the source of failure is the ethics itself.

Let us consider, first, the practice of selfishness in the smaller circle of friends and acquaintances. The chances of success are very slight. Here every action is observed and estimated, patterns of behavior cannot long be hid, and the habit of craft, let alone violence, soon loses the secrecy it so desperately requires. The intended victims, recognizing the would-be victimizer, surround him with a *cordon sanitaire,* which, since it keeps him away from them, keeps him also away from the goals he sought to achieve. Thereafter no friendships for him are possible, and scarcely any associations, however formal and distant. It becomes plain that all those values he has lost by the practice of selfishness can be recovered only by the practice of the precisely contrary ethics.

We are speaking, it must be remembered, of men with whom selfishness is a conscious creed. We are not speaking of men who now and then (or even often) commit selfish acts. Selfishness is the satisfaction of desire at somebody else's expense, so that the one's gain is the other's loss. I suppose that everyone, at some time or other, has done things of this sort; but no one can be a Machiavellian unless he makes such behavior a rule of life. And if he makes it a rule of life towards family and friends and associates, he will speedily cease to have family, associates, and friends. For no matter how cleverly he conceals the motive of personal gain, the others can hardly fail to notice their own personal loss.

Conditions are rather different, however, when the ethics of selfishness is practiced in the larger circle, that is to say, upon a national or international scale. Craft and violence need great areas in which to maneuver, and here for the first time such areas can be found. In the range of an entire society, considerable distance intervenes between exploiters and exploited. These latter, moreover, are often so absorbed in the immediate problems of living that they can attend only with difficulty to the activities of the former. Besides this, the distance between them is filled with various screens and road-blocks, which have a good deal the effect of masking the real exercise of power and of preventing close observation. We can learn from the Nazis, if from nowhere else, how every kind of institution in the community — educational, civic, ecclesiastical — can be interposed between the groups in just that way. And while, in the smaller circle, a lie can scarcely be maintained for days, a social superstition, in the larger circle, can be made to last for a century.

The same is true of violence. We have now, though with painful effort, largely got beyond the habit of individual, personal violence, such as prevailed, say, in fourteenth-century Florence, where every house was a fortress armed and manned and liable to invasion. We got beyond it, I am afraid, not because we thought violence morally wrong, but because it became recognizably self-defeating. On a social scale, however, it is possible to array violence in the garb of law enforcement and of national defense. I am far from saying that violence has never been justifiably so used, but I do assert that not infrequently these pretexts have been fraudulent. Use of the police and armed forces against labor shows what can be done in the name of "law enforcement," and intermittent warfare for the possession of colonies, over the past century, shows what can be done in the name of "national defense."

On this larger scale, the ethics of selfishness have certainly a greater chance of success. The Machiavellian man, now able to commit "comprehensive injustice" because he controls the apparatus of state power and the instruments of communication, cannot readily be defeated or even opposed. If, further, he successfully divides his victims, setting them against one another on the basis of fictitious and imaginary grievances, he may look forward to a prolonged retention of power. Yet even here there may very well be nothing more than mere prolongation, with failure waiting inescapably at the end. When I was first in Italy, in 1924, shortly after the murder of Matteotti, the fascist regime was more than a little shaky; but its defenders of course predicted for it a strong and continuing life, much like Hitler's brag of a thousand years. As time went on, nothing appeared to disturb the accuracy of this prediction. But, for all that, there came at last a day when justice, returning after a long absence, paused in a square in Milan to see the Duce hanging by his heels in the April wind.

It is true that Machiavellians sometimes escape their proper destiny; the logic of evil does not always contradict itself. But there are certain results which no Machiavellian can escape. Chiefly, he cannot escape being

Machiavellian. Every tyrannical act which brings him gain brings also the deterioration of his character. He is condemned by his own ethics to the hypocrisy of professing virtue and practicing vice. This cleavage splits his character at its foundation, and the resulting personal instability is constantly increased by the rapacity of his own appetites, which, accepting no discipline, make all of life a clamor and tumult. Greed fevers him like an ague; and the final death of his body, though it occur in quiet and in admiration, is the collapse of a charnel house upon the inhabiting bones. If, therefore, there seems any attraction in being a Nazi bigwig or a Ruhr industrialist, it must be remembered that in order to be one of these, you have to *be* one. You cannot have the gains without the character. In order to enjoy gold and garments and ample Saxon mistresses, you have got to be a man who makes, or permits to be made, gas chambers and crematory ovens. The gains seem hardly worth the degeneracy.

The most ironic aspect of the ethics of selfishness is the fact that, instead of being realistic and practicable, it is in a curious way idealistic and perfectionist. It shares the difficulties of all ethical systems whose values are so abstract and rigorous that they contradict one another when plunged into the flow of events. Let us take an example. Machiavelli says that "he who is the cause of another's becoming powerful is ruined; because that predominancy has been brought about either by astuteness or else by force, and both are distrusted by him who has been raised to power." [13] Now, of course, Mussolini did just this in assisting the consolidation of Ger-

13 *Ibid.,* p. 27 (Chapter III).

man fascism, and his policy had precisely the result which Machiavelli forecast. Are we to suppose that the disciple merely "forgot" this injunction of the master? Of course not. The policy was necessitated by the play of power politics and by the general anti-democratic character of fascism. In other words, Mussolini had to sacrifice this injunction, in order to obey other Machiavellian injunctions. The principles conflicted, and he had to choose. Had he chosen otherwise, he would have met a different disaster; but it would have been disaster nevertheless. The profound trouble with Machiavellian principles, then, is that you cannot practice them all at once. In any given situation you must refrain from doing certain things which you need to do in order to survive as an industrious tyrant. Machiavelli himself confesses that "prudence consists in knowing how to distinguish the character of troubles, and for choice to take the lesser evil." [14] But when you are forced to choose a lesser evil instead of a positive good, it is because events have put it out of your power to do more than stave off catastrophe. The catastrophe, indeed, is partly of your own making, for your use of craft and force over a long period of time inevitably creates and unites against you the forces necessary for your overthrow. The Nazis appear to have believed an Anglo-American-Soviet coalition impossible because of ideological differences, but their own acts gave the three nations a common interest in their destruction. Nazi policies did more to promote collective security against Naziism than all the efforts of far-sighted idealists before the war.

[14] *Ibid.*, p. 181 (Chapter XXI).

END OF A PROBLEM

Our criticism of the ethics of selfishness has thus far dealt with its workability. There seems to be no question that only a few people (perhaps 1 per cent of the population) can really get away with it at all, and that, of these, not very many maintain their success to the end. The theory itself cannot, without self-contradiction, be applied to events; and the practice of it depraves and disintegrates the character of the practitioner. Mussolini was fond of crying, "It is better to be a lion for a day than a sheep for a century!" But when, at the end of his day, he faced his executioner in the Como hills, he manifested a rapid conversion in favor of the sheep.

But the test of workability will not finally decide the merits of social-mindedness as against selfishness. There is ill-success in the practice of both. We have got to face a much larger question, the question why the one is *better* than the other. We have to try to show that an act which benefits society, though it may injure the doer, is better than an act which injures society, though it may benefit the doer.

It is a peculiar problem. Ethical theory has existed since the fifth century B.C., and in all that time nobody has ever contrived to prove that his definition of goodness is the only possible definition. The controversy has been varied but ceaseless, and the failure has been complete. These facts would seem to suggest that the problem cannot be solved in the old way, but must be opened to a new. Perhaps we can try.

Let us ask, first, how the problem happens to arise. It isn't just a fanciful affair, a puzzle to be worked on for sport or entertainment. If a man has to decide whether to seek gain for himself *or* gain for his fellows, it can only be because circumstances are such that he cannot do both. If he could do both, if the two were never incompatible, the problem could not arise. He could then gratify his wishes with the happy knowledge that he was injuring nobody, or that he was actually helping others. There must, therefore, be certain social circumstances which make one man's gain a loss to others. These circumstances are chiefly two: (1) a scarcity of goods and services, and (2) the exploitation of one group of men by another group. Let us look at these further.

(1) Scarcity means that there are not enough goods and services to satisfy the normal wants of *all* members of society. It means that there are not enough houses, clothes, food, medical care, education, and so forth, for everybody to have as much of them as he wants or even as much as he needs. From this insufficiency it follows that the possession of these things by some people entails the lack or loss of them in others. Those who have, not unreasonably want to keep; and those who have not, with equal reason want to get. There ensues a competition, always vigorous and sometimes violent, which would never exist in a society of genuine abundance. For what would be the point of taking food from another's mouth, if there were so much of it available that you, on the one hand, wouldn't need to take it, and he, on the other, could easily replenish his loss?

But as things are now, most people don't get all they need, still less all they want. They see no reason (for there is no reason) why they should be deprived. They see other people grasping, some of them successfully. It looks as though it were "human nature" to do so. Perhaps they had better get in there and grasp too. If they begin to philosophize about this, the first thing you know they will talk like Machiavelli: "The wish to acquire is in truth very natural and common, and men always do so when they can." [15] Success will bring a semblance of security, whereas failure will bring poverty, disease, and death. Under such conditions, what arguments can persuade men toward social-mindedness? As Lincoln Steffens once observed, it was not the serpent which corrupted man; it was the apple.

(2) Exploitation means the appropriation to oneself of the products of other people's labor without full compensation. The exploited person works part of the time for himself and part for somebody else. In the ancient world (and in the Old South) slaveowners enriched themselves upon the labor of slaves. In the Middle Ages the lords did the same with their serfs. In modern society, employers make a profit upon the labor of their employees.

Now, the interests of these groups are opposed. The employer cannot exist at all unless he makes a profit, and he cannot be secure unless he makes a large profit. But whether he increases his profits by lowering wages or raising prices, the effect on wage earners is to lower their standard of living. If, on the other hand, they improve their living standards, they do so at the expense of profits. It is a mistake to suppose that either group acts out of mere personal greed. Given the system, the

[15] *Ibid.*, p. 25 (Chapter III).

employer has to do what he does, or he will cease to be an employer; the employee has to do what he does, or he will cease to be at all. The one seeks to maintain his social role, the other simply to maintain himself.

In economic conditions of this sort, it is very difficult to urge the superior merit of social-mindedness. Humanitarianism, personal reform, and the dawning of an inner light may mitigate the conflict somewhat; but the conflict itself cannot be removed unless we remove also the conditions which produced it. This brings us within sight of our answer.

How does one solve a problem? If the problem is merely theoretical, one can solve it by analyzing it into its parts and assembling those parts into a coherent system. If the problem is, however, practical, one solves it by performing those acts which will put the problem out of existence. Suppose I have the "problem" of getting to New York. I solve it by taking a train or bus or motor car, that is to say, by doing those things which will get me there.

Now, for twenty-five hundred years, people have been treating the problem of selfishness *vs.* social-mindedness as if it were purely theoretical. And they have been reaching no answers. They have failed. They have failed, because the problem is not in fact theoretical but practical. Its solution lies not in the construction of new ethical philosophies but in the creation of a new society. Every program, every policy, every act which leads toward that new society is a contribution to solving the problem.

When mankind has attained a state in which goods and services abound and exploitation has ceased, there will be no social reason why your welfare should be incompatible with mine. Selfishness, having no longer anything important to do, will wither away, taking our problem with it. The ultimate philosophical justification of social-mindedness must be that it alone can give the entire problem a solution. The ultimate condemnation of selfishness is that it renders a solution forever impossible.

Can we reach the goal? Well, maybe not you and I, who are aging under the strains of the present world. Our best hope will be to move Leviathan a little, so that our children and their children can begin to see dawn. But though we do not, mankind certainly can reach the goal. Even before the harnessing of atomic energy, abundance was a very possible thing. Now it must seem that the possibilities are without limit. And exploitation itself need not exist forever. The human race, which abolished slavery and serfdom, which learned and practiced political democracy, cannot be eternally thwarted of control over its entire social destiny. It may appear a fabled and Utopian dream, but dreams far more fabled and Utopian have come true.

The dreams men dream in sleep are mist and shadow. The dreams men dream while waking can become the substance of a world.

CHAPTER IX THAT ALL
PROBLEMS ARE
MERELY VERBAL

THE NINETEEN-THIRTIES began in hunger and ended in blood. The lines of men before soup kitchens gave way to lines of pickets around factories and stores, and these in turn gave way to lines of troops moving into battle. The nineteen-thirties, a decade conveniently marked in time, were part of a vaster epoch of social change, which had existed before them and continues to exist after them. Nevertheless, they had a nature of their own, and they generated doctrines appropriate to it. Among these was the belief that all problems are merely verbal. This doctrine is not, I think, very widely diffused throughout the population, most of which, indeed, could not possibly survive by any such notion. It is, however, common enough among the intelligentsia — a social class in which membership is voluntary and is apparently attained by simple declaration of arrival. If any readers feel themselves outside this class, they may dispense with further reading, and thus remain in profitable ignorance of at least one social superstition. But if they know themselves to be members, then I am bound to think that the discussion will be useful.

When Hitler entered Austria in 1938, he drove into exile, among other talented intellectuals, certain members of a philosophical school known as the *Wienerkreis*. This school, the Vienna Circle, developed in the mid-nineteen-twenties, basing itself on the work of Ernst Mach in the nineteenth century and on the philosophical criticism of Hume in the eighteenth. The school was primarily interested in logic and scientific method. It believed that most, if not all, of the major philosophical problems had arisen from an inaccurate use of language, and it therefore set itself the task of removing from philosophy all ambiguities of syntax and definition. Such was the origin of Logical Positivism.

The lives of the founders have not been easy. Moritz Schlick was murdered by a student, before *Anschluss*. The war itself pursued Wittgenstein to England and Carnap to America. Moreover, the Positivist movement, which had preceded them westward, had taken a form they perhaps did not intend. Its newer devotees had begun to treat social problems as if these, too, were purely verbal, as if the struggle against fascism involved no more than a definition of terms. While "the round earth's imagined corners" flamed with horror and sacrifice, there grew soberly under new hands what Carnap had called "*der logische Aufbau der Welt.*"

Why, at such a time and for so long a time, should one interest oneself in rearing "the logical structure of the world?" I am not suggesting that the task is unimportant; rather, the task, even if imperfectly achieved, would throw much light on all other problems. But when men assert, as these do, that such is philosophy's only task, that philosophy itself is only "the critique of language," [1] then we may well inquire why so faint and diffident a theory has prospered in so violent an age.

The answer would be something like this. Suppose you are living in the midst of a disaster which involves the whole community. If you think that society can recoup its losses, you will find yourself committed to several philosophical assumptions, such as that the universe is not static and hence that social change is possible, or that society can be an object of knowledge and, by that knowledge, be controlled. But if you hold that the disaster is beyond repair, your philosophical views are modified accordingly. You may decide to endure things patiently, and thus embrace stoicism; you may decide upon a cautious pursuit of pleasure, and thus embrace epicureanism; you may decide that all accepted values are in fact contemptible, and thus embrace cynicism; you may persuade yourself that knowledge is quite impossible, that we cannot even be sure we are unhappy, and thus embrace scepticism. All four of these views flourished in Greece after the Macedonian conquest. They form an ideological pattern for all times of general catastrophe.

If, however, a society finds the means of recovery, these philosophies begin to disappear, partly because they have no longer any use and partly because the daily experience of people will seem to contradict them. The solution of social problems convinces men that they do have knowledge; hence scepticism fades. Solution

[1] Ludwig Wittgenstein: *Tractatus Logico-Philosophicus*, Harcourt, Brace & Co., New York, 1922, p. 63.

means a greater abundance and a better distribution of goods; hence there are more pleasures available, fewer shocks have to be endured, and the accepted values tend to be confirmed. Epochs of expansion are alive with confidence and large in ideas. The gains of each new day confound the sceptics; success charms cynics out of their cynicism; pleasure seekers slough off their ill-borne caution; and stoics exchange patience under adversity for eagerness under hope. There is a brilliance lighting all prospects; and it would never occur to anyone to think that philosophy, hovering over a renascent world, is but the breath of speech about speech.

Yet if recovery delays and will not come round the expected corner, if, on the contrary, a slow, morose deterioration sets in, the dynamic of philosophy moves in another direction. On the one hand, we have a social crisis which endangers us all; on the other, we have perplexity and frustration in our search for remedies. Perhaps this is due to our not having searched far enough; nevertheless our failure is plain. We begin to think we were looking for the wrong kind of solution. We are confused: perhaps our confusion issued from misty syntax and unclear definition. We are unhappy: perhaps if we knew how the word "unhappiness" is to be defined, we should discover that we are happy after all. There is no money in our bank account: perhaps if we really understood the syntax of "there is" and the negativity of "no" we should find ourselves rich. All perplexity is frustrated speech. All problems are merely verbal.

The beauty of this solution is its ease. Anybody of reasonable intelligence can do it or understand it when it is done by someone else. There may have to be trips to the library in search of the larger dictionaries, the treatises on grammar, and the considerable bulk of Korzybski's *Science and Sanity,* which Mr. Stuart Chase says he read "completely through three times, and portions of it up to a dozen times." [2] The whole enterprise is a little like increasing your circle of friends by counting the names in a telephone directory.

When so gentle a solution is placed beside so terrible a problem, the contrast is spectacular. Social catastrophes are extremely violent, whereas nothing can be calmer than semantics. Men, it seems, must be mad to kill one another over mistaken syntax and cloudy definition. Every devout semanticist regards himself as an island of sense in an ocean of absurdity. He frames his sentences correctly and establishes the meaning of each word. If violence engulfs him, well, he cannot help that. His abstention from the conflict is not only permitted, it is enjoined, by his philosophy. He is commanded to escape.

It is doubtless a long way from the sophistications of Wittgenstein to their applications by Mr. Chase, but the passage is direct. What Wittgenstein exhibits as critique of language Mr. Chase exhibits as social program. From the disciple and amateur we learn the new meaning of the master and sage. It will be found in Mr. Chase's discussion of the Spanish Civil War, that clear and terrible fire whose light made plain where everybody stood. Mr. Louis Fischer had written in the *Nation* of March 27, 1937, as follows:

[2] Chase, *The Tyranny of Words,* Harcourt, Brace & Co., New York, 1938, p. 94. Mr. Chase goes on to add, with charming wistfulness, "Large sections are still blank in my mind. A book on the clarification of meaning should not be so difficult to understand."

At this moment a brazen invasion of Spain is going on. The fascist powers, in undisguised violation of their own signatures, of every canon of international law, of every principle of decency and humanity, are trying to crush the Spanish people and their democratically elected, legally constituted government. Apparently that does not matter to us. We sit idly and contentedly, denying Spanish democracy the means to defend itself. Neutrality followed to its logical conclusion has made America effectively pro-fascist.

Mr. Chase quotes this passage, and on it makes the following observation:

Thus we find an emotive content similar to that of 1916, similar slogans, a similar call to cherish democracy. Mr. Fischer, I take it, is prepared, if necessary, to go to war to defend Russia. I am not. I am one of the greatest idle and contented sitters-by you ever saw.[3]

Remember the historical context: German and Italian troops were in Spain, trying out the new weapons, testing the new tactics, and, above all, winning an advantageous position for the future world war. The fall of Madrid was followed in a little more than a year by the fall of Paris. Another year, and the invasion of Russia began; six more months, and there were planes over Pearl Harbor. The world hung, for a dreadful moment, within the grasp of Axis fascism. Spain had been the first line of defense, and Mr. Fischer's plea was for a defense of that line. Yet Mr. Chase could see nothing but "an emotive content similar to that of 1916." Accordingly, he professes himself "one of the greatest idle

[3] *Ibid.,* p. 340.

and contented sitters-by you ever saw." Such is the proper, the inevitable, conclusion of a belief that all problems are verbal. Such is the social program (if sitting-by can be called a program) which that belief is intended to justify. Upon that belief and the sitters-by whom it has engendered lies part of the responsibility for the death and the agony of recent years.

Thus the semantic philosophy, like Milton's Belial,

> . . . with words clothed in reason's garb,
> Counselled ignoble ease and peaceful sloth,
> Not peace . . .

The effect upon the history of our times has been exactly that of witch doctoring upon disease. A medicine man is bound to believe that his failure is due to an error in the incantation. He has therefore to improve his language, sharpening and rearranging the words. Yet all this does nothing to stay the progress of bacteria. On the contrary, it assists that progress, because it makes impossible the intervention of genuine medical treatment. German and Italian fascism could not be destroyed by the mere assertion that "fascism" is a vague or meaningless term. On the contrary, the more meaningless the term was said to be, the more the movement itself thrived, since people cannot be organized against an enemy they are told is nonexistent. The future state of man will be as absurd as desperate, if the fascist remnants throughout the world are permitted to multiply again, on the excuse that there are no persons corresponding to the term.

Unfortunately, just this result is becoming observable. Whenever a man or a movement exhibits all or most of the usual fascist ideas and is named accordingly, some semanticist is sure to arise and pronounce the naming meaningless. The left wing has its labels, he will say, no less than the right; and both sets of labels lack content. Such "impartiality" is mere show. In reality it protects the fascists by enabling them to escape public identification, and it injures the anti-fascists by an accusation of word-mongering. It is now scarcely possible to gather men together on behalf of human welfare, without someone's blocking the whole program by a complaint of "semantic confusion." If we were to apply to the semantic philosophy one of its own favorite tests, the operational, we should find that its real meaning, abundantly demonstrated in practice, is defense of things as they are.

The theory is, indeed, a source of general paralysis, not creeping but swift. It invades all areas of thought and action, and everywhere it immobilizes. If the effect of its criticism were to enlighten men rather than to leave them in doubt and indecision, there could be no objection. But, as things are, the semanticist attack on logic has subverted all the techniques of acquiring knowledge, and the attack on ethics has deprived men of the rational ground for making choices. How, then, can a man act, if he must remain wholly unsure what circumstances he acts in and what values are to mold his decision? To avoid the paralysis, we shall have to repel the attacks. This is the main business of our discussion.

THE ATTACK UPON LOGIC

The villain in the semanticist drama is no less a person than the Father of Logic himself, Aristotle. It is, I suppose, one of the penalties of greatness to be abused by later and lesser intellects. With Aristotle, however, the inevitable penalty has been compounded, because he had the ill luck to undergo a sort of secular canonization during the Middle Ages. All the faults of scholastic philosophy have therefore been attributed to him, and the man who did rather more observing of facts than most of his contemporaries has come to be regarded as the great exemplar of men who do no such observing at all. In the seventeenth century Lord Bacon led an anti-Aristotelian movement on behalf of empirical science, although the basic principles of scientific method were laid down by Aristotle himself. In the twentieth century Count Korzybski proposes a complete regeneration of science under the universal heading, "Non-Aristotelian Systems." [4] We shall find, upon analysis, that the Count's complaints touch Aristotle just about as closely as the Viscount's.

In Korzybski's view, the root of error is the law of identity, which he understands to mean "Whatever is, is." Now, says he (and Mr. Chase after him), everything in the world is a process, and therefore whatever is is in the act of becoming something else. But if it is becoming

[4] Korzybski's symbol for these systems is $\overline{A}$, pronounced "A-bar." The bar indicates the negation of everything indicated by the symbol beneath it. Thus $\overline{A}$ = Non-Aristotelian. The device has been borrowed from the Boolean Algebra.

something else, then it cannot be what it is — certainly not always, nor even at any given moment. Mr. Chase's examples are calculatedly familiar:

A rocket is always the same rocket. True for words, but not for that non-verbal event in space-time which blazes in glory and falls a charred stick as we watch it; not for a mushroom full-blown today and underground yesterday; not for a rose, withered now and lovely a week ago; not for an ice-cream cone five minutes in the sun.[5]

"Change and decay in all around I see"! In the world of space and time this is certainly true. What I wonder is: Who are the thinkers who have ever denied it? The nearest ones would be those rather early Greeks, Parmenides and Zeno, who held that the evidence of our senses gives opinion rather than knowledge, or the more recent Hegelians who distinguish between appearance and reality.[6] Parmenides can perhaps be convicted of arguing from logic to fact, since he says that "thought and being are one." But before we ascribe such a view to the "infantile," or Aristotelian, period, as Korzybski does,[7] we had better reflect that Parmenides had a contemporary and an opponent named Heraclitus, whose account of the nature of change is far more accurate and profound than anything provided by the semanticists. And we may remark, also, that both our critics seem to be arguing without benefit of dates. Parmenides and

[5] Chase, op. cit., p. 228.

[6] It is interesting to observe that Mr. Chase believes Zeno's paradoxes to be a "sardonic thrust at the absurdities of formal logic" (Op. cit., p. 73). The historical tradition is that Zeno was supporting Parmenides's concept of a static universe.

[7] Alfred Korzybski: Science and Sanity, The Science Press, Lancaster, Pa., 1933, p. 194.

Heraclitus belong to the late sixth century B.C.; Aristotle
(and with him formal logic as such) belongs to the
fourth century B.C. Between them lies the whole flowering of Greek philosophy, and early in that flowering
stands a man, Protagoras, who is the true historical ancestor of the semantic philosophy itself. Zeal for a new
philosophy flames hotter the more ignorant we are of
the old.

Whatever errors there may have been in man's early
philosophizing, the law of identity does not now have
the meaning Korzybski gives it, and did not have that
meaning even in Aristotle. As applied to terms and
statements, the law asserts that, throughout any given
stretch of reasoning, each term and each statement must
retain one and the same meaning. Clearly, it must; the
alternative is chaos. Suppose that Korzybski's "Ā" means
one thing in the first chapter, something different in
the second, something yet different in the third, and so
on. What conclusions could Korzybski draw about the
virtues of "Ā"? None, for he would be talking about
one thing in the premises and another thing in the
conclusion.

Does this logical requirement correspond to the nature of the world around us? It does, and indeed it must,
for otherwise there could be no correspondence between
the world and our statements about it. What reference
could "Ā" have, if the philosophies it denotes suddenly
ceased to be non-Aristotelian, or (more paradoxically
yet) at one and the same time possessed and did not
possess the character of being non-Aristotelian? Rockets,
mushrooms, roses, and ice-cream cones are undoubtedly
processes, but each of them is a particular process with

its own special nature and history. Each of them is exactly what it is, and is not other than it is. This is the whole meaning of the law of identity. I think we may defy semanticists to alter it.

The attack upon the law of contradiction fares no better. Now, contradictory statements exist always and only as pairs, and they are any two statements which cannot both be true and cannot both be false. Thus, for example, "There are no rosebushes in my garden" and "There is at least one rosebush in my garden." These statements cannot both be true; yet one of them must be, since if it is false that there are no rosebushes in my garden, there must be at least one rosebush there, and if it is false that there is at least one rosebush in my garden, then there cannot be any there.

An attack upon the law of contradiction might take the form of denying that such pairs of statements exist. But, on such a view, what would become of Korzybski's and Chase's arguments? They are both attacking a certain theory which they call Aristotelian. This theory, they say, is false. Now, suppose someone asserts that this theory is true. Korzybski and Chase have got to deny this statement; but, if the law of contradiction does not hold, their mightiest efforts will be in vain. They may heap argument upon argument on behalf of the statement "This theory is false"; but, unless the statement "This theory is false" *actually contradicts* the statement "This theory is true," Chase and Korzybski might as well save their ink. Unless contradiction is possible, denial is impossible; and it will not even be possible to deny that denial is possible.

Well, perhaps Chase and Korzybski don't mean this.

They are fond of distinguishing between what is possible for words and what is possible for things. They might say that, though verbal contradictories exist, real ones do not; in other words, that there are no situations in the world of space and time which exclude other situations. I find this view hard to comprehend. Every situation in the world of space and time excludes, simply by existing, all the situations which might have been but are not. You are, let us say, a full-time student at X University in the year 1945–1946. This state of affairs excludes both your being a full-time student elsewhere in 1945–1946 and your not being a full-time student at all. The statement "You are a full-time student at X University in the year 1945–1946" expresses the actual objective fact. The statement "You are not a full-time student at X University in the year 1945–1946" expresses the eliminated possibilities. The contradiction between the statements is an accurate reflection of the incompatibility of the facts.

With this in mind, we may pass to a discussion of the law of excluded middle, which arouses in semanticists a special horror. This law has to do with the second aspect of contradictory statements, namely that they cannot both be false, *i.e.* one of them must be true. In all such circumstances you have just two alternatives; you cannot have both, you must have one, and you cannot have any third. It is one or the other, thus:

Either

    Aristotle is guilty of all the errors charged to him,

Or

    Aristotle is not guilty of all the errors charged to him.

Either

You are a full-time student at X University in 1945–1946.

Or

You are not a full-time student at X University in 1945–1946.

Chase and Korzybski call this structure "two-valued." Korzybski is willing to admit it as a "limiting case." This admission evidently occurs in a part of the book which Chase read only three times, for Chase is unwilling to admit the structure at all. As against the "two-valued" and the yet more primitive "one-valued," our semanticists urge the "many-valued" structure as infinitely superior. Such a structure alone is capable, they think, of recording the marvelous variety of possible events. The world is so full of a number of things that Chase and Korzybski are happy as kings. Here is a set of examples from Mr. Chase:

One-valued: Contemporary events make communism inevitable in America.

Two-valued: Events make either communism or fascism inevitable in America. (This is the vicious "either-or" pair.)

Many-valued: The American Government may evolve into one of a variety of political forms, some of them more dictatorial, some less so than the present government.[8]

Let us take a look at the second (or "vicious") example. I will grant that the alternatives there set forth are more than a little hair-raising. That quality, however, is purely esthetic, and we are concerned with the

[8] Chase, *op. cit.,* pp. 234–235.

logic of the structure alone. "Events make either communism or fascism inevitable in America." Now, it happens that "communism" and "fascism" are opposites, but not contradictories; they exclude each other, but they do not exhaust between them all the political possibilities. It is therefore erroneous to assert that you must have one or the other. But, plainly, the error lies not in the either-or relation, but in the choice of terms which are thus related. Indeed, it is the very integrity of the either-or structure which reveals the error in the choice of terms. Mr. Chase's example, so far from proving that structure "vicious," proves only that he cannot tell the difference between contraries and contradictories. And as if to strengthen this latter revelation, the third example, which purports to illustrate the many-valued structure, actually illustrates the two-valued: "some of them more dictatorial, some less so," the third possibility ("equally dictatorial") being by implication eliminated.

It is clear, therefore, that Mr. Chase is totally unaware of the logic which actually exists in his illustrations. The connections which he has in mind and which he mistakes for logical ones are really connections of quite another sort. They are connections in his feeling, not in his thinking. He sets up two alternatives, fascism and communism. He knows he doesn't want either, and he imagines that his readers don't want either. The emotional recoil from two specific alternatives he transforms into a recoil from all pairs of alternatives, contradictories included. It is a remarkable example of how nothing is immune to the influence of ideology. Because Mr. Chase opposes both fascism and communism, we are to abandon the basic principles of rational thought.

"Because thou art virtuous, shall there be no more cakes and ale?"

The social reasons for attacking logic are perfectly obvious. Indecisive people, or people who want to appear liberal while avoiding the results of liberalism, have an extreme distaste for the either-or construction, because in practical life it presents them with problems they cannot evade. Abstaining from one alternative has the effect of enforcing the other, and this condition is intolerable to men who wish to abstain from both. In their agony they dream of other possibilities; and, when these prove nebulous, they begin to reflect, very philosophically, that nothing is really this or that. "Either-or" is a hoax of the logicians, a conspiracy by dogmatists.

But these desertions of logic on behalf of political needs must end in disaster. If we abandon the either-or construction, we shall lose the means of rigorous discrimination among choices. The world becomes a plate of noodles, which, turn it how you will, is still noodles. If we abandon the principle of contradiction, all statements will be reduced to a level of equal validity, and it will be impossible to distinguish any of them as true from others which are false. Such a nightmare world, in which all rational criteria have been thrown away, is full of lurid gleams and strident voices. You cannot think, for there is no method of thinking. There is nothing to do but feel. Thus the way is prepared for a swift passage into fascist ideology. One understands more clearly why semanticists sat by during the Spanish Civil War.

THE ATTACK UPON ETHICS

A large part of our lives is spent in debating whether such-and-such an act is good to do, whether this other act should be abstained from, whether so-and-so's policies are justifiable. Questions like these are moral questions; they can always be recognized by the presence of words like "good," "bad," "right," "wrong," "ought," "should." When you use such words, you are not merely stating a fact; you are evaluating something, passing judgment on it. For example, to say that "One atomic bomb is capable of destroying fifty thousand people" is to state a fact. To say "It is a bad thing to destroy fifty thousand people" is to evaluate the fact, to judge it according to certain standards.

Human experience seems to show that everyone finds the moral life somewhat burdensome, except perhaps those people who contrive by one means or another to set themselves up as censors, from which eminence they are able to prescribe law rather than obey it. Ethics is by no means a purely negative discipline, yet it does seem inordinately fond of prohibitions. One harried mortal, whom morality had strained beyond endurance, was heard to cry, "Everything I like is either illegal or unhealthful or immoral!" Every honest man, I think, will hear in his own heart an echo of that complaint.

Well, if human beings have been lecturable by moralists, they have also been inventive of compromises with morality. In adjusting the standard to the wish all men are pretty skillful; and if intelligence tests were based upon that sort of wit, the number of genius-intellects would be found enormously increased. Not until the twentieth century, however, had it occurred to anyone to criticize ethical theory on the ground that value-judgments are syntactically confused.

For this ingenious effect we must turn away from Chase and Korzybski to a certain British adaptation of Logical Positivism, made in the mid-'thirties. Now, the early Positivists had suggested that all statements might be divided into two great classes: the meaningful and the meaningless. Meaningful statements are (1) those which are tautological — *i.e.* their predicates are definitions of their subjects — and (2) those which can be tested by possible sense experience. Thus, "A triangle is a three-sided rectilinear plane figure" is a meaningful statement, because its predicate defines its subject; and "Smith is wearing a brown suit" is meaningful, because it can be tested by a glance at Smith.

When applied, for example, to ethics or theology, this principle has remarkable effects. "God is a Triune Spiritual Being" would be a meaningful statement, for that is the definition of God, at least according to the Athanasian Creed. But "God exists" is a meaningless statement, since no such being can be the object of any possible sense experience. Theologians, who were long hardened to objections that their statements were false, were left breathless before this new charge that they had, for the most part, been saying nothing at all.

Even more startling is the effect of this notion upon ethics. We said, a moment ago, that the statement "One atomic bomb is capable of destroying fifty thousand people" is a statement of fact. It is verifiable by sense experience (though I hope never to verify it), and

Logical Positivists would say that it is meaningful. But our other statement, "It is a bad thing to destroy fifty thousand people," is a statement not of fact but of evaluation. I can observe the killing, but I cannot observe the badness. I am talking, not about the event, but about my attitude towards it. The word "bad" adds nothing to the factual content of the statement; it merely evinces my feeling about the fact. It is as if I had said in a tone of horror, "One atomic bomb is capable of destroying fifty thousand people!"

Now, suppose we have another man who thinks such destruction excellent. This, too, would be an evincing statement, as if he had said in tones of satisfaction, "One atomic bomb is capable of destroying fifty thousand people!" Most of us will quite naturally suppose that the two men have contradictory ethical opinions which they can rationally discuss — although, if I were the first man, I should prefer to take the second to the nearest psychiatrist. But, according to the new theory, no question of truth or falsity exists between the horrified gasp of the one and the delighted sigh of the other: there is no disputing about grunts. Mr. A. J. Ayer, the "*enfant terrible* of Oxford," puts the case thus:

Another man may disagree with me about the wrongness of stealing, in the sense that he may not have the same feeling about stealing that I have. . . . But he cannot, strictly speaking, contradict me. . . . There is plainly no sense in asking which of us is in the right. For neither of us is asserting a genuine proposition.[9]

[9] Alfred J. Ayer, *Language, Truth and Logic*, Oxford University Press, New York, 1936, p. 159. Mr. Ayer received his appellation in the *New Statesman and Nation* for March 27, 1937.

So now we know where we are: Jones says that stealing is morally wrong, Brown says that stealing is morally admirable, and both Jones and Brown are uttering sounds of very limited significance.

Well! But suppose that instead of "stealing" (an illustration which smells damply of the academic cloister) we take something less obvious and trite. Let it be the sort of happening which verbalists have done so little to prevent. Ella Winter tells of a ten-year-old Russian boy, who came to a hospital for treatment. Under anesthesia he suddenly began to relive the experiences of three years before, when the Nazis captured his village and hanged his uncle. The things he had never described poured from him:

"Don't cry," he sobbed, "don't cry, Grandmother. Go away. I don't want Uncle Vasya like that. Look what the Germans have done! Split open his whole head. . . . God sees everything. . . .

"When they took him down and buried him, look how he is all stiff, you can't even put him in the coffin. I will lie down with him in the coffin. Oh look, what a good Uncle Vasya.

"I will never forget Uncle Vasya [crying bitterly] . . . I will kill the Germans. Hurry up, Russians, kill the Germans! I want Uncle Vasya to be alive. Let God return him from the grave. Granny, don't cry or the Germans will kill you. . . .

"Grandmother, your heart can break with sorrow." [10]

[10] Ella Winter, *I Saw The Russian People*, Little, Brown & Co., Boston, 1945, p. 208.

I will pass over what the Nazis did to Uncle Vasya, whose only crime was rescuing a wounded Russian soldier. I will pass over what the Nazis did to other children, whose tongues they cut out, whose ears they cut off, whose bodies they used for target practice. I will even pass over that horrible pile of infants' shoes at the Maidanek death camp. I will turn to those philosophers who maintain that moral judgments express no more than personal feeling, and ask them to consider Vitya's wild cry: "Grandmother, your heart can break with sorrow." Then, having caught the attention of these somewhat timid moralists, I will say, "Gentlemen, I consider it demonstrably true that it is evil, vilely evil, to use children thus. Have I asserted a genuine proposition?" And the moralists in question will answer, "No, you have not." Then I shall have to say, "Gentlemen, I have a son of about Vitya's age, and my son has friends of about that age, and some of my friends have children of about that age. I do not think that the welfare of children can be a matter of personal taste."

It is at once absurd and fitting that at just that moment of history when the most exquisite torments have been inflicted and the greatest agonies endured there should exist a philosophy which holds moral judgments to be capable of no proof. One might think that philosophers of such mind would recoil from the consequences of their theory and re-examine the postulates which had generated such folly. For the consequences are that one cannot *rationally* choose (*i.e.* choose on the basis of argument) between death camps and liberation; one can only "evince" approval or disapproval. One cannot demonstrate that fascist practices are evil; one can only express dislike of them. No philosophy would better please the fascists themselves, since moral questions could then be safely left in the hands of the police.

The absurdity of all this arises from a peculiar philosophical bias. Ayer's view is that factual statements and tautological statements are the *only* meaningful ones, and consequently that, if ethical statements are to mean anything, they must merely express a psychological fact. But no proof is ever given for this "only"; it remains, from first to last, a simple assumption. It is an assumption which results from taking science and mathematics seriously, while indulging an emancipated scepticism toward ethics. The sense of what is triumphs over the sense of what ought to be.

Thus men like Ayer will seem to take ethics rather frivolously. I do not mean that they are morally frivolous; when they leave your house, you don't have to count your spoons. They are philosophically frivolous, however, because they simply pay no attention to what an ethical statement actually asserts. When I said, "It was an evil thing for Nazis to torture children," I was certainly doing more than asserting that the Nazis did torture children. Ayer would say that the "more" which I did was to grunt my personal disapproval. Well, I will allow the grunt, but I must insist that my original assertion contained still more than the fact plus the grunting. It contained the further assertion that everybody ought to disapprove the torture of children by the Nazis (or, for that matter, by anybody else). For the whole point of ethical statements is their claim to be binding upon *all* men. This claim upon all cannot possibly be exhausted by the grunts of any *one*. Therefore, ethical statements contain more than Ayer is willing to admit, and this additional content is in fact their proper meaning. They are therefore meaningful in a sense which makes them susceptible of argument and hence of verification.

It may be worth while to add that if Ayer's Positivism is true, then the statements which express its main tenets are themselves meaningless. These statements are not definitions. If, then, they are to be meaningful, they must (according to the theory itself) be verifiable by some sense experience. But how can you verify by sense experience the statement that all meaningful, non-tautological statements must be verifiable by sense experience? You cannot. As a matter of fact, sense experience *alone* will not tell you whether you have exhausted the meaning of any statement whatever, for, in order to tell a thing like that, you would have to compare the given sense experience with the given statement, the meaning of which you would have to know already.

We have, therefore, a theory which is reduced to meaninglessness by its own tests. On behalf of this theory, we are asked to abandon all moral judgments, to surrender, that is to say, every rational means by which good may be chosen and evil shunned. I think we shall require more than a frightened and self-defeated theory to lure us in any such direction. We may leave it to the verbalists to analyze gasps and breathings. For our part, let us continue to seek a better future for mankind.

THE ATTACK UPON SOCIAL CONCEPTS

Having thus indulged an excursion upon strange seas of thought, we may return to more familiar subjects. The damage done by the attack on logic and ethics is hidden, but the damage done by the attack on social concepts is obvious and great. Semanticists are full of admiration for science; they invoke it with a solemnity which was once reserved for religion alone. Nevertheless, it will not be difficult to show that, if the views of semanticists are correct, there can be no science of anything. And especially, there can be no science of society.

Any science is a system of *general* statements about the world. The statement which expresses the principle of gravitation, for example, does not confine itself to the two balls which Galileo is said to have dropped from the tower of Pisa. It asserts, rather, that, assuming a vacuum, all objects fall at the same rate. A science, therefore, deals with classes and kinds, not with individuals alone.

In the second place, a science deals with systems, with organizations, of things. In order to explain the behavior of any individual member of a system, it has to describe the nature of the system and the individual's relation to it. If we were to consider the heart in isolation from the lungs and the circulatory system, not very much could be known about so solitary an organ.

Now, if a science is to be really a science, its statements must correspond accurately to that portion of the world which it describes. But if classes and systems do not really exist in the world, most of the statements of any science will have nothing to correspond to. The science will then be locked within its own statements and will be pure fancy and artifice. No scientist, so far as he is a *scientist*, can fail to assume as a basic fact that classes and systems are as real as the individuals composing them.

This proposition, however, the semanticists deny. Their view is that individuals are real, but that classes and systems are abstractions. This *is* their view, despite the fact that they have carved in the granite dogma certain passages of escape. Korzybski, for example, says that on nonverbal levels "we deal exclusively with absolute individuals, in the sense that they are not identical." [11] Now, an absolute individual would be one which had no connections whatever with anything else; and we are said to deal with this "exclusively." But all this intransigeance of language melts away when "absolute" is defined as meaning merely that the given individual thing is not identical with others. Of course it isn't, and no one would suppose that it was. This obvious, indeed platitudinous, fact serves as an escape corridor when the fortress is stormed. For the essential question here is not whether individuals differ from one another, but whether, by the possession of common qualities, they form real classes.

The semanticists also give faint recognition to the presence of systems in the world by their concept of space as a "plenum." "When we have a plenum or fulness," says Korzybski, "it must be a plenum of 'something,' 'somewhere,' at 'some time.' " [12] But there is very

[11] Korzybski, *op. cit.*, p. 405. It happens that Aristotle also held the individual to be basically real. If Aristotelianism is "infantile," what are we to say of the semantic philosophy?

[12] *Ibid.*, p. 229.

little system in this plenum, which speedily resolves itself into a sequence of individuals related like the knots in a string:

All our experiences and all we know indicate definitely that ordinary materials ("objects") are extremely rare and very complex special cases of the beknottedness of the plenum; that the organic world and "life" represent extremely rare and still more complex special cases of the material world; and, finally, so-called "intelligent life" represents increasingly complex and still rarer cases of "life." [13]

In this passage the beknottedness of the plenum seems somewhat overmatched by the besottedness of the language, but it is nevertheless quite plain that Korzybski ignores the fact of things interacting with one another. Without this notion the term "system" is meaningless. Everything has been explained away into what Mr. Chase more poetically calls "a mad dance of atoms." The lunacy, however, is not in the atoms. They are not so mad as to avoid combining with one another to produce systems great and small, and thus to produce the world.

The effect of this relentless atomizing of the universe is to unsettle confidence in our knowledge of it. The old, deadly schism between "appearance" and "reality" is introduced once more; and the ordinary reader, as modest as he is unwary, begins to distrust even the most obvious teachings of experience. His enemies vanish beneath a transcendental disguise, only to reappear in the end miraculously, like Birnam Wood before Dunsinane. Let us observe how Mr. Chase accomplishes the process of dissolution, from philosophy to politics:

[13] *Ibid.*, p. 480.

There are no dogs-in-general in the world of experience, but only Rover$_1$, Rover$_2$, Rover$_3$, some gentle, some neutral, some vicious.[14]

There is no entity "mankind." Call as briskly as you may, "Hey, Mankind, come here!" and not an Adam will answer.[15]

No profit system exists as an entity in the real world. Instead one has to study the behavior of Adam$_1$, Adam$_2$, Morgan$_1$ and Morgan$_2$.[16]

Semantically there is no "party" as an entity. The referents of the term are individual voters more or less controlled by local bosses.[17]

Well, what does fascism mean? Obviously the term by itself means nothing. In one context it has some meaning as a tag for Mussolini, his political party, and his activities in Italy. In another context it might be used as a tag for Hitler, his party, and his political activities in Germany. The two contexts are clearly not identical, and if they are to be used one ought to speak of the Italian and German varieties as fascism$_1$ and fascism$_2$.[18]

To which let us add some remarks by Mr. Bernard DeVoto, who wrote admiringly of Mr. Chase, regretting only that Mr. Chase did not go further:

He [Chase] says that "more than one-third of the people in America are underfed, inadequately housed, and shoddily clothed." He has never counted them, no one has ever

[14] Chase, *op. cit.*, p. 51. The subnumerals are a semantic affectation which purports to emphasize the individuality of individuals.

[15] *Ibid.*, p. 102.

[16] *Ibid.*, p. 277.

[17] *Ibid.*, p. 347.

[18] *Ibid.*, p. 188. But if "there is no 'party' as an entity," how can Mussolini and Hitler each have had one?

counted them, and his statement is not meaningful but emotionally useful. The only word in it that can be operationally examined is "underfed," and an inquiry by nutritionists (granting they could agree on tests) would possibly reveal a certain percentage of "blab." "Inadequately housed" is open at both ends— inadequately by what scale, in relation to what facts, in relation to what specifications and persons? "Shoddily clothed" is meaningless though it appears to refer to garments.[19]

There is no such thing as "truth." There is no such thing as "social justice." [20]

So now we see it all: there are no dogs-in-general, no mankind, no profit system, no parties, no fascism, no underfed people, no inadequate housing, no shoddy clothes, no truth, and no social justice. Such being the case, there can be no economic problem, no political problem, no fascist problem, no food problem, no housing problem, no "garment" problem, no scientific problem, and no social problem. By the simple exhalation of breath, Messrs. Chase and DeVoto have conjured out of existence every major problem which has vexed mankind throughout the entire history of the human race.

Of the five terms which Chase proscribes as meaningless, one ("dogs-in-general") is a class name, and the others are names of systems. Since classes differ very markedly from systems,[21] we may divide our commentary accordingly.

[19] In *Harper's Magazine*, 176: pp. 222–223 (January, 1938).
[20] *Ibid.*, p. 224.
[21] Individuals belong to classes by virtue of common characteristics. Individuals belong to systems by virtue of constant interaction with one another. "Party" is both a class name and the name of a system.

(1) It is remarkable that Mr. Chase, while denying the existence of dogs-in-general, nevertheless contrives to call his three dogs "Rover." The sub-numerals indicate that they are different dogs, but "Rover" indicates that all of them are dogs. How does Mr. Chase know that all of them are dogs? Because they all possess the essential canine characteristics. Mr. Chase appears to think that, though individual dogs exist, the class of dogs is merely an abstraction in his mind. But how can this be? $Rover_1$ will go right on resembling $Rover_2$ and $Rover_3$, whether Mr. Chase has a mind or not. The dogs are in the class and the class is in the dogs.

Let us put the case another way. Suppose you have upon your pantry shelf a jar of pickles, and suppose that on that jar there is a label which says PICKLES. According to Mr. Chase and the other semanticists, the pickles are real enough: there is $Pickle_1$, $Pickle_2$, $Pickle_3$, and so forth. But pickles-in-general is an abstraction, a sort of mental sign referring to the individual pickles exactly as the label PICKLES does on the jar. Well, I submit that no housewife has any such notion. She is not concerned with the pickleness that is in Mr. Chase's mind; she is concerned with the pickleness that is in the pickles. If it is not there, she has been wantonly deceived by her grocer, who was, perhaps, a semanticist.

(2) Now for the terms which signify systems. Mr. Chase says that there is no entity called "mankind," that if you were to summon mankind to you, no one would answer. Well, naturally. You might also cry out, "Hey, United States Army, come here!" Not a soldier would answer. Can we then infer that there is no entity called "The United States Army"? Obviously such reasoning

is nonsense. What Mr. Chase has done is to assume that a system will behave like one of its members. An individual man would doubtless answer if you called, "Come here!" Mr. Chase expects the same behavior of "mankind," that is, of men taken collectively. Not finding that behavior, he infers the nonexistence of the system. His assumption was, of course, false: what is true of a part is not necessarily true of the whole. Logicians call this error the Fallacy of Composition, and it was first identified by Aristotle. Who, then, is more "infantile," the philosopher who discovered the fallacy or the writer who continues to commit it?

"No profit system exists as an entity in the real world." Mr. Chase urges us to study the behavior of various Adams and Morgans. Very well, let us study it. If $Adam_1$ goes to work in a factory, he enters a system of relationships so intimate that the product which comes off the assembly line cannot be supposed the work of any one man; it issues from the *collective* labor of hundreds of men. If we assume $Morgan_1$ to be an industrialist rather than a banker, then we know that he markets the products which $Adam_1$ has helped to make. $Morgan_1$ must sell the products for an amount greater than the costs of production, among which are $Adam_1$'s wages. The difference between the income on sales and the costs of production represents $Morgan_1$'s profits, and without these he cannot continue in business. Thus $Adam_1$ and $Morgan_1$ are members of a system which will operate only so long as profits are made. No profit system exists, then? Well, perhaps it is only a system by which people make profits.

The assertions about "party" and "fascism" are

equally ludicrous. There are, to be sure, individual Democrats, but there certainly is also an entity known as the Democratic Party — an organization with an apparatus of functionaries, an organization capable of putting on campaigns. There are, to be sure, individual fascists; but there is also fascism — a definite, describable social and political system. Without this, indeed, it would be impossible to identify fascist$_1$ or fascist$_2$, for the individual fascists are fascists precisely because they strive to bring into existence, or to maintain in existence, that very system itself. If the term "fascism" means nothing by itself (in the same sense in which any other term has meaning by itself), then we can never recognize any regime as fascist, nor can we combat any movement to establish such a regime. The effect of Mr. Chase's argument is to blind us to our enemies.

As for the remaining "meaningless" terms, I confess I would enjoy imposing on semanticists their own operational test. If, like Mr. DeVoto, they find no meaning in "underfed," "inadequately housed," and "shoddily clothed," then I think it would be pleasant to watch their behavior on an unemployment allotment of, say, five dollars a week. And when, after months of this, they come to us with obvious symptoms of malnutrition, with bodies enfeebled by exposure to the elements, and on their backs the rags of ancient clothing, we may justly remind them that it was they who "proved" that no one can be ill-fed or ill-clothed or ill-housed, because all these are meaningless terms. And such is their passion for this preposterous dogma that I rather wonder whether they would not go away convinced and satisfied. At any rate, so long as the operational test is imposed only on other people, the semanticists will see no reason to change their minds.

In general, the social views of semanticists are what you would expect of men who are unable to perceive either the effects of poverty or the conspiracies of fascism. Korzybski's ethics is clearly that of an aristocrat, who hates above all things "commercialism," that is to say, the influence which capitalism has had upon art, science, and invention.[22] Chase is a smiling, and DeVoto a rather grim, conservative. Both of them find in semantics a means of combating the great anti-fascist movement of the past fifteen years. In this they are altogether correct, for the semantic philosophy has no other social reason to exist.

An attentive reader will also discern in the writings of some semanticists a faint murmur of racism. Ogden and Richards, whose *Meaning of Meaning* first made semanticism fashionable, tell a story which they call a "darky anecdote." [23] They also quote with obvious approval the sneering remarks of a certain Ingraham:

We do not often have occasion to speak, as of an indivisible whole, of the group of phenomena involved or connected in the transit of a negro over a rail-fence with a melon under his arm while the moon is just passing behind a cloud.[24]

Korzybski tells us that the Aristotelian system was a semantic response "of the white race of more than two

---

[22] See the remarkable Table of Standards, Korzybski: *op. cit.*, pp. 555–557.

[23] C. K. Ogden and I. A. Richards, *The Meaning of Meaning*, Harcourt, Brace & Co., New York, 1923, p. 347 *n*.

[24] *Ibid.*, p. 131.

thousand years ago." [25] Evidently he believes that systems of thought are determined by the racial origins of thinkers. That appears to be the meaning, also, of the following passage:

. . . When we explore the objective level . . . we must try to define every "meaning" as a conscious feeling of actual, or assumed, or wished, *relations* which pertain to first order objective entities, psycho-logical included, and which can be evaluated by personal, varied, and racial — again unspeakable first order — psychophysiological effects.[26]

We must exempt Mr. Chase from any such charge, for he shows himself not lacking in a certain militancy against racism. But we have, at any rate, two semanticists who are contemptuous of Negroes, and one who regards race as a determinant of thought.

Lastly, we can learn something of these men by the authors they praise. Korzybski is lavish of compliments to Spengler,[27] whose work the Nazis drew upon, and who himself joined the Nazi Party. Chase repudiates Spengler, but falls instead into a citation of Alexis Carrel, the collaborationist, and of *Man, the Unknown,* which was in its day an important contribution to fascist ideology in America.[28] I do not for one moment suppose that these facts suffice to make fascists out of Korzybski and Chase; but they do show that our two authors either do not recognize fascism when they see it,

[25] Korzybski, *op. cit.,* p. 555.

[26] *Ibid.,* p. 23. Except for the three dots to indicate omissions, the punctuation and italics are Korzybski's. I say "appears to be the meaning," because it strikes me as improbable that this passage can be clear in anybody's mind, including the author's.

[27] *Ibid.,* p. 47.

[28] Chase, *op. cit.* Carrel is cited as an authority on page 194. The repudiation of Spengler is on page 222.

or find some of its ideas congenial. In any case, the facts corroborate empirically what we deduced by theoretical analysis — that there is a decided kinship between the semantic philosophy and the whole world of fascist and reactionary ideas.

If the nineteen-thirties began in hunger and ended in blood, we must strive to prevent the nineteen-forties, which began in blood, from ending in hunger. But we shall never succeed in this task unless we recognize that the real world sets us real problems, and that the real problems are susceptible of real solutions. We have to repair a ravaged world, to feed and clothe and house its people, to liberate the yet oppressed, to deal justly with millions who have never known the touch of honest hands. It is inconceivable that even the smallest of these mercies can be visited, if we permit ourselves to think that the words which express them are meaningless and vain. Nor shall we succeed by imagining the contrary folly, that problems can be solved by a simple adjustment of language.

There is a problem of language, to be sure; but that is not our main concern. There is a need for speech of clarity and precision, but neither is that our final goal. What we shall find is that our speech will grow clearer in proportion as we solve the objective, nonverbal problems; and that, so far as we fail to solve them, our speech will remain halting and obscure. It is precisely for this reason that semanticists cannot make themselves intelligible; and the semantic philosophy, a tower of confusion, warns us forever that men who forsake the care of humankind will lose all understanding from their hearts and all vision from their eyes.

CHAPTER X THAT WORDS WILL NEVER HURT ME

In the beginning were no words. The marvelous articulations of vowel and consonant, which are so expressive in our use, were creations of man, not gifts to him. Presumably our apelike ancestor and many generations of his progeny came no nearer to speech than the vague sound of air expelled along the passages of nose and throat. Such sounds may have resembled one another, but they lacked convention; that is to say, they lacked the social agreement which could make them generally intelligible. The spoken word was not early, and the written word was late indeed.

However language arose (and its origin is wholly conjectural), the lack of it must have sadly lamed our remoter ancestors. They could point to things, but relations among things must have been hard to indicate. One can see a hairy finger pointing to this or that tree. Yet it would be less easy, by grunt or gesture, to convey the notion that this tree is to the left of that; and it would perhaps be impossible to convey the notion that trees in general form one class among many botanical classes. We have observed in the previous chapter that there are several modern gentlemen of very advanced views who share, in precisely these respects, the difficulties of primitive man.

Since communication was thus generally restricted, so must deception have been. It is possible, of course, that a stoical primitive said "Yowie!" when he felt "Ugh!" and thus diplomatically concealed his own dissatisfaction. It is likewise possible that gestures can have been misleading. But until the full development of language, the arts of reasoned guile and fraudulent persuasion can hardly have been practiced. The existence of vice is a sort of tax which men pay for being civilized. It attests at one and the same time their imperfection and their perfectibility.

Language, indeed, is not a merely passive instrument of deception, a mask which cannot conceal unless it is used. Language can deceive even when its user is moved by the plainest honesty and is making obvious effort to say what he really means. Words and the syntax which connects them are both notoriously tricky; this is the sole fact behind which Chase and Korzybski have performed their legerdemain. As I write these pages, I am haunted by the knowledge that many a sentence which I fancy to have molded to my thought will convey a rather different meaning to the reader. The other meaning has escaped me, but the reader very reasonably accepts it, for it is there.

Ambiguity can lurk in the most innocent-seeming syntax, the briefest sentences, the simplest words. Professor Quine suggests the following phrase as an example:

Pretty little girls' camp.[1]

If you have the patience to spin the possible meanings out of this you will find that there are five — more meanings, that is to say, than words:

1. A pretty camp for little girls;
2. A pretty and little camp for girls;
3. A camp for girls who are pretty and little;

and, taking "pretty" in the sense of "rather,"

4. A rather little camp for girls;
5. A camp for rather little girls.

The second meaning is probably the one intended, but any of the five is possible. The presence of so much variety renders unsure even the likeliest choice.

If there can be so much obscurity in language apparently simple, how much more obscurity will there be in statements which have a complicated syntax and an abundance of formidable words! Philosophers are supposed to be especially addicted to this vice, but a fair analysis would show that they are not really more so than any other victims of erudition. I can name you five economists, ten political scientists, and a dozen theologians whose linguistic opacity no philosopher can hope to rival. Such talents are impressive. They even find a place in schemes of organized persuasion, where the speaker wears his own obscurity like a mantle, and, thus adorned, postures among the prophets. The memory of Mr. Hoover's speeches on the gold standard, dur-

[1] Willard Van Orman Quine: *Elementary Logic*, Ginn & Co., Boston, 1941, pp. 30-1.

ing the campaign of 1932, lingers with me yet as a model of this kind of utterance. No ray could disclose, no key unlock, the secret of those sentences. Across a vast and slumbrous gulf of sound, one heard dim struggles with unutterable thoughts.

So long as we think it important to say what we mean and to know what other people mean, accuracy in the use of language will be prized; but besides the inaccuracies to which all men are subject, there is the deliberate effort by some to use language as a screen which can hide actual meanings and actual purposes. To the ambiguity of innocence is therefore added the ambiguity of deceit. Evil can move in the guise of honest error. Knaves, when hard pressed, can pass themselves for fools.

There would be some harm in the honest misuse of language, since communication, which is its main purpose, would be defeated. But where malice and deceit are working, the harm is great indeed. A belief that "words will never hurt me" doubtless begets a cheerful patience under insult, but in these violent and troubled years the sticks and stones which are to break my bones will follow not long afterward. The verbal artillery of disputants employs at least as many abusive epithets as rational arguments; and these epithets have the power to ruin reputations, to deprive men of their livelihood, and even to incite physical violence against the victim. Worse still, perhaps, is the fact that such epithets sidetrack discussion, exhaust it upon irrelevancies, and thus prevent action upon the main theme. It is therefore one of the first steps not only toward knowledge, but toward safety, to recognize the commonest abuses of language and to secure ourselves from committing them or suffering the commission of them by others.

THE MANY-SIDED WORD

Words are visual or auditory signs, which have surprisingly many characteristics. To call them "signs" is to say that they refer to something other than themselves, and that this reference is their meaning. Words can refer to things, events, relations, qualities, and quantities: "chair," "explosion," "brotherhood," "amiability," and "five" will illustrate each of these groups respectively. Under the scrutiny of modern science and philosophy the distinction between "thing" and "event" has disappeared. We can retain the distinction, however, as representing a difference of emphasis: sometimes (as with the term "chair") we want to emphasize the stability of the object, and sometimes (as with the term "explosion") we want to emphasize the velocity of change.

All meanings are fixed ultimately by social convention. There is no purely logical reason why the term "chair" should refer to those articles of furniture which hold the body in a sitting position; the only reason is that English-speaking people have agreed to call them that. The agreement is, of course, nothing rigid. Language is always in flux, with old words leaving, new words entering, and old meanings metamorphosed into new. The makers of dictionaries can slow down, but not withstand, these changes. With dictionaries, as with governments, the people have the final say.

If words had nothing but their agreed references, the only problem would be to keep those references precise and to make sure that they change with our increasing knowledge of the world. But words take on associations in addition to their dictionary meanings, and the associations are sometimes vague and ambient mists which, concealing the established reference, can be mistaken for that reference itself. In narrow and parochial minds, for example, the word "foreigner" has had its core of meaning quite wrapped round with uneasy notions of strangeness and peril, so that the word suggests not someone born in another country, but someone whose purposes are subversive and dark. Before we smile too loftily at this error, we had better be sure how we ourselves stand toward the phrase "alien isms." The literal meaning would be "theories originating abroad and now current in our country"; but "isms" is satirical jargon, almost slang, and "alien" evokes the old nameless dread. The phrase is peculiarly absurd in America, because hardly any theories are historically indigenous here. Offhand, I can think of only one: the concept of the Happy Hunting Ground, which the Indians seem to have invented and which the early settlers turned into a horrible reality.

The associations which thus encrust the literal meanings of words have several sources. Words can acquire, for example, the emotional tone of the things they refer to. "Don't say 'spinach' to me!" cries the harried victim of dietetics, and we know that the word has begun to acquire the loathing which the vegetable itself excites. Transformations like this are private and personal; but when it is normal and common, when it is the feeling most people have toward a given object or event, the word will receive that new flavor as an accomplished social fact. Euphemisms bear excellent evidence of this process. What happens with them is that a word or phrase has acquired the distastefulness of its reference, and is remodeled (or abandoned) in the hope that distastefulness will vanish at least from the symbol. "Funeral undertaker," the original name for that profession, became so far unsavory as to require reformation into simple "undertaker." However, the slicing off of "funeral" gave but a temporary respite, and the practitioners of that useful, though melancholy, craft were driven in the end to call themselves "morticians." Behind the conspicuous error of this etymology they seem likely to live protected for a long time to come.

Other trades and professions have not been slow to perceive how one may rise in the world's opinion by exchanging a lowly and familiar name for one more elegant, or hopefully believed to be so. Thus hairdressers became "beauticians," tooth-pullers "exodontists," and janitors "custodians." [2] I dissent a little from Professor Robertson's view that these changes issue from American pomposity. They show much more, I think, an eye for the main chance and the influence of admen. Pomposity is by no means a national trait with us; it appears, when it appears at all, genially and in moments of exceptional élan. Some years ago, when I was living in an under-

[2] These examples are borrowed from Stuart Robertson: *The Development of Modern English*, Prentice-Hall, New York, 1934, p. 445.

heated apartment, I was told by my landlord that the furnace was "carrying all she could carry." Since the look of the furnace seemed to verify this assertion, I suggested he might call in a plumber. But matters lingered in that delay which landlords require for reaching a decision, and I finally called in a plumber from down the street. My man arrived at our rendezvous in the cellar straight from close communion with a bottle, and breathing out such vital breath as far surpassed the furnace temperature. He examined heater, pipes, and gauges with a vastly knowing air; and then he said, rocking back and forth in elaborate dignity, "Tell Mr. Blank that you called in your heating engineer — your heating engineer, sir — and that your heating engineer says the fire will burn better if it has more coal."

One need not quarrel with these gentle efforts at elegance, though false etymologies make the purist wince. It is far more important to observe how men of small scruple can profit by the fact that words have associations as well as meanings, that the associations can be made to obscure and even eclipse the meanings, and that in general the associations arouse either approval or disapproval in the minds of other people.

LANGUAGE AS ABUSE

A propagandist is very often a man with a bad case. If it were not so, he could afford to state his views with proof and argument. He could afford, indeed, to state what his views really are. Since, however, the views are unpalatable and the arguments unconvincing, he can persuade only by suggesting that he means something else, by substituting adroit verbal maneuvers in the place of proof. The honesty and general "rightness" of any debater is in direct proportion to the amount and the rigor of argumentation he displays. The test is perhaps not perfect, but it is very usable, as readers will find if they apply it to columnists and orators.

Setting candor aside as injurious and proof as unobtainable, the intriguing gentleman begins to woo us in the only way wooing can ultimately be done. There may be a serenade of music and a seductive lowering of lights, but sooner or later there must be speech. There may be martial sounds and an invigorating blaze, but, again, sooner or later there must be speech. And what will speech consist of? It will consist of such words as can associate what *he* wants with what *we* like and what he does not want with what we detest. And all this without our really knowing what the things in question are.

Let us look at an example. The Housing Authority in a certain American city proposed to level a block of slum dwellings and to erect on that site a modern housing project. It is no secret, of course, that this kind of thing deprives the slum owners of rentals, and introduces the federal government as an unwanted competitor in real estate. It is also no secret that people would rather live in modern housing projects than in slums. The propagandist's problem is to keep these people living in slums where they do not want to live, paying rents which they do not want to pay to landlords they would rather not have. He solves the problem thus:

As a good American citizen, I am opposed to the un-American methods of depriving people of their right to own homes in the place of their choosing. The Authority would take from the people their homes — and offer them pigmy-like houses to rent. You are being handed a luscious peach, but in reality it is a lemon. This thing is Communistic. It makes for restrictive families, birth control.

These words, which were uttered by a clergyman, offer us no proof of any sort, but simply suggest what we "ought" to believe. The work of suggestion proceeds somewhat thus:

1. I am a good American, and therefore (by implication) desire what is best for you, am on your side. No good American would lie; therefore you can believe me when I say I am a good American. (The inference is a trifle circular.)

2. It is un-American (*i.e.* you ought to disapprove it) to move people out of the slum dwellings they "choose" to live in.

3. These dwellings may look like slums to other people, but they are "homes" to you. You "own" them. The Authority wants to tear them down and build "pigmy-like" houses, which will lack the spaciousness of your one-room flats.

4. The peach and the lemon: it looks good, but you won't like it.

5. The project is Communistic — not Communism exactly, but "istic," *i.e.* something very much the same. (Here we have the infallible incantation which is to exorcise all progress.)

6. The pigmy-like houses will incite you to limit the size of your families, whereas your one-room flats are a constant invitation to fecundity.

The passage is, of course, double-talk. It is not meaningless, as one might be led to think. On the contrary, the meaning can be deduced from the fact that the speech is directed against public housing; and the meaning would therefore be, "I want the housing situation to remain exactly as it is now." The effort is to arouse a similar wish in others by associating slum clearance with things vaguely, but perhaps ardently, disapproved ("un-American," "pigmy," "lemon," "Communistic," "birth control"). The tactic involves some risk, for the obvious excellence of a program may neutralize the opprobrium of the words used against it. Indeed, many people have learned to recognize a good policy by the presence of just such words upon the lips of opponents.

By far the most potent weapons of abuse are the words connected with political radicalism. Once upon a time, when the middle class was in revolt against the aristocracy, "Jacobin," "atheist," and "republican" were epithets of this sort. The Jacobins were, of course, the left wing of the French Revolution; "atheist" meant anyone opposing the dominance of the feudal Church; and "republican" meant anyone opposing monarchical government. Except for "atheist," these epithets are dead, because the struggles which gave them life are now long past. "Atheist" retains some power, since there still exists a connection between politics and organized religion. That power steadily diminishes, however, because the persons answerable to the name can be found in all political groups.

In our day, the comparable words would be "Communist," "Red," "left-winger," "anarchist," and "Socialist." "Red" is a broader term than "Communist," and "left-winger" than "Red"; and there seems to be a kind of euphemistic flavor about the broader term. In America, anarchism has ceased to exist as a political movement; and the label, lacking a source of life, has been used very little since the days of Emma Goldman. The Socialists still exist, but have become respectable through opposition to the Soviet Union and to Communists generally. Indeed, since 1914, when the European Socialists abandoned their internationalist creed and supported the war policies of their respective governments, the term "Socialist" has lost a good deal of its old flavor of revolutionary change. The consequent effects are interesting. The Nazis were able, without too obvious absurdity, to style themselves "National Socialists." It is inconceivable, however, that they should have called themselves "National Communists." For how could they put in their own title a name which they employed as the supremely abusive epithet?

Such considerations show the character of our problem. We are not dealing with the kind of verbal abuse which men employ merely in the heat of argument. If you assert that the earth is spherical in shape, and I say, "Nobody will believe that, you fool!" we are both talking on a personal level where the silliness is plain and the damage slight. But if you assert that the wages of labor ought to be raised, and I say, "Nobody ought to say that, you Communist!" then we are talking on a social level where the silliness is by no means plain nor the damage slight. For if I am a political writer, the chances are that I didn't call you a Communist because I hated you personally, but because I wanted to isolate your views and render them ineffective. In politics, abusive language is very carefully employed, and even the angry tone of its utterance may be wholly simulated. The purpose is to separate the victim, perhaps from his job, perhaps even from his life, but certainly from his fellow men.

In every printed or spoken medium examples abound, some "gross as earth," some adroit. Here is one in which the liberal and reforming policies of the New Deal receive their baptism of red fire:

> To sum up, then, Mr. Roosevelt has permitted the demoralization of the American Merchant Marine at the hands of the Communistic Harry Bridges. He or his radical friends conceived and he forced through the utterly Communistic undistributed profits tax; which, if it continues to stand, will prevent corporate private enterprise from going to its own assistance in future depressions. He forced through the Wagner Labor Disputes Act, which has brought dismay, distress, and disaster to both employers and employees. . . . His associates have been the radicals and have included some of the most Communistic-minded men of the day. And his speeches, especially his acceptance speech of 1936, suggest clearly the Communistic origin of his plans. I unhesitatingly submit this data as tending to show that the President is communizing the United States.[3]

These remarks were addressed to an audience whose ample flesh must have quivered with alarm. It is always terrifying to have such things presented "unhesitatingly," even though there is only a "tending,"

[3] Mervin K. Hart: "This American System," in *Vital Speeches*, Vol. IV, p. 24. (February 1, 1938) . The speech was doubtless vital, but for whom?

an inclination, a tilt, as it were, in the policies under attack. Yet if a majority of Americans had felt any comparable alarm, they would have voted the New Deal out of office and thus have forgone the benefits of unemployment compensation and social insurance generally. This was, of course, the effect hoped for. That it was not the effect achieved must remain a tribute to the national intelligence, which declined to accept weakness and poverty for fear of a word.

The smearing of good policies need not be done with such raw and vulgar colors. It can appear in the quieter hues of science and high political theory. The *Science News Letter* for November 12, 1938, shows what surprising results economic theory can yield:

Gradual increase of taxes permits a nation to "approach communism at pleasure, always clinging formally to the principle of the right of private property," Dr. K. G. Hagstrom, Swedish actuary, says in a report to the Econometric Society. "If the 'Supported Party,' consisting of those receiving dole, relief, pensions, 'ham-and-eggs,' and old age or unemployment benefits, should reach a majority, it is entirely possible for them to impose taxes on the working part of the population that would plunge the country into a communistic state without any sort of revolution, bloodless or otherwise," he claims.[4]

Here, again, we can judge the real meaning from the intended effect. The authority of statistics and of a Swedish actuary (a Ph.D. at that!) is directed against old-age pensions, unemployment relief, social insurance, and in general against any measures on behalf of com-

[4] The *Science News Letter,* Vol. 34, No. 20, p. 310.

mon men. A remote and highly improbable consequence will suffice, it is hoped, to deter men from satisfying their most obvious immediate needs.

I will add a final illustration, which serves to show that more sophisticated audiences require a greater elegance in abuse. This passage is directed against the Wagner Act, and it asserts that compulsory collective bargaining violates the principle of "voluntarism" which is essential to "democracy." Thus:

> England and the United States are similar in that both countries are democracies and that the principle of compulsion has never been accepted by any preponderant element in either country. In Russia, Germany, and Italy — that is, in the Fascist countries — the principle of compulsion is accepted. In Great Britain and the United States, the principle of voluntarism is binding — that is, a man may join or not join an organization and the law must protect him in his choice. This is fundamental in a democracy. This principle defines the basic social distinction between a democratic and a Fascist state.[5]

The concern here manifested over a workman's right to choose his own union is peculiarly touching, since by the exercise of that "right" a minority of workmen could prevent any one union from representing all the workers in a given plant, and thus seriously impair the union's power as a bargaining agent. This, of course, is just what Mr. Sokolsky intended. If the weakening of unions can be made to appear "voluntarism" and the strengthening of them "compulsion," then we may be

[5] George E. Sokolsky: "The Law and Labor," *Atlantic Monthly*, Vol. 159, p. 438.

brought to bestow approval and disapproval accordingly. By way of clinching this result, Mr. Sokolsky hints that the Wagner Act is fascist, although it is of the essence of fascism to destroy unions and to leave workmen defenseless against extreme exploitation. If the fascist label is to be applied, it fits Mr. Sokolsky's proposal much more aptly. Finally, as if confusion were not great enough already, Mr. Sokolsky places under the fascist name the Soviet Union, a nation in which Labor exercises both economic and political leadership. This device seems to be a polite version of the old "Communazi" tag, a preposterous telescoping of two words which had nothing in common except the letter n. The Nazi bigwigs showed their own opinion of this tag by an embarrassing preference for surrendering to the Anglo-American forces rather than to the Red Army.

LOGIC AND THE RED LABEL

The red label, whether plastered or implied, is obviously a potent negative force. It is so, because it concentrates within a few syllables the bitterest of hatreds, the most panicky of fears. Communists who are true to their principles do, of course, propose to socialize the means of production, and thus they arouse unbounded wrath in the present possessors. These, in their turn, retaliate with all available weapons. Hence arises the fear of being called "Communist," for the victim is well aware that where the label goes, penalties may swiftly follow.

It is true that an exceptional spirit can grapple with the word, tear loose the opprobrious meaning, and use the word thenceforward as a symbol of glory and sacrifice. Such a spirit, as it seems, was Gabriel Péri, the one-time editor of *L'Humanité*. A leading French Communist, he was one of the first to be arrested, and during his imprisonment the Nazis many times offered him freedom in exchange for the betrayal of his comrades. Against this greatest of all lures he proved unyielding, and at last his execution was set. The evening before his death, in gloom and in agony, he searched his conscience, for when a man dies on behalf of principle, he wants to be sure that the principle is right. At such a time, doubts strike more feelingly than ever they do in the fancies of habitual sceptics. What Péri wrote, that night, was this:

Let my friends know that I remain faithful to my life's ideal; let my countrymen know that I shall die in order that France may live. I have made a last examination of my conscience: the result is positive. . . . If I had to begin my life again, I should take the same path. Tonight I still believe that my dear friend Paul Vaillant-Couturier was right in saying that Communism is the youth-time of the world and that it prepares "tomorrows of song." I feel myself strong in the face of death. *Adieu, que vive la France!* [6]

Whatever one may think of the principles for which Gabriel Péri died, there is a remarkable difference between the *tone* of this passage and the tone of those I

[6] Taken from the pamphlet *Ceux de Chateaubriant*, by Fernand Grenier, published in London by the Communist Party, 1943, p. 30. The translation is mine.

have previously quoted. When a man reckons up his last account and sets aside all solicitations of ease and happiness, his speech cannot be trifling nor his words irrelevant. With these depths of thought and feeling no propagandist can be acquainted. The last words of smearers are seldom recorded: they have not the voice for it. Yet I fancy that if some final squeak be heard, there is laughter among the martyrs.

If either we are incapable of Péri's heroism or, through disagreement with his principles, are unwilling to exercise it on their behalf, what then can we do? We must surely do something; otherwise we permit the smearers to blight discussion and paralyze action as they please. The usual practice is to deny the charge with some indignation; but this method wastes time upon a logically irrelevant issue, and is, moreover, rather less than convincing. The red label will never lose its effectiveness as abuse until the public at large clearly understands the accurate, literal application of the term "Communist" to people and to programs. Let us see what this would mean.

(A) *WHAT PEOPLE ARE COMMUNISTS?*

Political classifications have to be based upon the set of opinions held by the persons who are to be classified. It is the sharing of identical opinions which establishes membership in the class. Membership in a given organization will not suffice, for it may be that the organization does not profess all the opinions which its name would suggest, or, though professing them, does not enact them into policy. In the end, as investigating committees well know, it is the opinions themselves, together with action based upon them, which are decisive.

Following this procedure, then, we can say that the term "Communist" will properly designate those people who accept the content of Marxist theory as applied by Lenin to the period of the Russian Revolution and by Stalin to the post-revolutionary period. The content of this theory may be summarized thus: (1) that only a system of social control over the land and the means of production can resolve the antagonisms of existing society and release to mankind the abundance which modern technology makes possible; (2) that such a system can be reached only by a conquest of political power by the working class in collaboration with the farmers, the professionals, and some at any rate of the small proprietors; (3) that the workers, once having in their hands the machinery of state power, must use it to end the existence of capitalists as a social class (which is not the same thing as ending their personal existence) ; and (4) that all these events can occur within a single nation — that is to say, socialism does not need to be achieved everywhere in order to be achieved anywhere.

This is the body of ideas which distinguishes Communists from liberals and conservatives (both of whom support capitalism), from Socialists (who deny the seizure of power doctrine), and from the followers of Leon Trotsky (who deny that socialism can be built in a single nation). Given the century-long development of Marxist theory, with all the schisms and inner conflicts which have occurred, one can tell pretty accurately what characterizes the various groups. It is, however, a much subtler problem to decide what the term "Communist" would mean as applied to a single legislative measure or to a political program other than the one just described. If the program were such as to bring the nation to the very edge of socialism or to the actual building of it, then there can be no doubt that the adjective would be properly applied. But what of programs and measures which fall far short of socialism, which in fact were not conceived with any such intent?

(B) *WHEN IS A PROGRAM COMMUNIST?*

There is a sense in which smearers call anything "Communist" which they happen not to like. But the more adroit among them are aware of the need for some show of reason in applying the term. Accordingly, they often base their application upon the fact that the given program is supported by Communists or that the program is an effort at some kind of collective action. Both grounds are wholly insufficient, and we have now to see why they are so.

The Communist attitude toward nonsocialist programs was set by Marx himself in the *Manifesto,* Part IV:

> The Communists fight for the attainment of the immediate aims, for the enforcement of the momentary interests of the working class; but in the movement of the present, they also represent and take care of the future of that movement.

Therefore, from the fact that Communists (in the sense just now defined) support a given piece of legislation nothing can be inferred except that they judge it to be in the interests of Labor. The smearer intends you to think that the legislation means socialism now or very shortly, and that that is why Communists support it. But surely socialism would be a very, very remote effect of legislation, for example, like the Wagner Labor Relations Act. The only connection between the two would be that the Act preserves enough political and economic power in the labor unions for them to set about the establishment of socialism at some later time. If the smearer means to say that the unions, thus protected, will inevitably move toward socialism, then he comes near to talking Marxism himself, and, like all unskillful painters, he displays upon his own features the paint he was daubing elsewhere.

It seems plainly illogical to describe a political program in terms of a section of its supporters, especially when that section is small. An accurate description would have to base itself upon the actual creators and sponsors of the program and upon the larger goals which they intended the program to achieve. By this test it becomes obvious that the New Deal was not conceived in Marxist terms at all. It was conceived in the philosophy of political liberalism, which seeks to provide economic opportunity for everyone within a system of private ownership of the means of production. No one in his senses has ever seriously believed that the Roosevelt administration, together with its supporters in Congress and in the American electorate, was Communist or even -istic.

Now, what about programs which involve collective action? Can they properly be called "Communist"?

There can be no doubt, of course, that all socialist action is collective action, for under socialism the production and distribution of goods is planned by and for the entire national community. But is all collective action socialist action? All whales are mammals; are all mammals whales?

There are people who appear to think so. All the measures for unemployment benefits, works projects, health insurance, government control over wages and prices have at one time or another been denounced in just this way. Yet the truth is that capitalist nations have often resorted to programs of collective action, without ceasing to be capitalist. They have done so with enterprises like the postal system, which are necessary but not profitable enough to excite "individual initiative." They have done so on occasions of great emergency, such as wars, when nothing less than the collective effort of an entire people can bring victory. If all collective action is socialist, as some propagandists seem to imply, the conclusion would follow that capitalism cannot serve its most essential needs without behaving in a socialist manner.

If our analysis has been correct, then no political program or legislative measure can be called "Communist" merely because Communists support it or because it involves collective action. All programs and measures short of socialism will be logically free of that adjective, unless they have been articulated into a larger program for the establishment of socialism, and are so regarded by a majority of their supporters. In all other circumstances, the application of the term will be either a blunder or a smear, from which the perpetrator can escape only by arguing that *everything* done collectively or done in the interests of Labor leads inevitably to socialism. Smearers, therefore, must confess themselves mistaken or dishonest or something rather pink. It would be interesting to know which of these alternatives they would choose.

LOGIC AND EMOTION

Having thus observed the paradoxes which can arise when words are used solely for the sake of the feelings they excite, we come to the final question: ought we to use emotional language, and, if so, how ought we to use it? Quite a few writers, attempting to avoid both error and chicanery, have apparently come to believe that nothing but the most unemotional language should be employed. Instead of writing (as was said of Oscar Wilde) at the top of their voices, they write in a manner scarcely audible. They permit themselves no rhetoric, no exhortation, not even a faint professorial witticism. A vast neutrality descends upon their prose.

Surely this is the opposite extreme, and no less erroneous. It rests, apparently, upon a belief that since a single word is capable of being neutral, a prose style made up of such words will exhibit a comparable neutrality. It does nothing of the sort. On the contrary, such a style could be accurate in expression only on the assumption that everything we write about has the same significance for human life — a significance which, the language being neutral, would have to be zero. Absolute neutrality flattens everything: "the lone and level sands stretch far away."

There is, moreover, much doubt whether a neutral style is really attainable. Words, being used by men and only by men, are marvelously mingled with human interests. All attempts to escape this fact by inventing a living vocabulary out of dead languages end by producing a false and odious jargon. Nor is the impartial language of science proof against a similar contagion. The mixture of awe and gratitude which in the eighteenth century grew over the Newtonian universe now reaches out to touch Einsteinian Relativity. I have seen Pasteur's rabbits and Mendel's peas in a church window. Even the cold nonverbal equations of mathematicians and physicists cannot wholly repel the heat of human feeling. Since atomic energy will either benefit mankind or destroy it, and since we cannot predict which of these it will do, an alternating passion of hope and despair suffuses the apparently neutral statement, $E = mc^2$. There are, I dare say, even physicists who wish that such a statement had never been formulated.

Well, if a purely neutral language is either impossible or false, and if emotional language is capable of fraud and deceit, what language are we to use? What shall be the criterion of the accurate use of words? I think we shall have to say that a word is used accurately (1) when its literal meaning does in fact embrace the objects to which the word is applied, and (2) when its emotional character corresponds to the feelings which those same objects, viewed without prejudice, would generally excite. Thus any program which could help to bring us abundance of goods and ease and peacefulness of social life is a program which would inevitably excite the approval of most people. The words employed to describe such a program ought therefore to be words which will convey the approval of the majority.

By this sort of standard we can at once perceive what falsification results from words like "bureaucracy," "regimentation," "collectivism," "totalitarianism." When these are applied, as indeed they continually are, to legislation which is plainly in the public interest, they misrepresent both the nature of the legislation and the emotions it would normally arouse. The unfavorable feeling of the word supplants the favorable feeling of the thing. The reverse can be achieved by phrases like "private enterprise," "individual initiative," "free labor." As these are commonly used, they forestall an unfavorable reaction to the thing by introducing a favorable reaction to the word.

I suppose that the moral of all this is a little platitudinous. With words, as with knowledge generally, there can be no substitute for constant analysis of fact. Unless we school ourselves to avoid that laggard language which perpetuates old feelings as it perpetuates old ideas, and to make our speech correspond with fact both in thought and in feeling, the present will always lie just a little beyond our comprehension, and the future will be hopelessly obscure. This problem really falls within the larger problem of how we are to act, not as creatures of impulse and emotion, but as rational men. No one, so far as I know, has improved upon Spinoza's remedy, which was to control emotions by an understanding of them and of the world.

*　　*　　*

Some years ago, a friend of mine was invited by a Gallup poll taker to give his definition of "free enterprise." " 'Free enterprise,' " said my friend, "is a euphemism under which businessmen conceal their thirst for profits." There was a pause while the poll taker wrote this down. Then the poll taker said, "What's a euphemism?"

Such is the fate of words. They are measures of our ignorance as of our knowledge: they are sources of darkness as of light. But though they are elusive as the breath which bears them, perhaps we may put our faith in this: that men who understand the world will be masters of the word, and men who are masters of the word have the rudiments of mastery over the world.

CHAPTER XI

THAT YOU CANNOT BE FREE AND SAFE

IN THE land of social mythology the inhabitants, as we must now realize, manifest a behavior which custom renders familiar even as reason renders it strange. There exists, however, one more device not yet described within these pages — a device which might be called (after Bradley's famous phrase) "a spectral ballet of bloodless categories." I have saved discussion of it to the end, not because it possesses any exceptional relish, but because it is best displayed in a trinity of concepts which summarize all social thought. The concepts are Liberty, Equality, and Fraternity; and the device consists in treating them as if they were counters upon a checkerboard.

There is something about abstract ideas which makes them an invitation to mendacity. It is not that they are general and may thus refer to a multitude of individual things. It is rather that, being abstract, they have lost a direct reference to things; and so long as they are kept in that state, they cannot tell us what precisely were the things they once referred to. Yet, like flowers under refrigeration, they retain the scent and loveliness of their true species. We continue to admire them, not knowing any longer the garden from which they came or the climate in which they grew. If, then, some lying florist claims as his little own these blooms which prospered in far larger gardens and under vaster skies, we may well be deceived into thinking that they are really his.

Deception arises from the fact that when social concepts are maintained as abstractions, they can be arbitrarily defined. A small group of men can seize the concept, fasten upon it an interpretation favorable to themselves, and propagate the new meaning through every avenue of speech. The concept, however, retains its social tone. There results then a merging of the social tone with the new and twisted meaning, and people begin to accept as valid for all society what is really but the secret interest of a special group.

Nowhere, I suppose, is this more obviously true than in the concept of freedom. It is perfectly natural for the rulers of a society to believe that freedom lies in their own unhampered activity. If they can persuade the other members of society to accept this definition and to regard freedom as a good thing, then they will have done all that is necessary for the public justification of their rule. Something of this sort has actually been achieved by the monopolists and cartelists, who have covered their whole range of economic behavior with the honorific title "free enterprise." There are other titles, too, now stale beyond any refreshment. These have been repeated so often that the users of them seem like mechanical men, equipped with a robot vocabulary of perhaps a dozen phrases. But repetition, while it bores some people, convinces others; accordingly, every use of such a phrase is like the laying of stones in a wall, to keep the concept away from outsiders.

Nevertheless, abstractions are not without danger to the rulers who use them. The very indefiniteness of reference which enabled them to seize the concept enables the people to seize it also. There develops a process by which *all* the members of society interpret the concept in terms of their own experience: they begin to think of freedom as involving some control by themselves over the national economy — a definition few rulers would approve. When the prestige of the old idea begins to invest the new meaning, the rulers find that they have unwittingly provided the whole population with a battle cry. They have raised up enemies, have organized them, and have even provided a vocabulary for proclamations.

It now becomes necessary to manipulate concepts with more agility. If the people seize upon a certain concept as expressive of their immediate needs, that concept must be countered by another. If, for example, the concept of equality expresses what the people want, as it came to do at the end of the eighteenth century, then the rulers try to replace it with another concept which is no less praiseful but a good deal less democratic in meaning. Thus we hear the cool voice of Jeremy Bentham, observing that "Equality ought not to be favored, except in cases in which it does not injure security; where it does not disturb the expectations to which the laws have given birth; where it does not derange the actually established distribution." [1] In other words —

[1] From *Principles of the Penal Code,* excerpted in D. O. Wagner: *Social Reformers,* p. 50.

and you must always express Bentham in other words — equality is laudable enough, provided it in no way affects the existing distribution of property.

What sort of equality would this be? The sort that obtains among wage earners. It decidedly would not apply to competing entrepreneurs, each of whom is to get what he can; still less would it apply to the relations of workers and employers. "If the condition of the industrious," says Bentham, trotting out what was even then an ancient nag, "were not better than the condition of the idle, there would be no reason for being industrious."

The incentive of acquisition, fortified by security in the property acquired, is thus held necessary to make society operate at all. Even the powerful charms of liberty, equality, and fraternity do not suffice to overcome what Bentham calls "the natural aversion to labor." The right of property alone suffices to do that — a right which presents "ideas of pleasure, of abundance, and of security." Thus the dazzling goals of three revolutions (in Britain, in America, and in France) give way to other goals more suited to the times. Men are to be less free, less equal, less brotherly than had been wished, in order that incentive may sharpen appetite, and security crown endeavor. Sweet commerce! How bold of enterprise when everything was still to be gained, how fat and timorous when everything was still to be kept!

Security, however, is an abstraction like the others, and it has suffered their fate: it has been captured by the people. During the last fifteen years especially, security has been the concept most adequately embodying the needs of populations racked by depression and war.

It has come to mean such things as unemployment insurance, old age pensions, and national programs of medical care. In short, it has come to mean at least the partial reorganization of society for the benefit of all the members, as against the old purpose of profit for a few. The capitalists on whose behalf Bentham once opposed the concept of security to the concept of equality are now obliged to oppose the concept of freedom to the concept of security. They cannot appear so nakedly as to say, "We think it just and right that society should be organized for our benefit alone." On the contrary, their apologists must try somehow to make out that it is better for *society* when things are organized that way. Accordingly, they have evolved the doctrine that you cannot be free and safe at the same time, and that, of the two, it is better to be free. Perhaps it would be unkind to ask, "Better for whom?"

THE LURE OF ADVENTURE

Apologists to whom these grateful tasks are assigned are by no means limited to writers and lecturers. They can be found also among educators, who have in their care the informing of our youth. Indeed, the more philosophical the doctrine to be formulated, the more likely it is that an educator will be called upon. He is invariably a man of calm and vegetative intelligence, who sees life steadily and sees it whole, or has heard at any rate that, according to Matthew Arnold, he ought to do so. He understands the niceties of prose as fixed by the Department of English, and he is acquainted with the larger generalizations as these are assembled in Bartlett. He speaks, perhaps, like this:

In over-emphasizing the rights and privileges of the individual without regard to his responsibilities we have been led into the error of substituting security for liberty as the object of social effort. The restoration of a sense of responsibility to this and succeeding generations, a renewal of our faith in the innate worth and importance of the individual, and a determination to preserve this conception in American life, are necessary to a continuance of the principles upon which the American Republic was founded, and by which it was developed. . . .

It should be remembered that in the life of the nation as in that of the individual *security* is the by-product of a well-ordered life. It is something which eludes those who set it up as a goal to be sought. It is like happiness which comes to the individual whose life is effective but which is never found by one who makes it the object of his search. . . .

In the life of nations as well as in that of individuals concentration upon *security* as the goal of paramount importance means stagnation and defeat. . . .

Too great caution and too much concern over making certain that *profits* will accrue from efforts contemplated mean stagnation in business and industry. Likewise the concentration of labor on its right to collective bargaining, on the length of its hours, the amount of its wages, and the type and certainty of employment, has slowed the wheels of progress.[2]

[2] O. O. Carmichael: "Liberty vs. Security," *Vital Speeches*, Vol. 4, p. 670. This is an address delivered at a banquet of the New York State Bankers Association, June 26, 1938, at the Saranac Inn, Upper Saranac, New York. The italics are Dr. Carmichael's.

I have often marveled at the ability of banqueters to proceed directly from the assimilation of food to the assimilation of ideas, for the longish interval after coffee evokes in me nothing so much as a disposition to sleep. Dr. Carmichael's audience, however, proceeded not only to the assimilation of ideas but also to a renewal of their faith in the innate worth and importance of the individual. I think we must salute these talents as incomparably athletic. It may be that the achievement was somewhat less great than it seems, for the speaker was assuring his audience that the innate worth and importance of the individual is different from, and indeed opposed to, collective bargaining, shorter hours, higher wages, and full employment. An interpretation of this sort makes it easier for bankers to renew their faith in the innate worth and importance of the individual. Under such circumstances, the innate worth and importance of the individual becomes a kind of Jack Horner concept: "What a good boy am I!"

There must have been comfort, also, in the ingenious argument by which security was shown to be impossible of attainment by planned effort. Like happiness, so the argument runs, security is an accompaniment of other conditions, and cannot be a goal in its own right. To this, I suppose, one might reply that if a is an accompaniment of b, it would certainly be possible to pursue b and, on attaining it, get a also. And if what would thus be attained would be a state composed of a and b, there seems to be no reason why we should not say that, of the two, we are more interested in a. Nor is there any reason why we could not plan for b precisely because it is accompanied by its more desirable partner. Dr. Carmichael's argument is one of those which hopes to have its conclusion remembered and its premises forgotten. For if people can be persuaded that security cannot be a goal, it is obvious that they will not work for it.

The classic argument for the incompatibility of liberty and security is to be found, however, in the last two paragraphs. This argument holds that security produces "stagnation." Once people are secure, it is believed, they will relax their labors and will even grow lazy and indolent. Visions of a new Sybaris begin to float before the mind, together with sobering recollections of a people pampered into defenselessness. The attainment of security puts an end to incentive, and without incentive no one can be brought to work.

Now, curiously enough, this argument *against* security is the same argument which Bentham used *in favor of* it. He held that if men are not secure in their possessions, there will be no incentive to acquire them, and thus no work will be done. Dr. Carmichael holds that if men are secure in their possessions, incentive disappears, and thus no work will be done. Bentham and Carmichael have between them constructed a giant dilemma, of which the alternatives are security or insecurity, and the common consequence is universal idleness. Such a result is manifestly absurd in a society like ours, which exhibits a real, though uneven, technological development.

You cannot, of course, make the same argument work in two opposite ways. If security is genuinely required in order to excite men to labor, and if the labor of men is demonstrably worth exciting (as I have no doubt it is), then security is beyond doubt one of the desirable social goods. If, on the other hand, security discourages men from labor, and if the labor of men is demonstrably worth exciting, then security is beyond doubt an undesirable social evil. It will be necessary to decide between these views: Bentham and Carmichael cannot both be right. Or if, by introducing chronology, you try to save both sides, you will have to explain why Bentham was right in his day but is wrong now, and why Carmichael would have been wrong in Bentham's day but is now right.

One other means of reconciliation exists: we can suppose that Bentham and Carmichael mean different things by security. When Bentham says that security is desirable because it protects the property-owner, he is saying that security is a good thing for capitalists to have. When Carmichael says that security is undesirable because it unduly emphasizes collective bargaining, shorter hours, and higher wages, he is saying that this sort of security is disadvantageous to capitalists. On this interpretation, both Bentham and Carmichael are seen to have a common standard of value, which is the welfare of capitalists. The apparent conflict between the two disappears, and we find that their agreement would have been perfectly obvious if only the term "security" had not chanced to change its meaning.

Let us examine one more version of the argument. On October 8, 1945, Dr. Irving Langmuir, associate director of the research laboratories of the General Electric Company, appeared before a Senate joint subcommittee. The subject was legislation granting federal aid to scientific research. Dr. Langmuir was worried that the incentives which lead scientists to conduct research might be blunted by certain governmental practices:

We have inherited from our past (personal liberty, freedom of thought, free enterprise, patents, etc.) a system of incentives more effective than that existing in any other nation, but the obvious necessity of government control of some features of our capitalist system has frequently led to attacks on the capitalist system as a whole, attacks on its good as well as its bad features. Let me give a list of some of the things which are now tending to restrict or even suppress incentives. In giving this list I do not at present wish to favor or oppose any of them. I want merely to call attention to the effects they are having upon incentives.[3]

Dr. Langmuir's list contained the following: antitrust laws, taxation, civil service laws, preference for war veterans in employment, social security laws, and attacks on the patent system. That is to say, he placed in this list almost every kind of legislation limiting the actions of monopolies and conferring some benefits upon ordinary men. In brief, the incentives which make scientific research possible must in the end be those which make monopolies possible. Again:

The pioneering spirit in the United States shows signs of dying out; we now talk about a thirty-hour week — the right to a job. We attach too much importance to security and too little to opportunity.[4]

Listening to such apologetics, one would suppose that the pioneers were motivated solely by dreams of gallant adventure. As a matter of fact, the pioneers were very sensible men who did not leave their homes until forced

[3] *New York Herald Tribune,* October 9, 1945, p. 12.
[4] *Ibid.*

out by economic failure or by the prospect of tangible gain. They were, for the most part, untouched by the folly of pursuing adventure for adventure's sake. They sought something, of course, as the goal of all their risks and labors. What they sought was security, the security they had not found at home.

It is very curious. The pioneers labored in order to get security, but we are to abandon security in order that we may labor like pioneers. The pioneers took risks in order that their children might be safe; but we, their children, are to abandon safety in order to take risks like the pioneers. We are to imitate the pioneers, by frustrating the purposes they strove to satisfy. The argument is standing on its head.

SECURITY AND IDLENESS

It is remarkable that the security which "endangers" freedom, which "suppresses" incentive, is always the security of workers, of farmers, or of small businessmen. One never hears that any of these sad results issue from the security of corporations, from the safe flowing in of profits. No, it takes something like the thirty-hour week or the prospect of full employment to put freedom in peril. But whose freedom would suffer thus? Not that of the workers, who, with certainty of employment and a thirty-hour week, would be freer than ever in their lives before. Not the farmers and small businessmen, who, with all wage earners employed, would have a steady market for their products. The only "freedom" to be lost would be that of the large employers, who thus could not hire and fire as they please or make the working hours as long as they please. What the large employers would lose the rest of society would gain.

If, therefore, security is defined in terms of social gains for the great majority of people (and Dr. Langmuir so defined it), the only kind of freedom which can be opposed to it must be the freedom of those who lose when the majority gains. But then "freedom" turns out to be a word masking the special interests of a small exploiting class. Once this fact has become obvious, the concept of freedom will no longer serve to pass off the special interests as identical with the general welfare. A freedom which means unrestricted profits is certainly opposed to a security which means full employment and the thirty-hour week. But who will maintain that such a freedom can exist for society as a whole?

There remains one last argument which might, on social grounds, justify the freedom of capitalists as against the security of everyone else. This argument is to be found in both Dr. Carmichael and Dr. Langmuir, and it holds that security paralyzes action by removing incentives. Expressed in economic terms, the argument asserts that people will not produce goods unless they have an incentive for producing them, that a state of security is one in which they have no such incentives, and that therefore a state of security is one in which they will produce no goods.

The argument is uncommonly naïve because it quietly assumes that the motives which lead capitalists to produce goods are the only motives which can do so. It is, of course, altogether characteristic of capitalists that they are never interested in the production of goods as such, but only as a means of making profits. Destroy the opportunity for profits, and you deprive capitalists of any reason for producing goods. This is not a congenital blindness in them; it is a blindness which results from their having to play a certain social role. It is, if you like, their own peculiar kind of industrial disease.

At any rate, the notion has become a basic part of capitalist apologetics: men cannot be brought to produce goods simply for the sake of possessing the goods they have made. There must, it is held, be some added incentive, such as immediate or future profit, the hope of rising in the world, the enticement of fame. These are strenuous and masterful incentives, which suggest toil from early to late, honest brows wreathed with honest sweat, and at last a peak of public renown on which the exhausted man flings himself, a shattered hulk too feeble to enjoy his prize. By contrast, full employment and the thirty-hour week suggest nothing more active than a life of comfort and of ease, in which the laborer labors mildly for thirty of the week's hours and loafs or sleeps for the remaining hundred and thirty-eight. Such a life (which is everyone's secret desire) is readily justified by reason, but the mores are still against it, and will, I should imagine, remain against it so long as a fifty- or sixty-hour week is profitable to the managers of mores. Perhaps there will even be a restoration to all hymnals of the hortatory chant,

> Work, for the night is coming,
> When man works no more.

In other words, a dead laborer is no source of profit.

The supposed conflict between security and incentive vanishes the moment we realize *that security is itself an incentive.* To be secure is to be protected against everything which can threaten one's economic position, one's life, one's prospects of happiness. To be secure is to know that one shares fully in the goods and services one has helped produce, that one labors today without danger of unemployment tomorrow, that one can keep one's family and one's friendships inviolate, that one can look toward an old age free from poverty and degradation. All these goals serve as very powerful incentives; indeed, they are what people really want, so far as wants are normal. It is these goals which excite, it is these goals which brighten, the always effortful and sometimes odious toil of man. The facts are almost majestic in their humanity. But — setting them for the moment aside — if security were not an incentive, on what basis would insurance be sold?

In the second place, security is not a static condition which, when we attain it, leaves us nothing more to do. On the contrary, security has to be maintained in existence by the united labor of the whole society. If people shirk this task in any considerable numbers, security will vanish. This is true even within the lives of individual men. Take, for example, our two learned apologists. By any reasonable standard, they may be said to have security, as such things go in the contemporary world. What form does their security take? It takes the form of a salary contract, which is capable of being terminated. To maintain the security our apologists have to maintain the contracts. To maintain the contracts they have to provide the services (and what services!) which the contracts demand. If they don't provide the services, they lose the contracts; and if they lose the contracts, they lose their security (or, at any rate, must find it elsewhere). Thus security in the present and in the future is certainly one of the things which excite their labor.

If security is itself an incentive, and if security is a condition which has to be maintained, then it follows that we can work to achieve it and, on achieving it, can work to keep it in existence. But if this is true, then security is not necessarily incompatible with incentive and cannot be a source of universal idleness. The goals of full employment and of a thirty-hour week are capable of *producing* work rather than stifling it. Indeed, such goals, because they can be shared by multitudes, are probably more powerful and more universal incentives than the unlikely prospect of "rising from the ranks."

Such being the case, we may wonder how the notion ever arose that security begets idleness. Partly the idea is just sheer invention, but there is one social phenomenon which somewhat corresponds to it. If we ask where in our society idleness and security do go hand in hand, we shall find that the answer is, in the leisure class. The members of this class have invested sufficient funds in various commercial enterprises to enable them to live comfortably or, it may be, luxuriously upon the interest. Such income is, by definition, unearned — which is another way of saying that those who receive it do not have to work for it. Their security is perfectly compatible with their idleness. It is not, however, compatible with the idleness of other people, who have to work partly to maintain themselves and partly to enable the coupon clippers to clip.

There is thus only one social group in which security can be considered a possible source of idleness. If, as our myth tells us, security is a bad thing because it makes men idle, then we should have to begin by taking security away from the coupon clippers in order to get them to do some work. Let the gander bathe in the goose's sauce: if we are to forgo full employment and the thirty-hour week on behalf of incentives, then let us first bestow upon the leisure class the beneficial rigors of insecurity. Let us tax away their unearned income, and turn them out to fare as best they may by the honest toil they so much admire in other people. If we do this, we shall hear such a howl as never shook heaven before, and within one day a whole army of editors, commentators, and columnists will fall to proving that security is more important than freedom and that idleness (at least in certain people) is a conspicuous ornament to society. "For 'tis the sport to have the enginer hoist with his own petar."

Of all the myths we have examined, the one which tells us that we cannot be free and safe is the one most obviously invented for a special use. What the rulers of society have in mind is their own freedom and their own security, not ours. If we tell them that we wish to be free, they reply that they intend to be secure; and if we tell them that we wish to be secure, they reply that they intend to be free. In other words, *their* freedom is compatible with *their* security, but both are incompatible with *our* freedom and *our* security. Perhaps this is true. But if it is so, then the theorists who propagate the doctrine ought not to blame others for suggesting that there exists a conflict among classes. This conflict is the burden of their own song, and is but faintly concealed beneath an engaging tune.

LIBERTY, EQUALITY, FRATERNITY

If, as we said at the beginning of this chapter, liberty, equality, and fraternity are a trinitarian whole, security might well be the name of the essence embracing them. You can see this by running over in your mind all the examples of insecurity you can think of. You will find that they resolve themselves into three main types. Men are insecure (1) because they are irrationally limited instead of being rationally free, (2) because their conditions of life are grossly unequal, and (3) because group conflicts (*i.e.* the lack of universal brotherhood) keep both life and life's achievements in constant peril. It would seem, therefore, that if men can ever succeed in being free, in being equal, and in being brothers, they will at last know what it means to be secure.

It is an adorable trinity, too. Not even the fraudulent uses to which these concepts have been distorted can diminish their charm as sovereign social ideals. Their central content, sublimely stubborn, defies all arbitrary change; and the more the world falls short of them, the more obvious it is what values are being lost. Nor has cynicism the power to corrupt such ideals.

It is quite true, of course, that they are most frequently upon the lips of men who are bent on destroying them, the true believers keeping them more silently at heart. But the lip-service and the betrayals exist because some men are exploiters and others are exploited, because these groups are in conflict, and because the conflict can be resolved only by the end of exploitation itself. But the end of exploitation would be the beginning of actual brotherhood, the end of unequal powers would be the beginning of equality, and the end of extreme privilege for a few would be the beginning of genuine liberty for all.

Thus even the enemies of our three ideals cannot conceal or misinterpret them without showing us very plainly what in fact they are. Nor can we misconceive the ideals without being tossed by the very logic of our desires into an awareness of our misconception. It is surely the most genial of all paradoxes: the more we mistake the ultimate social truths, the more we are obliged to know them truly; the more we are deceived by rulers, the more apt we are for shedding the deception — provided, that is to say, the rulers have not succeeded, as the Nazis did with their people, in paralyzing the exercise of reason.

Moreover, the three ideals are joined, simply as concepts, by the fact that the meaning of each involves the meaning of the others. You cannot begin to exhaust the content of any one of them without discovering that you are talking about all of them. Would it, for example, be possible to conceive of a free society in which large or small numbers of men lacked the minimum requirements of freedom? It would not, of course. But if a free society were one in which everybody possessed the minimum requirements of freedom, then everyone in that society would be equal in the possession of those minimum requirements. The equality of that possession would be, in fact, the very thing which demonstrates the society to be free. Or would a free society be one in which large or small numbers of men found that their essential needs were thwarted of fulfillment by the activities of other men? Again, it obviously would not. But if a free society is one in which everybody satisfies his essential needs not only without interference by other men but with their help, then such a society would be thoroughly co-operative and would deserve to be called a brotherhood. Its fraternal character would, in fact, be the very thing which proves it free. As for equality and fraternity, I should suppose the connection between them so plain as to need no laboring. For a brotherhood of fundamentally unequal members is inconceivable, and an equality of members which, however, belonged to no brotherhood could not possibly exist.

Yet, although the three ideals are thus intimately joined, the development of industrial society has tended to sunder them; and although their content is plain enough to him who searches it out, it has been largely vulgarized by that same development. A group of men whose social role consists in taking profits from other people's labor can have no profound belief in equality and fraternity as desirable ideals. Their whole position is founded upon an inequality of economic status, which is the most important inequality of all. The actions they are obliged to take as profit-makers force them into competition with one another as well as with the men upon whose labor the profits are made. Thus for profit-makers co-operation has only an incidental, not a basic, use; and accordingly for them fraternity can scarcely be an ideal.

Such men, I imagine, must often have cursed the fate which imposed upon their revolutionary ancestors the necessity of espousing such ideals. In the ancestors the choice was a stroke of genius, for the slogan of "Liberty, Equality, and Fraternity" was exactly the one needed to mobilize all sections of feudal society against the aristocrats; it consolidated all victims and their grievances, and it left the aristocrats isolated and helpless. But after the various revolutions, when the note came due (the metaphor seems appropriate), the victorious middle class was disposed to pay it not with legal tender but with bullets and bayonets. What Tennyson from his British Parnassus saw as "the red fool-fury of the Seine" was the attempt of the people to collect payment and the refusal of the debtors to pay.

And indeed they haven't paid yet. Industrial capitalism has been in existence for about one hundred and fifty years, during which time it has enormously increased man's ability to produce and now has crowned all previous triumphs by the control of atomic energy. But after all that time and the release of all those productive forces, what state do we find the world in now? Europe is a continent devastated from side to side. Much of Asia is in ruins. Five hundred million people are said to be starving, and of the world's remaining millions not very many have more food than they need. In short, after one hundred and fifty years of industrial capitalism, the most productive society in history up to its time, most of the human beings on earth cannot satisfy their simplest economic needs.

Moreover, we stand amid the havoc of our latest war, perfectly aware that there may very well be another. The search for markets and for raw materials, which has driven capitalist nations through a century of conflicts, remains compulsively alive. The protection of foreign investments continues upon the colonial peoples the same oppression they have long endured, and reduces nations which once owned colonies to the level of the colonies themselves.

Yet, because history moves unevenly, gathering into its new stages some portion of its past, real gains are easy to overlook. The Second World War destroyed one formidable tyranny, the fascist Axis. It also released some few countries from the domination of foreign capital. Accordingly, we must conclude that, during recent years, we have moved somewhat closer to our trinitarian ideal. The progress was difficult and violent, but it was nevertheless progress. We should, I suppose, be failing our duty to the future if we thought that what brings pain to us could never bring benefit to our children.

Hope is as eternal as history, out of which, indeed, hope springs. But we shall not find it in that portion which is given over to the fevered intrigues of kings and emperors, prelates and lords, monopolists and foreign ministers. For these spend part of their allotted time in demonstrating their social uselessness, and part in resisting oblivion. Such contributions as they may have made to human advance were made unwittingly, as incidental to their own well-being.

On the contrary, hope dwells in the submerged classes and populations and in the leaders whom these produce. Just as the recent future turned out to lie, not with the Nazis, but with the peoples they oppressed or hoped to oppress, so the next future lies not with men ambitious of empire, but with those other men upon whom empire is built. Their freedom, once gained, will set the world free; their rise to equality and brotherhood will make us all one.

And here we can perceive the grossest deception which results from a belief in the "natural inferiority" of certain peoples. By this belief we make ourselves unable to learn from them, since we consider that they have nothing to teach. There is the danger that, while they struggle on after liberty, equality, and fraternity, we, for our part, may grow more and more despondent over such ideals. While they, by learning from their struggles, get more of the truth, we shall be sinking deeper into our illusions. And, of all illusions, the greatest and most deadly is despair.

In the sixteenth century, the Araucan Indians, a South American tribe now scarcely remembered, fought with the utmost gallantry against the invading Spaniards. One of their captains, being seized by the Spaniards, had both his hands cut off to render him useless for further combat. When he returned home, he explained to his people that the Spaniards had done all this out of fear, for fear (as he said) "produceth cruelty, the companion of cowardice."

Thus encouraged he them to fight for their lives, limbs, and liberty, choosing rather to die an honorable death fighting, than to live in servitude as fruitless members of the commonwealth. Thus using the office of a sergeant-major, and having loaden his two stumps with bundles of arrows, he succoured them who, in the succeeding battle, had their store wasted; and changing himself from place to place, animated and encouraged his countrymen with such comfortable persuasions, as it is reported and credibly believed, that he did more good with his words and presence, without striking a stroke, than a great part of the army did with fighting to the utmost.[5]

One can imagine this heroism transplanted to the twentieth century and described by our racist sages as the incurable rebelliousness of inferior peoples. But there is a lot to be learned from it.

"Fear produceth cruelty, the companion of cowardice." This was the secret of fascist barbarity, and it remains the secret of similar ghastly enterprises still observable in the world. Cruelty is a contagion spread from dying tyrannies, great or small, which endeavor, as they vanish, to make everything vanish with them. The fear from which it issues is the fear of losing power, and the cowardice which is its companion is timidity before a better world. Men who seek by cruelty to continue in the old way are men afraid to try a new.

But we, if we are to fear anything, ought rather to fear the old ways, the old intolerances and crimes, the old myths which once obscured our vision. We are cast upon the future without reluctance and even without regret, as finding there the substance of desire. If the

[5] From *The Observations of Sir Richard Hawkins*, quoted in J. A. Froude: *Short Studies in Great Subjects*, Oxford University Press, World's Classics Series, p. 319.

present rulers of earth can be persuaded into peace and fraternity, we shall do all we can to bring them thither. But if they continue to offer us nothing but tears, then we, the peoples of the world, must take the world and mold it to our wish. Either way, we shall come much nearer than before to that securer condition of man in which, by common control of our entire social destiny, we liberate all talents and energies, cast out all barriers of unequal privilege, and show ourselves at last a present and enduring brotherhood.

Now, therefore, since the struggle deepens, since evil abides and good does not yet prosper, let us gather what strength we have, what confidence and valor, that our small victories may end in triumph, and the world awaited be a world attained.